Air Travel Partnerships

While change in the aviation sector is hardly a new phenomenon, going forward the rate of change will accelerate due to the emergence, convergence, and intersection of powerful internal and external forces. To deal with the accelerating change in the marketplace, stakeholders in the travel ecosystem need to deepen collaboration that is productive to (1) building adaptable, resilient, and lean businesses, (2) achieving growth and innovation, (3) elevating traveler experience to a much higher level, and, at the same time, (4) reducing the impact on the environment.

Undoubtedly, while some innovations implemented by different aviation business sectors—to become more adaptable, more resilient, and leaner as well as to improve customer experience—have been adding some value, the innovations being introduced have been transactional, fragmented, and incremental. What is needed is a step change in proactive collaboration among different stakeholders in the air travel ecosystem at the holistic level, to co-create value for travelers in terms of experience (relating to simplicity, convenience, and speed) and for businesses to adapt in order to reduce costs and increase profit margins.

This book focuses on four types of organizations within the air travel sector: airlines, airports, aircraft manufacturers, and travel intermediaries. It provides a framework, tools, and insights to enhance collaborations by design in an age of increasing uncertainty.

Air Travel Partnerships is essential reading for all executives and senior managers within airlines, airports, and air transport supporting industries.

Nawal K. Taneja, whose work experience spans more than five decades, has worked for and advised major airlines and related businesses worldwide. His experience also includes the presidency of a small airline that provided schedule and charter services with jet aircraft and the presidency of a boutique think tank that provided advisory services to the air transportation community throughout the world. Within the academic community, he has served on the faculties of the Massachusetts Institute of Technology and the Ohio State University. He is a Fellow of the Royal Aeronautical Society of Great Britain.

Air Travel Partnerships

How to Create Greater Value through Collaboration

Nawal K. Taneja

Routledge
Taylor & Francis Group
LONDON AND NEW YORK

Designed cover image: lvcandy/Getty Images

First published 2025
by Routledge
4 Park Square, Milton Park, Abingdon, Oxon OX14 4RN

and by Routledge
605 Third Avenue, New York, NY 10158

Routledge is an imprint of the Taylor & Francis Group, an informa business

British Library Cataloguing-in-Publication Data
A catalogue record for this book is available from the British Library

ISBN: 9781032776019 (hbk)
ISBN: 9781003483960 (ebk)

DOI: 10.4324/9781003483960

Typeset in Galliard
by Newgen Publishing UK

Dedicated to Angela, Matthew, Sophia, and Ravi

Contents

Illustrations

Figures

Tables

Foreword

Stephen Brobst

Chief Technology Officer, Ab Initio Software

Data sharing is the key to successful collaboration

Inter-company collaboration to create a seamless end-to-end experience for consumers of travel services is a critical success factor that has yet to be achieved by most players within the industry. The missing component, in most cases, preventing effective collaboration between enterprises is data sharing capability. It is impossible to effectively collaborate between two enterprises without an underlying mechanism to share information. There are many different scenarios for which this is a critical capability.

For example, there is a strong dependency between an airline and the airports from which its flights depart and arrive. The airlines have strong visibility regarding the number of passengers that will depart and arrive at specific times for each airport in which they are served. Moreover, the airlines know how many of these passengers will require passport control versus those that are flying domestically. Understanding peaks and valleys in demand for services such as security processing, passport control, terminal to/from aircraft shuttle transportation, retail services, etc. will help airport partners staff more appropriately relative to passenger traffic. No Personally Identifiable Information (PII) need be shared from airline to airport to make this happen; aggregated and anonymized data with passenger counts by nationality and flight details is sufficient to achieve the objectives.

Sharing information from the airline to the airport is particularly important when there are abnormal variations in demand due to events that may not be easily visible to the airport itself. Having the right staffing level within an airport can make a huge difference to passenger experience, but this requires robust information sharing from the airline to the airport. In addition, the airport must have underlying technology capable of consuming the information, analytic capability to derive appropriate prescription of actions, and the business processes in place to take those prescribed actions.

Inter-airline data sharing is also essential. Much progress has been made in recent years to create better flight experiences between alliance partners in the industry. The ability to share data has created the opportunity to package a richer set of travel options for passengers and better handling of baggage, re-scheduling, and overall customer service. Sharing data among partner carriers has made handling of disruptions less impactful on passengers. However, there are still gaps. The impact analysis for understanding the implications of one disruption in one airline is often not carried through to all of its partners in a timely manner. This is a situation that can be remedied with appropriate investment in (near) real-time sharing of data and alignment of business processes for taking actions.

As Nawal Taneja points out throughout this book, and in particular in Chapter 5, from a passenger perspective, the holy grail of collaboration is to enable booking and seamless consumption of multi-modal travel experiences. To do this, the collaboration model needs to extend beyond inter-airline partnerships. Many journeys start and end with some combination of train and/or car services. However, in today's world, there is a distinct chasm between ground transportation and air transportation for most passengers. A select few airlines (mostly within Europe) have extended the flight experience to trains to yield a more robust travel experience, though these extensions are still mainly between major airports.

The nirvana of a truly frictionless travel experience would be door-to-door, including all modes of transportation necessary to make this a reality. In a single booking. This goal state requires data sharing far beyond current best practices. Extending booking to encompass a door-to-door travel experience would involve creation of new partnerships and much more sophistication in search engines and booking processes.

Moreover, owning responsibility for recovery after an unexpected disruption in transportation in any mode along the journey must be executed in a seamless way from a passenger perspective, as discussed in detail in Chapter 3 of this book. Airlines have long dealt with disruptions related to weather, congestion, mechanical issues, crew constraints, and so on. Analogies to these same issues exist for trains, buses, and automobiles. Disruption recovery protocols, including appropriate data exchange, will need to be extended to these new modes of transportation.

To be effective in realization of this vision, data sharing must be capable of happening in (near) real-time. The travel ecosystem is highly dynamic in nature; keeping up to date on any changes that occur in the context of passenger journeys is critical. Publish and subscribe protocols must be established across disparate operation systems embedded within each partner in the travel ecosystem. A set of Application Program Interfaces (APIs) with defined service levels and data contracts must be established and extended within the industry across all players. Intelligent agents leveraging AI/ML technologies will consume data services across enterprises for real-time scoring to prescribe next best actions to guide the passenger journey.

It is clear that we must adapt business processes to create frictionless passenger experiences from end-to-end, from door-to-door. To make this a reality, we must construct a data operating model that facilitates sharing across an expanded set of industry players and adapts to changes via new information.

Players in the travel industry should identify internal and external opportunities to implement API-based data sharing.

By leveraging a collection of Open Travel APIs it is possible to create an ecosystem of industry partners that has the potential to radically disrupt the travel industry. Success requires standardization of APIs within the industry and may require regulatory pressure to accelerate adoption, such as has been the case with Open Banking APIs. The benefit of improved passenger experiences will drive the design of next-generation travel services with innovative co-creation across industry partners with business and IT stakeholders leading the charge in unison.

Lexington, Massachusetts, USA

Foreword

Kyle B. Clark

Founder and CEO, BETA Technologies

Operating electric aircraft at both large and small random airfields across the United States and Canada has been fun, and comedic at times. Often on the tarmac corporate jet pilots will wander over to our odd-looking planes and start asking questions: "So it's electric, but is it ALL electric?", "How far does it go?" The questions from the control tower are even more telling of the nascency of aircraft electric motors. It's not uncommon for the tower to ask if we are ready to go, noting the propellers aren't turning at the runway hold short line. Demonstration flights are a challenge because someone needs to point out the quiet plane approaching for a flyby. It is indeed silent.

The aviation world is changing. Many are resisting it, some are embracing it, while still a small segment of us is devoting our lives to leaving the world a better place in an area we care deeply about. In this book, Dr. Taneja outlines the present status of these efforts with an open mind and fair representation to both the most optimistic futurists and the pragmatic technology developers.

I find myself in the categories of "dedicate my life to this" and "pragmatic engineer" alongside some amazing entrepreneurs offering creative solutions for all the technical, operational, and regulatory challenges in fielding electric aircraft. Thought-leading aircraft operators from both traditional airlines and small early-stage aspirational operators have drawn out equally insightful adoption and utilization strategies. We are exceptionally lucky to have landed at this time in aerospace.

It isn't surprising that about a decade ago, many engineers at UPS, DoD, Amazon, and airlines, as well as my mentor Dr. Martine Rothblatt, concurrently did the simple math to say that the battery, motor, and controls technology had reached a performance threshold that enables fuel-free commercial flight. This was the first step. In order for electric aviation to work, we first needed to show that the basic physics work and the level of technology to exploit these physical principles is at a mature enough state to do so reliably and efficiently. Second, the regulatory and commercial environments needed to be developed.

As a student of the aviation industry, I was very intrigued when I heard Dr. Taneja speak on the concept of "incentive for change." Aviation has had small incremental changes, but no major transformational changes. Strict regulations are often blamed for this stagnant business and technology environment in aviation. I often hear "the FAA/EASA has no incentive to allow new technologies." This is hand-waved by technologists that are looking for an excuse or a scapegoat that isn't themselves or their customers. Regulations are simply not return-seeking — rather, the regulations are designed to provide a minimum standard. Airlines, operators, and militaries are, however, return-seeking and in many cases seeking economic returns.

The opportunity for the move to electric aircraft is fundamentally economic, but the adoption is accelerated because of the potential sustainability of electric aircraft. Most importantly for high-cadence operators, the ratio of CapEx and OpEx is flipped up-side-down from traditional aviation. Although the vehicles will cost similar amounts, the recurring cost of operation of electric aircraft is significantly lower than combustion aircraft, due to both the obvious energy/fuel cost reduction and, almost as important, the drastic drop in maintenance costs. Controlled combustion is a nasty business. Yet we have nearly perfected it with wonderful (albeit expensive) solutions of materials science and well-oiled overhaul processes. Electric motors and solid-state inverters don't get hot, don't produce corrosive gasses, and in many cases don't require any liquids, filters, or pumps, and have no sliding metal-to-metal contact. In the simplest form there are two bearings and an electromagnetic field between the rotating rotor and stationary stator. The very first physics principles of operation are different, so we should expect a different outcome.

Developing electric aircraft is hard. Making one take off and land vertically is harder. It is even more challenging to industrialize the process of repeatedly building these aircraft in a highly regulated industry. There is little sense of humor in aerospace for off-point designs. This demands rigorous engineering, multidisciplinary optimization models, and validating tests. Aircraft must be light, reliable, and high performance, with high safety margins, all while being low cost for operators.

I have seen many different technological insertion strategies and Dr. Taneja outlines several in this book. My thoughts on this are that one must simply have a logical technological insertion strategy that respects the time needed to develop and integrate that technology. It is a mathematical fact that a bunch of numbers less than one (element probability of success) multiplied together makes a number much less than one (net probability of success). Through multiple vehicle developments, I have learned to minimize the introduction of new technologies, carefully selecting ones that have high returns, but low risk and cost of development. Because much like aircraft operators need to be fiscally acute, we as developers need to do the same.

The pace of development in most technical fields is at a high and accelerating rate. The electric aircraft industry is no exception. In a handful of years, the industry has gone from small models and sketches to full-scale aircraft flying routinely in controlled airspace. This maturity step is often overlooked because, to a layman, a flying aircraft is a flying aircraft. In R&D experimental test flights everything is controlled. The weather is selected. Test points are modeled and simulated. The electric aircraft now flying in class C, B, and in the Washington DC FRZ are under the direction of Air Traffic Control (ATC) for speed, altitude, direction, and reasonable rates. A broad envelope of performance must be cleared by the vehicle developers and the regulators before this is allowed. We should all watch closely for vehicles that make this important step.

Flying in all weather conditions and at night will further differentiate those that are developing working aircraft from those developing demonstration aircraft. I was flying one of our electric aircraft Instrument Flight Rules (IFR) at night over the mountains of Vermont and New Hampshire just a few weeks ago, as part of our continuous cargo operational demonstrations. These experiences are very visceral reminders of the importance in a working aircraft of icing management, interior and exterior fog, navigation instrument immunity, and lightning strike protection. I don't believe a Visual Flight Rules (VFR) aircraft can be a working aircraft with any high utilization rate, a must for exploiting the benefits of low recurring cost of operation. Lightning does strike airplanes and designing for immunity is core to the basic architecture of electric aircraft, not something that can be "added later on."

Critics of battery electric aviation often ask, "Why don't you develop a fuel-cell hydrogen or diesel hybrid aircraft?" After a bit of head cocked stare, I typically draw a block diagram of a battery electric aircraft. After agreeing to the basic blocks, together we walk through and add the components needed to create a fuel-cell or diesel/gas hybrid aircraft. This brings on the realization that, in nearly all cases, the aircraft would need all the systems an electric aircraft needs — and then some. So, the fundamental platform for hybrid or hydrogen fuel-cell aircraft is an electric aircraft. As you will read Chapter 5 in this book, I think it is important to note this as it is a part of the technology insertion strategy.

We are in an amazing time for aviation. New technologies have opened doors to drastically improved operational economics and performance flexibility. We have set the table with a technology platform change that has unknowable potential to be built upon, likely including hybrid, hydrogen, autonomy, and other fascinating business models.

The leaders of the Advanced Air Mobility industry are now in the execution phase of industrialization, which will be followed closely by closing Type and Production Certification. Operational deployments have started first with the military and by early 2025 we will see several small operational commercial deployments. Some operators will be a part of the leading group pulling the industry forward, and others will draft off of their success. There are merits to both strategies, but I'm quite sure I know which group is more exciting and will leave their fingerprints on aviation forever.

Leahy Burlington International Airport, Vermont, USA

Foreword

Kevin E. Cox

Chief Executive Officer, Ferrovial Vertiports

Over 110 years ago, the world's first scheduled commercial passenger flight took off from St. Petersburg to Tampa, Florida, carrying a single passenger. In 2024, commercial airlines are expected to set a milestone and exceed pre-pandemic levels by carry over 9.4 billion passengers around the globe. The complexity of moving over 25.7 million passengers a day is difficult to comprehend, let alone to deliver upon, but that is exactly what airlines, airports, regulators, and various other service providers are expected to do in an ever-changing, complicated, and demanding environment.

In a similar trajectory, global investment in, and the development and deployment of, innovative technologies is occurring faster than at any time in history, setting the stage for transformational forms of air transportation to fundamentally change how we move to, through, and between cities.

Having spent my entire career in the aviation industry, I have had the honor of serving in executive leadership positions at some of the largest and most complex organizations, including one of the busiest airports in the world—DFW International Airport; the largest airline in the world—American Airlines; the largest FBO network in the world—Signature Aviation; and one of the largest aviation marketing, distribution, and fueling companies in North America—EPIC Fuels. Today, I have the distinct honor of working for Ferrovial, one of the largest and most successful infrastructure companies in the world who is at the forefront of investing, developing, and ultimately operating the critical infrastructure, which will be essential to bring this promising form of advanced air mobility into reality.

This diverse background provides me a unique perspective on how each element of the aviation ecosystem is critical to the overall success of the industry as a whole and how interdependent they are in order to ensure a safe, dependable, and customer-centric form of transportation. In short, we are at a real crossroads where the ever-growing complexity of the aviation ecosystem is confronted by the promises and challenges that technology can deliver to our industry.

Who is better positioned to tackle this tipping point in our industry than the prolific writer, educator, and trusted advisor—Nawal K. Taneja. With 15 acclaimed publications spanning all facets of our industry, he confronts, analyzes, and argues in his latest book that our collective success is tied to developing more holistic and resilient partnerships through real and thoughtful collaboration. This, his 16th publication in the series, ***Air Travel Partnerships: How to Create Greater Value through Collaboration***, delves deep into our industry.

He argues that the basic objective of delivering lean, innovative, and profitable businesses designed to elevate a traveler's experience has remained the same for decades; however, he challenges us to take the "revolutionary leaps" that will be necessary for us to develop meaningful partnerships founded on "proactive collaboration." He encourages us to avoid the inherent pitfalls of claiming that we are collaborating across our company and across the industry, while in fact reverting to our long-held tendencies of refusing or fearing to share data with others.

He challenges each of us in the industry to understand the real problems that have historically held back collaboration and postulates that truly holistic collaboration can only be achieved through a new lens focused more broadly across the aviation ecosystem, yet laser focused on the customer experience.

In the book, he focuses on four types of organizations within the air travel sector: airlines, airports, aircraft manufacturers, and travel intermediaries. For each, he provides a framework, tools, and insights formulated to enhance collaborations in an age of increasing uncertainty.

Topics discussed in some detail include the effective management of disruptions, potential transition from conventional interlining to self-connections and virtual connections, new segments of travel (Mobility-as-a-Service, eVTOLs, small electric airplanes for regional markets, and multimodal travel), and transformative technologies.

The book also provides real life examples of business transformations through collaborative partnerships in four other sectors: healthcare, automotive, telecommunications, and financial.

In summary, Nawal's latest publication is well worth immersing yourself in, no matter if you are new to the industry or a veteran, as it represents the ongoing contemporary thinking of its author and challenges each of us across the industry to rise to the occasion and deliver on the promise of the future.

Southlake, Texas, USA

Foreword

Scott DeFoe

Strategic Growth Initiative Director, Solventum (formerly 3M Health Care); Former Sr. Program Director, Strategic Innovation, Medtronic

As we stand on the brink of an era characterized by rapid technological advancement, partnerships emerge as pivotal components in the strategic arsenal of companies aiming to navigate the accelerating pace of change. Nawal Taneja illuminates the significance of forging and nurturing partnerships in the face of these evolving market dynamics. I whole-heartedly agree with Nawal in believing that partnerships are poised to become more strategically important as companies prepare themselves for the accelerated rate of change enabled by advancing technology including data science and predictive analytics, GenAI, LLMs, and digital twins.

Strategically establishing, deepening, and judiciously focusing on partnerships are essential to preparing companies to successfully navigate the accelerating change in the marketplace. As Nawal discusses in this book, partnerships will enable air travel providers to address important business imperatives including (1) building adaptable, resilient, and lean businesses, (2) achieving growth and innovation, (3) elevating traveler experience to a much higher level, and not to mention, (4) reducing the impact on the environment. Legacy competitors will need to extend their historic core competence and establish access to new resources (time, talent, infrastructure, customers, data, etc.). Partnerships are an attractive option uniquely poised to achieve this in a timely and affordable manner.

Based on my experience, when weighing options, it is essential to seek partners and areas of collaboration that are (a) important and (b) urgently timely for both parties. It is also vital to identify strategic initiatives that can be delivered better together than either side could realize independently. Aligned interests and motivation should unlock synergies and increase the probability of impactful success.

In particular, as the utility of AI models is improved by greater amounts and more diverse sources of data, data aggregation across partnerships provides an attractive opportunity to pursue win–win–win outcomes for partner companies and their customers. There are three basic categories of opportunities to solve business problems using AI. These distinct categories of applications include customer facing, functional management, and strategic business insights. With sales and marketing as one example, this function's applications include demand generation, sales enablement, customer segmentation, customer service, etc. AI can be used to identify and track behavior patterns that are elusive for even the most experienced human minds. Examples in healthcare and air travel would both include the management of customers, operations, and support functions (maintenance team schedule planning, etc.). I am particularly impressed by the incredible trajectory of AI-enabled solutions offering both vital insights to internal business processes and innovative new product features.

Generative AI holds the power to revolutionize the realms of air travel and healthcare work in several ways:

- Automation: It can handle various human tasks like customer support, content generation, and composing emails autonomously.
- Augmentation: Generative AI aids humans in enhancing their decision-making processes, facilitating quicker and more informed choices.
- Acceleration: It swiftly navigates through vast amounts of data, distilling and presenting its core insights efficiently so that they can be activated by humans at the desired moment in time.

While the final application of AI may seem straightforward, its success hinges on the robustness of the underlying AI stack, consisting of three fundamental elements. (1) The infrastructure layer encompasses crucial components like computer hardware and cloud platforms, providing the necessary backbone for AI operations to thrive. (2) Foundation models, whether open source or proprietary, form the bedrock of AI capabilities, serving as the building blocks upon which specific applications are constructed. (3) These applications, ranging from novel organizational structures to innovative partnerships and embedded use cases, represent the tangible manifestations of AI's transformative potential in various domains.

Many predict that the future will increasingly rely on data-driven approaches, acknowledging data as our most precious resource, often likened to currency or raw material. The rapid proliferation of smart devices and sensors, capable of capturing various forms of data such as images, sounds, and text, has expanded exponentially, unlocking opportunities previously unimaginable. When coupled with advancements in technology that automate analysis and extract timely insights from this data deluge, the outlook for the future appears exceptionally promising. AI applications are poised to further enhance a virtually unlimited array of data-driven decision-making processes, much like how Google Maps revolutionized navigation and Amazon transformed the shopping experience.

Not all data is created equally, however. The best data scientists or AI capabilities cannot "spin straw into gold." They cannot compensate for data that is inadequate – incomplete, unstructured, or riddled with errors. They may also be prohibited from using ideal data sources due to copyright or privacy limitations. As a result, data that is readily available, repeatably structured, and reliably accurate will enable the insights necessary to generate great value.

Satisfying the seemingly insatiable appetite that AI has for data will drive currently separate siloed data sources to be aggregated. Large volumes of this rich high-quality data will be coveted and are worth investments or are functions of new collaborative partnerships.

The air travel and healthcare industries feature a series of parallel challenges and corresponding solutions. Each depends upon a complex ecosystem with partnerships collaborating in and around vital infrastructure hubs of airports and hospitals. It both cases, customers value a seamless journey with predictable outcomes (on-time arrival and return to full health) and minimal complications. The proliferation of detailed data enables service providers to know these customers from a distance and more intimately than ever before. Digital transformation and aggregation of healthcare data across the multitude of times and places where it is collected remains elusive. Air travel is similar if one considers related data collected and stored by potential partners. AI will be a key tool in building adaptable, resilient, and lean businesses. AI-enabled innovation promises to improve both the workforce planning required to complete tasks that require particularly expensive/scarce specialized skills (e.g. mechanics for air travel and surgeons for healthcare) at the top of their license and tools (aircraft digital twins and robotic surgery).

Framing an AI Initiative in Healthcare using the Seven-step Business Model Canvas approach.

1. *Business problem*

In healthcare there are serious resource constraints and many unknowns concerning the efficiency and effectiveness of therapy delivery options competing for adoption. There is currently a lack of clear, adequately powered, and real-world data to inform selection of the most valuable options. AI will enable healthcare stakeholders to effectively analyze the overwhelmingly voluminous and complicated outcome data better than human experts have and to expertly tailor prescribed therapies on an individually customized basis.

2. *Business value*

Healthcare providers and suppliers that furnish clear compelling real-world evidence (insight derived from quality data) demonstrating that their offerings provide superior outcomes will be rewarded by markets (ability to charge a premium and or gain market share).

3. *Data strategy*

The surgical procedure involves scheduling the procedure time and selecting key surgical technique options; surgical tools are chosen based on their features, including the presence or absence of anti-microbial properties; the surgical infrastructure, including the room and its features, is taken into account; patient outcomes, such as survival rates and quality of life measures, are evaluated; and finally, the costs associated with all these factors are considered.

4. *Objective function*

One example of delivering a seamless patient journey is *freedom from infection* acquired during a surgical procedure or hospitalization. Features that could be used to predict outcomes include infrastructure (operating room design and features), surgical techniques and procedure times, and utilization of products (anti-microbial features, etc.).

5. *Modelling approach*

Mathematical regression techniques could be used to isolate the healthcare delivery variables that are predicted to economically impact infection rates so that best practices can be clarified and replicated by providers and rewarded by payers across healthcare practices.

6. *Model training*

As best practice hypotheses are developed and tested, new outcomes can be compared to both predicted outcomes and the previous standard of care to confirm cause and effect.

7. *Customer value*

More efficient utilization of constrained healthcare resources and improved outcomes for patients. Freedom from complications like infection.

A multitude of air travel business problems parallel these healthcare examples and could be modelled using a similar business canvas.

Pillars of my innovation and strategy philosophy:

- Begin with a compelling vision – know how your business and customers would be better after strategies have been successfully implemented. Prioritize the biggest impacts.
- Customer-centric begins with unmet needs and desired outcomes.
- Observe behavior. Note customer choices. Discover *why*? Begin but don't end with asking.
- Design thinking … Innovators define solutions to address important needs and deliver desired outcomes.
- Strategic plans are staffed and funded to achieve objectives. If adequate resources are not identified it is a strategic aspiration, not a strategic plan.
- Focus – the most important decisions may be the paths not taken and the discipline to stay the course unless the situation analysis changes.

True disruptive innovation fundamentally alters barriers that constrained utilization by enabling jobs to be completed at lower cost, with less expertise, or with less infrastructure. AI has already enabled and accelerated disruptive innovation by Netflix (displacing traditional brick and mortar media delivery) and Amazon (displacing traditional brick and mortar shopping). Companies like Netflix and Amazon have now conditioned customers to expect to be known and understood better. Their platforms leverage deep customer insights to provide unprecedented levels of individual customization. They engage with their customers almost instantaneously. Automation allows this customization that is affordable even at a grand scale. Jobs to be done for the customer … personalized recommendations, aid evaluation, potential solutions, and activate the choice that best satisfies their needs. Proliferation of detailed data enables us to know customers from a distance. By establishing strategic partnerships, air travel providers have a similar opportunity to solve longstanding business problems and create better value while improving the customer experience.

Begin with customer focus. Develop bold technology-enabled strategies. Stay focused to deliver successfully. Establish partnerships to do all of this better, faster, and cheaper.

In his insightful discourse, Nawal Taneja underscores the imperative of cultivating partnerships strategically to equip companies with the agility and resilience necessary for success amidst dynamic market landscapes. He delves into the multifaceted benefits partnerships offer, elucidating their pivotal role in fostering adaptable, resilient, and lean businesses while driving growth, innovation, and enhanced customer experiences across industries such as air travel.

Through compelling problem statement examples and strategic insights, Nawal navigates readers through the intricate terrain of partnership development and provides an inspiring call to action that should add to his legacy as a leading driver of air travel innovation by offering a roadmap for companies seeking to thrive in an era defined by relentless innovation and change.

Minneapolis, Minnesota, USA

Foreword

Frederic Deschamps

Former Senior Executive, Hertz, Expedia, Hilton, and Delta Air Lines

It's been an interesting journey to work at airlines, hotels and car rental businesses over the last 30 years as the travel space has once again reinvented itself. The main enabler is no doubt the advent of massive and cheap availability of data and computing power coupled to massive communication capability. It has allowed us to analyze where we used to estimate, and to test where we used to choose. Overall, we went from "we have experience with that" to "we have data for that".

The consequences have been far-reaching. What I observed across all three travel verticals is the ability to analyze accelerated innovation. Because large-scale testing became possible, like Expedia does, making it possible to run a continuous test bed of the booking path. Or because ideas can be de-risked by calculating the likelihood and value of success, like Hilton evaluating their loyalty pricing scheme prior to deployment. As a result, operations are more efficient than ever and able to take what used to be secondary concerns like waste and environmental footprint explicitly into account. Commercial activity is driven by ever better insight into the consumer to the point of anticipating needs and behavior. Areas that were already data-intensive, like revenue management, are now powered by streaming rather than batch data and processes. It all adds up to newer and faster operations and capabilities.

Ubiquitous and inexpensive data has also increased competition. Gone are the days of premium air carriers and discount air carriers. With troves of fresh data to inform pricing decisions, airlines, hotels and especially car rental companies can be priced at a discount one moment and at a premium the next, depending on supply and demand. Car rental companies can also continuously re-optimize capacity, by adjusting car fleet deployment as demand reveals itself. Some airlines practice some form of dynamic scheduling either by swapping aircraft or adjusting departure times. With lots of affordable and reliable data available, small competitors can be as smart as large competitors.

But for all of the change data has enabled, the space that I'm familiar with of air, hotel and car has not changed structurally all that much. Every company that has made it this far has deepened its expertise and has collectively improved its industry by most measures of success. But multi-modal improvements, be it across modes of transportation or between transportation and corollary activity, have been slower to come by. And that has made sense, since improvements in shared spaces are by definition only partially beneficial to participants. But we may well be at a point now, where the next opportunity in shared spaces is larger than the next opportunity in each company's own space, a point made well by Nawal Taneja in this book. Here are a few examples of such areas.

Share the customer. Which is not the same as "turn over your customer". Conventional marketing wisdom used to be that you succeed when you "own the customer". But the practical application has mostly been to service repeated patterns in a customer's history with timed and hopefully relevant content. And most customers don't want to be "owned" that way; it remains a fairly transactional relationship. The time when consumers might agree to be "owned" is when they try something new, something that is not in their discoverable history. Because when faced with the unknown, a consumer might accept trustworthy help to save them time and effort. The signal that a consumer is about to try something new necessarily exists outside the company's perimeter. The most common reaction to such a signal is for the donor company to link the consumer to the receiver company and for any subsequent transaction to be the responsibility of the receiver company. This burdens the consumer with complexity with no off-setting benefit. Wouldn't it be better if the relevant functionality is seamlessly presented in one place? Branding and settlement would need to be figured out, which can surely be done.

This idea of a seamless customer experience is not new, but is newly relevant with the proliferation of information and choice. In the 1980s, Richard Ferris as Chairman of Allegis Corporation had bought United Airlines, Hilton International, Westin and Hertz Car Rental. The motivation was to meet all of the traveler's needs "under one roof", with the means available at the time. Today, this can be done virtually, by sharing the relevant information instead of making the consumer hop from one portal to the next. This is one of the central points discussed in this book.

Note that in this construct, every participating provider gets all of the data. The consumer history is now enriched, and each provider can get closer to correctly anticipating consumer needs that they can address. Sure, there would be data privacy and confidentiality issues to address. But customers who are trying something new will be glad to get the help if the help is good.

Use complexity with caution. In a world where data is abundant and data processing is cheap, it is tempting to solve problems by applying massive computing to address every possible factor. We end up slicing and dicing every aspect because we can. And while in the short term, introducing additional complexity can generate additional gains, cumulatively it can become paralyzing. Consider the case of car rental pricing. The car rental industry has more degrees of freedom than the hotel or air travel space. It starts with around 44 car types, vs 1–5 cabin types and 5–20 room types. Car rental has a long history of using aggressive segmentation with those 44 car types to try to gain a temporary price advantage. It usually works, for a while. But over time, the car types have lost their meaning to the consumer and controlling billions of prices without unintended consequences becomes challenging. While each additional segmentation made sense, cumulatively they have resulted in a bewildering set of choices beyond what most consumers are willing to consider. If the only solution to a problem appears to be to do something complicated, think twice before going down that path.

Share the talent pool. Most companies face a simple fact: money and time can eliminate any competitive advantage. I'm convinced that the only resilient competitive advantage for a company comes from its people and how they are organized. The travel industry has been roiled by so many disruptions that it has been difficult to have a steady people plan. But the time may have come, when having one is as important as any investment to secure a company's future. By 2030, Gen Z will be the largest generation in the labor pool. There are significant indicators that Gen Z is distinct and different than its predecessors in how it thinks about work. LinkedIn's research strongly suggests that values alignment is a determinant in where Gen Z'ers work and how engaged they are. The Gallup Workplace 2023 Report shows that 60% of today's workforce (including Gen Z'ers) is quietly quitting and 40% of those give "culture" as the main reason. So, work culture matters more than before, but how can that be operationalized? One way is to finally get serious about the work culture fit aspect of hiring. Skills assessments are fairly reliable, but for front line positions especially, cultural fit is difficult to assess at scale. There are tools available to do this reliably now, however. Imagine, if every potential employee had work values coordinates, in addition to skills coordinates, and could find a job they not only will be good at but will like and therefore will stay with. Companies would need to publish objectively measured work values; job seekers would need to publish theirs. The resulting better hiring would result in longer tenures, which help build institutional knowledge and turn jobs into careers.

By keeping things reasonably simple, by sharing the customers and sharing the talent pool, companies may find that the next best growth opportunity lies outside of their immediate perimeter.

In this latest book, Nawal Taneja skillfully explores these and other topics. This book is a great read in its own right and certainly a helpful read for practitioners who are looking to explore what lies ahead, why and how to prepare for it.

Minneapolis, Minnesota, USA

Foreword

David Franks

Investor & Finance Director, Protect Group

The importance of ancillaries in curating a customer-centric offer to develop airlines as retailers

It is a pleasure for me to contribute a foreword to Nawal's latest book, *Air Travel Partnerships: How to Create Greater Value through Collaboration*. I had the pleasure to meet and spend time with Nawal at the International Airline Symposium in Vietnam in February 2024. What shone through was his knowledge, passion and commitment for the airline industry, and the idea of fostering partnerships to drive lasting change through the embrace of technology. At the Protect Group, we firmly believe in developing trusted partnerships to deliver value for our partners and their customers.

As the airline industry moves steadily towards a world of offers and orders, it is essential to know who your customers are and how you add value through the products you can offer in your owned channels – web, mobile and NDC.

Ancillary selling as we know it really began with the advent of e-commerce and the rise of Low Cost Carriers (LCCs) such as easyJet and Ryanair, who unbundled the traditional all-inclusive proposition of Full Service Carriers (FSCs), stripped the offer back to the seat, significantly reducing the lead-in cost of a flight, then adding such items as seat selection and hold-baggage as optional extras. Not every customer flying needed a bag, and some were prepared to pay a little extra for better seats. These airlines were able to reduce costs and start curating an offer of products that customers were (and weren't) willing to pay for. The success of this approach is borne out by the success of these airlines, the growth of other LCCs, particularly in shorthaul markets, and the fact that FSCs started to unbundle their own fare products. They say imitation is the sincerest form of flattery.

At the same time, one thing we are increasingly conscious of is "ancillary fatigue" – the prospective passenger can be tired by having to look at so many alternatives and this friction could lead to a lost sale.

However, the central premise here, and it's our core principle at the Protect Group, is **know your customer**. By starting out with an unbundled proposition, LCCs set expectations low and built from there – the focus on price, and cost, was all-encompassing. FSCs, who had a quite different customer base, responded by reducing their proposition and then selling it back to the customer. It's worth noting the initial reaction from customers when the likes of British Airways and Lufthansa first removed inflight meals on shorthaul flights and started selling food and beverages onboard.

The ancillary products referred to above are what we know as "owned ancillaries". These are ancillaries that the airline produces itself, prices and merchandises to customers either in its direct or indirect channels. Other examples include priority boarding and inflight WiFi. As airlines developed as retailers, they began to offer additional content that they did not own – third party content. Typically, these were products associated with air travel, such as hotel accommodation and car hire. Often, these would take the form of a web redirect to a different website, or they would be included in the e-commerce channel, either in the booking flow or the post-booking environment. As tech capabilities have developed, airlines have become better at incorporating these products into their own channels and tailoring the offer to the customer, but we still have some way to go to deliver a truly curated offer that talks to a travelling customer's requirements on a specific journey.

At the Protect Group, we identified the lack of protection for tickets in industries such as music and sports events. We developed our business by offering embedded refund protection in the event that somebody was not able to attend for a reason beyond their control. As we grew in these verticals, we recognised that the majority of airline sales are in non-refundable and semi-flexible fare categories. With airlines rapidly developing their ability to integrate API content into their booking flow over the last decade or so, we began to offer refund protection in these fare families. Just because somebody is booking in a lower fare class doesn't mean they don't want protection – they're just more price sensitive about it. A family of four may have even more need of protection, but they're also less likely to be looking to buy four fully flexible tickets for a flight.

There are other new and exciting products being developed, including the popular CFAR (Cancel For Any Reason), but airlines and retailers need to think carefully about the products and services they offer. CFAR is a brand-new untested product not normally backed by insurance companies, instead relying on a non-insurer's balance sheet. There's no regulatory capital requirement and no external scrutiny of the liabilities incurred by the non-insurer provider. Any failure will reflect badly on the airline.

AI and machine-learning allow us to constantly optimise our price and product proposition, and as we work with airlines (and other online retailers), we take these learnings with us to refine our proposition to offer maximum value to our partners and their customers. Our data insights enable us to curate this offer. Moreover, with our dynamic widget, we are able to offer an airline the products that they need that are missing from their portfolio, in a single integration. As they develop their own data insights, this in turn will allow them to generate an a la carte offer for different customers in their booking flow, beyond the standard price points and optional extras that have typified airline retailing for too long.

Of equal importance is using technological advances to ensure that the customer receives the best possible servicing when availing themselves of services such as Refund Protect. We employ AI to optimise our refund processes, giving customers a fast and easy way to interact with us. The results are borne out in the experiences our partners and their customers have, and the Trustpilot scores we achieve – over 28,000 reviews at 4.8.

The best bit of all this? Not only are the airlines developing their retail proposition and improving customer satisfaction, they are also able to generate incremental ancillary revenue. It's a win–win that has the customer at the heart of the retailing journey.

London, UK

Foreword

Katsuya Goto

Member of the Board, Executive Vice President, All Nippon Airways Co., Ltd.

The aviation industry is currently undergoing a dynamic transformation fueled by the evolution of airline partnerships. I will explore, in this foreword, the changing landscape of airline collaborations and delve into the future of airline joint ventures, which are reshaping the industry and fostering innovation in the aviation ecosystem.

Airline partnerships have evolved significantly over time. Initially, partnerships were limited to codeshare agreements and interline collaborations aimed at expanding route networks and enhancing connectivity. However, with the increasing complexity of the global aviation market, airlines realized the need for deeper and more comprehensive partnerships.

In the ever-evolving aviation industry, global alliances have become powerful networks that foster collaboration and innovation. These alliances, such as Star Alliance, oneworld, and SkyTeam, serve as platforms for airlines to connect, cooperate, and expand their reach. Within these alliances, airlines began to form new strategic partnerships called joint ventures, taking collaboration to the next level.

Amid intense competition and changing market dynamics, a subject discussed at length in this book, airline joint ventures have emerged as powerful mechanisms for growth and sustainability. These joint ventures involve multiple airlines pooling their resources, expertise, and networks to create synergies and deliver enhanced services to passengers. Joint ventures allow airlines to tap into new markets, optimize fleet utilization, and provide seamless travel experiences, ultimately increasing customer satisfaction.

Airline joint ventures offer several advantages to both airlines and passengers. For airlines, these partnerships provide access to a wider customer base, increased operational efficiency, and cost savings through economies of scale. Joint ventures also enable airlines to coordinate schedules, optimize flight connections, and streamline customer services, resulting in a seamless and hassle-free travel experience for passengers. Moreover, joint ventures foster collaboration in areas such as technology innovation, environmental sustainability, and talent development.

As the aviation industry continues to evolve, the future of airline joint ventures looks promising. Technological advancements play a crucial role in shaping this future, as the industry embraces digitalization, artificial intelligence, and data analytics to enhance operational efficiency, revenue management, and customer experiences. Nawal Taneja discusses emerging technologies and their role in the management and operation of airlines at great length in this book, particularly in Chapter 6. And joint ventures allow airlines to share technological expertise, collaborate on innovation, and create new solutions that benefit the entire industry.

The airline industry is experiencing a transformation in how airline partnerships are structured, the theme of this book. This shift is driven by the introduction of Offers and Orders, the rise of Low-Cost Carriers (LCCs), and the advancement of Virtual Interline technology. These factors reshape airline partnerships and create new opportunities for collaboration and connectivity. Offers and Orders streamline the creation and management of airline offers, allowing for personalized bundles that enhance the travel experience and increase revenue. LCCs, with their low-cost model, bring new partnership opportunities and expand network connectivity. Virtual Interlines facilitate seamless connections between airlines without the need for physical codeshare agreements and provide more diverse and flexible travel options for passengers.

These changes present airlines with opportunities to enhance network connectivity, increase ancillary revenue, penetrate new markets, and deliver customer-centric experiences. By embracing these shifts and adapting partnership strategies, airlines can remain competitive and provide enhanced travel experiences in a rapidly evolving industry.

Furthermore, environmental sustainability is a growing concern in the aviation industry, and joint ventures play a vital role in addressing this challenge. By sharing resources and best practices, and investing in eco-friendly technologies, airline partnerships reduce carbon emissions, promote sustainable aviation, and support the industry's commitment to environmental stewardship.

Additionally, competition authorities closely monitor airline joint ventures to ensure fair competition in the industry. As the aviation sector becomes increasingly globalized, airline alliances and partnerships have become more common. However, this trend has also raised concerns about potential anticompetitive behavior. In response, competition authorities adopt a cautious approach, carefully reviewing and scrutinizing these joint ventures to maintain a level playing field.

The evolution of airline partnerships and the rise of joint ventures redefine the future of the aviation industry. These collaborations unlock new opportunities for growth, innovation, and customer-centric service offerings. Joint ventures enable airlines to forge strategic alliances, leverage synergies, and create a sustainable and interconnected aviation ecosystem. The future of airline partnerships is bright, with continued advancements in technology, expansion into new markets, and a shared commitment to providing exceptional travel experiences for passengers worldwide. As the industry continues to evolve, airline joint ventures will undoubtedly play a pivotal role in shaping the future of air travel.

Tokyo, Japan

Foreword

Subodh Karnik

Former Aviation CEO/Executive – ExpressJet, ATA, Delta, Fareportal, Jet Airways, ICF-SH&E, and others

Nobody wants customers to be unhappy – not Singapore Airlines nor Ryanair, not Changi nor Newark-in-a-snowstorm, and definitely not their travel agency. Everyone wants those enigmatic travelers not only to be "satisfied" but to have their expectations exceeded.

But today's travel comes with no guarantee that the disparate pieces that constitute the journey will work even remotely as planned. Be it instantly changing ticket prices, uncertain availability of airport parking, becoming a random selectee at security, scrambling to deal with an airport gate change, or the chaos at the baggage carousel – a traveler feels helpless and at the mercy of fragmented pieces of information as soon as they begin planning their itinerary. And they are convinced that when things go wrong, because of severe weather or an airline/airport operations hiccup, all stakeholders will simply pass the buck while leaving them stranded!

Decades of consumer research has pointed to two feelings that elude travelers: (a) being in control and (b) believing that travel providers will work together to execute a service recovery. Even the toughest type A road warrior laments that, as soon as they begin their travel journey, they feel like a pimply teenager on a first date or like someone getting on a roller coaster ride on a full tummy.

Why does a global air transportation system that flies more than four billion passengers in much the same way, not really work together to always deliver a seamless and reliable product to the traveler – let alone elevate their travel experience and meet their changing needs? Mood lighting in the airplane or the self-playing piano in the airport atrium do not obfuscate the fact that airlines, airports, travel agencies, and others do not, together, find ways to always deliver for the customer.

Nawal Taneja, in this latest book, addresses the core reasons for this lack of reliability and dependability head on:

- The first chapter lists the ten systemic reasons for this inability by the major providers – the aircraft manufacturers, the airlines, the airports, and the ticket distributors – to help the customer regain control.

- And then the book quickly gets to the underlying cause – namely the inability for these integral parts of the travel ribbon to COORDINATE, COOPERATE, and (even!) COLLABORATE in a manner that would provide a holistic solution to the traveler that is greater than the sum of its parts.

Throughout, Nawal avers that collaborative partnerships are fundamental to (i) delivering and even elevating the customer experience and (ii) a travel provider's ability to remain lean, resilient, and adaptable to the changing marketplace.

Across the various chapters, Nawal takes us from the tactical to the massively innovative: (a) Starting with the need for cooperating and sharing data between travel experience providers to make the journey seamless; (b) To discussing the focus on multi-modal and cooperatively designed elements of the journey – be it train stations at airports or the equitable sharing of gates to benefit the customer; (c) And eventually highlighting innovations that are in the works – eVTOL vertiports and such. The common theme in the broad canvas of his book is the essential need for all players to coordinate–cooperate–collaborate.

I can point to several attempts from my experience at such collaboration and customer control – some even successful: Intense discussions during an aircraft manufacturer's design phase on the importance of carry-on bags and their effect on the airport/airline process; Designing *Flight Bank*, a super-simple virtual coupon-book program for Hawaii–California commuters; Helping implement *World Business Class*, the first audio-video at-seat-on-demand IFE; Building a gating algorithm to minimize the number of 35-minute physical (terminal A to E) connections at Atlanta; and many others.

One down-to-earth area of cooperation–collaboration is worth elaborating. When we were designing the first modern global airline alliance, at Northwest–KLM, "Seamless Service" and "Global Reliability" were the laudable core tenets of the relationship. Over the years, the airlines successfully collaborated to make incompatible airport and operations systems exchange data in real time, instantly confirm a reservation and seats for the whole itinerary, align handling, boarding, and inflight procedures, even design the common business class mentioned above. So, today you can attach your special meal or wheelchair request to every segment of the multi-airline itinerary and even check current ETA/ETD on either airline's website. These were revolutionary developments 30 years ago – but are taken for granted today. Even with all the progress, however, all alliances have found it difficult to collaborate in one area that has meant countless sweaty palms and missed flights – the ability to check in at the airport, with bags, at the counter of ANY alliance partner. There are countless "reasons" why that has proven difficult – mostly attributable to the complexity of multiple airlines, airport baggage handling systems, security screening, liability issues, etc. But this has resulted in hundreds of daily occurrences of customers showing up at the wrong terminal ("but I booked my flight on Airline XX – how was I to know that I was supposed to check in with Airline YY at the other terminal?"). Alliance collaboration has come a long way – but with some ways to go.

After five decades of leadership in his field, Nawal Taneja can simultaneously be a visionary and a pragmatist! And he articulates the hurdles to progress – the need to "own" customer information, the divergent planning horizons of airports and airlines, real-estate (gates and such) as a competitive weapon, the practical ability to share and use data, and other topics. This book is thought-provoking reading for the practitioner as they navigate through their medium- and long-term plans and focus on how to collaborate with their partners to deliver a quality product and to develop corporate resilience and flexibility.

Atlanta, Georgia, USA

Foreword

Kerem Kızıltunç

Chief Information Officer, Turkish Airlines and Chief Executive Officer, Turkish Technology

As those who work in aviation, a dynamic and ever-developing industry, we are at a very important crossroads. With the convergence of new technologies, changing traveler demands, and the emergence of new competition, we are witnessing a profound transformation in the landscape of air travel. Nawal K. Taneja's newest book accurately captures these changes in a timely and insightful manner, providing stakeholders with a roadmap to navigate the complexities and capitalize on the opportunities this new era presents.

In this detailed study, Taneja touches on the main factors that force us to change and reveals what needs to be done to cope with change, in a relatable way. These drivers of change, along with the changing expectations of travelers and the rise of competition, have the potential to fundamentally alter the fabric of the aviation industry. The book states that the key to success is for stakeholders to embrace proactive collaboration. He convincingly argues that to provide added value, the key is to establish new partnerships that transcend existing boundaries, thus renewing old processes and enhancing the passenger experience.

New technological advances are the driving force behind transformation initiatives. The pace of progress in the fields of large language models, generative AI, and digital twins forces all kinds of companies, including airlines, to recognize these technologies, reshape their perspective and develop projects in areas where they can be applied. The main expectation in these new initiatives is to make more accurate decisions in a much shorter time by redefining and enriching the parameters in the decision-making stage. When we consider digital twins as an example, we see the potential to create a virtual copy of physical assets such as aircraft and engines. By doing so, monitoring these digital models in real time will help to optimize performance and allow prediction of maintenance requirements with a richer data set. Alongside these new technologies, legacy systems and processes are some of the most vital components in an airline's transformation journey. It is necessary to examine in detail what needs to be done to change the processes that have been in use for more than 60 years and to reshape them from the perspective of airline-specific strategies and ways of doing business. This is where this book comes into play and explains to the reader the best practices not only in the aviation industry but also in other sectors, with spot-on examples.

One of the aspects of this book that appealed to me most is its emphasis on the traveler experience. People are at the core of changes, and every successful change initiative has successfully addressed the human factor. In the world we live in, meeting customers' demands has become a vital phenomenon for companies to remain competitive. When we consider the increasing customer expectations, it is obvious that we need more value-oriented and sustainable criteria instead of the metric-based value judgments of today's world. As Taneja accurately puts it, travelers cannot be responsible for the complexity of current processes. All stakeholders in the travel ecosystem have a responsibility and a substantial role for a simpler and more environmentally friendly, sustainable future. To provide end-to-end friction-free and uninterrupted service to travelers, it is essential that all players in the travel ecosystem, beyond the airlines, contribute to the solution with a collaborative temperament. To improve end-to-end travel for travelers, stakeholders of all roles and responsibilities in the travel ecosystem need to come together and cooperate. Through collaboration between stakeholders in the travel ecosystem, empathy will be heightened in understanding the challenges faced by the parties in their respective verticals. In this way, more effective solutions fueled by synergy can be reached by providing transparency, especially in critical areas such as regulatory compliance and data sharing.

This book is a call to action to pave the way for change, as well as a guide to achieving a successful change. In addition to defining the drivers of change in a very tangible manner, it describes what needs to be done on the road to change. It encourages readers to generate ideas about proactive actions for addressing the challenges of change and share these ideas with other stakeholders.

At the point of solving such a multi-faceted, complex and multi-stakeholder equation, the insights of a seasoned and competent name like Taneja, resulting from his inter-industry knowledge and analysis ability, are invaluable. It is a must-read for those who want to take a leading role in this change by enriching their knowledge with useful information about current status and the actions required to embrace the future to take necessary measures before the next radical change disrupts us.

Istanbul, Turkey

Foreword

Anand Lakshminarayanan

Divisional Senior Vice President, Revenue Optimisation, Order Management & Airline Partnerships, Emirates Airline

Air travel partnerships is not a commercial requirement but a strategic imperative in the post-Covid new normal, as the airline industry is undergoing significant changes in recent years adapting to the evolving needs and higher expectations of travellers.

Airlines are increasingly using data and technology to personalize the customer experience, understanding clearly the customer needs through data analytics and predictive modelling, as opposed to providing customer experience based on airlines' perception. This includes personalized offers, targeted promotions, and tailored services based on customer preferences and behaviour. In order for the airline retailing to be effective and rewarding, there is a need to deliver consistent customer experience across the entire spectrum of the customer journey. Therefore, it is critical there is active collaboration between partners across the ecosystem to ensure the customer experience is seamless and consistent.

There is plenty of scope to introduce innovation across many domains to enrich the customer experience – these could be reducing the physical contact between the customers and service providers' frontline staff, instead using technology such as biometrics to ensure touch-free but efficient clearance of customers at every touch point,.agile recovery of lapses in customer service via quick and seamless information flow, use of artificial intelligence to study customer behaviour and expectations, and providing curated services based on insights to name a few.

The book touches upon very relevant topics that are currently in focus with airline CEOs – to deliver a top-notch customer experience in the very demanding post-Covid world. The book also emphasizes self-service by customers, which is the expectation of modern-day travellers who do not like to reach out to the contact centre of the service provider via chat or telephone, instead preferring to take greater control of their travel itinerary themselves electronically.

The author aptly touches upon the critical need to transform the collaboration between partners in the air travel ecosystem, moving away from the traditional practice based on fragmented and incremental steps towards improving coordination. This initiative entails unison of objectives, clearer understanding of the current failures in seamless customer experience, modern air traveller expectations which are more sophisticated, technology investment and high degree of data analytics, insights and agility in the handshake of customer data across the ecosystem, notwithstanding ring-fenced customer data privacy.

The inter-modal partnerships during pre-Covid days had moved away from the traditional air-to-air connections, shifting the focus to air–rail connections. This has further transformed in recent years as the industry is looking into expanding connectivity to coach, ferry, helicopter, and other travel modes. An interesting transformation is currently under way where airlines would soon be foraying into inducting eVTOL to provide first- and last-mile connectivity to customers, which not only provides novelty to traveller experience but also is expected to deliver cost-effective and timely connectivity between airports and final destinations in larger metropolises.

The author's depth of knowledge on industry transition and transformation is evident from a variety of functional domains he discusses in the book. It is pertinent to highlight that the author's best practice advocacies are not theoretical but practical and implementable. Dr Nawal Taneja is an exponent in the aviation industry and his immense contribution to the industry practitioners and followers is significant and invaluable. In this book, he has touched upon the topical subject that is in the wish list of many airline CEOs, as such a timely contribution to the industry.

Dubai, UAE

Foreword

Puneet Mahindroo

Group Director, Revenue Management and Distribution, COMO Hotels and Resorts, Singapore

In an era defined by rapid technological advancements and shifting global paradigms, the aviation industry stands at a critical juncture. *Air Travel Partnerships: How to Create Greater Value through Collaboration* by Nawal Taneja is a timely masterpiece that addresses the pressing need for innovative collaboration across the air travel sector.

The aviation world is increasingly complex and unpredictable, influenced by emerging technologies like generative AI, predictive analytics, and digital twins, alongside the evolving demands of travelers. These changes call for a fundamental shift in how industry stakeholders, including airlines, airports, and service providers, collaborate and innovate to enhance efficiency, customer experience, and sustainability. In my career, spanning two decades in the hospitality industry, in various hotel and corporate-level roles in marketing, revenue management, and distribution, I have dealt with similar developments and have seen the value of proactive partnerships to grow and innovate.

Nawal Taneja, with his profound expertise and forward-thinking approach, masterfully outlines the necessity for an integrative approach to problem-solving in this high-stakes industry. Based on my service as the Asia Pacific Chair to the HSMAI Revenue Management Advisory Board, the Asia Pacific Chair on the Board of Directors of Hotel Electronic Distribution Networking Association, and a member of the Leading Hotels of the World International Rooms, Revenue Management and Distribution Advisory Board, I can say that this book is not just a call to action—it is a roadmap for building resilient, adaptable businesses that can thrive amid uncertainties and capitalize on new opportunities. It delves into the complexities of managing disruptions, the potential of new travel modalities like eVTOLs, and the transformative impact of technologies that can create seamless, stress-free travel experiences.

The insights presented in this book are not isolated to the aviation sector; they resonate across various industries facing similar challenges of technological disruption and consumer-driven change. Through examples from the healthcare, automotive, telecommunications, and financial sectors, the book illustrates the universal relevance of collaborative innovation.

As we navigate this ever-changing landscape, *Air Travel Partnerships* serves as an essential guide for anyone involved in the aviation industry or any sector, for example, hospitality, where strategic partnerships are key to overcoming challenges and driving success. It inspires not just understanding and adaptation, but a proactive approach to reshaping the future of business and customer engagement in air travel and beyond.

This book is a beacon for all stakeholders in the aviation industry, urging them to look beyond traditional practices and to forge partnerships that can withstand and leverage the winds of change. Let us take this journey together, guided by the expert insights and visionary perspective of Nawal Taneja.

Singapore, Singapore

Foreword

Arjan Meijer

President & CEO, Embraer Commercial Aviation

The introduction of a new technology, or the acceleration of its development, often occurs following a period of acute shock. The oil crises of the early and late 1970s heralded a new era of conservation and sovereign energy policy. The 2008 collapse of international financial markets revolutionized digital banking services, and the 2019 global pandemic fueled e-commerce and gave sustainability a seat at corporate boardroom tables and product development desks.

The pandemic also radically changed commercial air travel, for airlines, their passengers, and the complex supply chain that serves them all. This includes Embraer, which manufactures small narrowbody aircraft that operate predominantly on short-haul flights. The changes are present in five areas.

Environment

The call for greener energy to power new aircraft has brought development, mass-scale production, and distribution of Sustainable Aviation Fuel (SAF) to the forefront. Suppliers are working with manufacturers to refine propulsion concepts using electricity, hydrogen, and hybrid concepts to curb polluting emissions. Policymakers and travelers are increasingly vocal about the urgency for more environmentally responsible aircraft to reduce the aviation industry's carbon footprint.

Greater Efficiency and Cost-Effectiveness

Supply chain disruptions forced airlines and manufacturers to review product, process, and procurement efficiency. New technologies helped reduce aircraft fuel consumption, maintenance, and operating costs. We have implemented sweeping changes in our own production methods and collaborated with our suppliers to make materials lighter, more durable, and less polluting. All these initiatives contribute to greater efficiency, and to keeping production costs in check. This, in turn, ensures the economic viability of an airline's operations and the continued sustainable growth of its network.

Technological Advancements

Smaller aircraft often serve as an ideal entry point for new technologies before being scaled up to, and adopted on, larger platforms. Post-pandemic, we are seeing greater use of composite materials in airframes and structures, and more widespread additive manufacturing. New low- or zero-emission propulsion systems will be first deployed on small narrowbody aircraft in the short-haul segment before eventually rippling out to the larger narrowbody and widebody types.

Maintaining Network Connectivity

Short-haul air service is vital to smaller cities, towns, and regional hubs. The shift to work-from-home arrangements has accelerated the migration of people from large urban centers, and has placed a new emphasis on maintaining efficient, cost-effective flights for these communities. Smaller aircraft are ideal for providing the right balance of frequency and capacity to connect passengers with airlines' broader networks. That connectivity, in turn, generates economic and social benefits.

Competition and Market Dynamics

New technology aircraft can disrupt the norm as airlines often find themselves compelled to modernize their fleets to stay competitive. Ultimately, all stakeholders in the aviation value chain benefit when new technology aircraft are brought to market: passengers enjoy a more comfortable onboard experience, airlines realize the economic upside of operational efficiencies, and the broader community benefits from cleaner and quieter aircraft. Embraer has already adopted many new technologies on our aircraft being delivered to airline customers today, positioning them at the fore of the industry's pivot to a more sustainable future.

Indeed, if there remains a lasting effect of the global pandemic on the aviation industry, it is the reminder of the importance of constant innovation, one of the main themes that Professor Taneja thoughtfully examines throughout this book. Our industry's agility, as well as its focus on ensuring an open and collaborative ecosystem for development, will ensure that the next generation of aircraft will continue to transform commercial aviation for the welfare of society and the planet.

São José dos Campos, São Paulo, Brazil

Foreword

Stefanie Neumann

Chief Executive Officer, Lufthansa Systems

In the rapidly evolving landscape of the airline industry, the need for collaboration has never been more crucial. As Nawal Taneja explores in his book, the future of aviation depends on the ability of stakeholders to work together in innovative and meaningful ways.

To truly unlock the potential of these partnerships, every collaboration in the aviation industry should be digitally enabled.

At Lufthansa Systems, we are specialists in the potential of digital innovation to transform the collaborative processes of various stakeholders within the aviation industry.

Artificial intelligence and machine learning have already been incorporated into our products. For instance, our innovations are utilizing these tools to assist decision-makers in the aviation industry in network planning and turnaround management. Given the crucial role of cost reduction and efficiency in our industry, it can be assumed that the number of data-driven solutions will increase in the near future.

These examples illustrate Taneja's insight into the significance of employing digital tools and data-driven insights to facilitate proactive collaboration.

The use of technologies that apply AI and data science will be essential to building an adaptable, resilient, and efficient business as we navigate the complexities and uncertainties of the modern aviation market.

Nawal Taneja's book provides a comprehensive framework for stakeholders to embrace the power of collaboration to ensure a brighter, more innovative future for the aviation industry.

Frankfurt, Germany

Foreword

Heather Passe

Former Senior Executive, C.H. Robinson, Regis Corporation, Carlson Hotels, and Delta Air Lines

The rate of change in the aviation industry continues to accelerate, and the only thing for certain is that more change is on the horizon. Aviation has always been fast-paced and wonderfully complex. That is why it attracts some of the brightest minds, people who desire the chance to tackle an ever-growing list of challenges. This is not a sector for the faint of heart. But, for those who relish this industry, they don't see themselves as gluttons for punishment; rather, each new day brings a gift, a cornucopia of unpredictable challenges and puzzles, with no easy answers, that beckon to be solved.

You either love this business or you sort of just hate it; and although I have been fortunate enough to have C-suite experience in a few different industries, I also happen to be one of the airline afflicted. Accordingly, I was happy to have the opportunity to read Nawal Taneja's new book, *Air Travel Partnerships: How to Create Greater Value through Collaboration*.

New technology, new traveler expectations, new competitors, and new service providers are all merely select examples of forces that are converging to impact the future of air travel. In his new book, Mr. Taneja argues that the aviation sector is going to need to deepen collaboration (internally and externally) if it plans to not just meet the onslaught of these changes, but to thrive. The premise of the book is that to build agile, resilient businesses that foster growth and innovation and delight travelers, requires collaboration among multiple parties within the travel ecosystem.

The case for collaboration is clear. Airlines are among the most complex business models. Add numerous forces of change, legacy systems, and legacy processes to the already inherent complexity, and airlines have some pretty tough puzzles to solve. There isn't a single complex business problem that doesn't require collaboration – collaboration internally across functions within an organization and externally across organizations. Tackling complex challenges requires finding top talent and bringing together colleagues (co-creators) with diverse skill sets and perspectives to achieve uncommon results – results that no one individual or organization could actually achieve alone.

Make no mistake about it, airlines are filled with bright people that have found ways to innovate and succeed, but many challenges still remain. For example, airlines that are truly using all of the data they possess to deliver holistic, seamless end-to-end experiences are few and far between. In a recent personal incident, a return flight of mine was canceled due to weather. Weather is not within the control of an airline, but how it handles service recovery is within its control, and it leaves a lasting impression (positive or negative) of the airline and the sector. In this particular instance, I wasn't warned my flight was canceled until I arrived at the airport. At that point, I stood in a sea of hundreds of angry people – all of whom were being serviced by two lone customer service employees. After over an hour of snaking through a hot, dirty room, filled wall to wall with people, I made it to the agent, who told me there was a flight I could take, but he didn't have the authority to book me on it. I asked about whether someone inside security might be able to book the flight. He said "perhaps," but the security lines were much longer than the one I had been in, and they were even shorter staffed inside security. While in line, I heard travelers saying, next time, they planned to book airline 'x' because the extra dollars they saved booking airline 'y' weren't worth it. With collaboration, an airline can build experiences and a brand that travelers prefer and drive growth for itself and the industry at large.

What if I (and the hundreds of other passengers) had been notified ahead of time and given meaningful options to rebook our flights ourselves? The self-service model using technology, data, and collaboration has profound implications for both traveler and employee satisfaction. Imagine how many incremental trips would be booked each year if travel journeys were stress-free? Or, how many more airline employees would be attracted and retained, instead of opting out after days like I described above?

Similarly, what if airlines used all of the data they have on customers' interactions with them to truly personalize the entire end-to-end experience – from shopping to booking to inflight travel and beyond. The online retailing and service recovery implications are almost limitless for airlines. Airlines are filled with distinct, expert-filled departments who are often weighed down by legacy technology and processes. These are some of the reasons why collaboration with multiple stakeholders across the value chain is critical for the next frontier of customer, employee, and shareholder value creation.

The aviation sector is incredibly innovative, resilient, and successful. It is estimated that global passenger volume reached almost nine billion passengers carried in 2023. Airlines take these travelers thirty thousand feet above the ground, safely, and in doing so, make the world a smaller, more connected, understanding place. In the next chapter of aviation, the airlines that also figure out the collaboration equation will be the ones who reap the spoils of today's rapidly evolving landscape.

Minneapolis, Minnesota, USA

Foreword

Stuart Waldron

Director, Open Travel Alliance, and Leader of the Travel Special Interest Group at OpenAPI; Former Senior Executive, Travelport, Amtrak, IBM

I will focus on a few points made in Chapters 1 and 7 of this book by Nawal Taneja. A key question in Chapter 1 is: "How can travelers take greater control of their trips?" In Chapter 7, the author discusses four basic pillars for the development of a productive collaboration within different stakeholders in the travel ecosystem. But first let me discuss the situation today with APIs.

In travel APIs today there is horrendous redundancy resulting in huge amounts of costly labor. The most used API is availability of services. There are more than 1000 bespoke availability APIs that do the same thing. There is no competitive advantage to how one availability API works with another, certainly not at the schema and behavior level. Each of those bespoke APIs cause the API consumer to write bespoke code to work with them. It is not just schema differences. There are also syntactical and semantic differences resulting in elements in the message that do not mean what one thinks they mean. Workflows are rarely documented and, if they are, usually they are out of date. At the GDS, where they must deal with all of this, it could take six months to onboard a new provider of travel products, instead of six weeks, or less. All deal with this problem, not just channels, as nearly all travel providers, which are API providers, are also API consumers. At a conceptual level the answer is simple. Think about open-source code efforts, and as a community, start creating and publishing open-source APIs that cover 80% to 90% functionality of the most common booking workflows. As well as OpenTravel, I also run the OpenAPI SIG-travel team. Using the specifications from OAI, there is a means for those that extend the open-source APIs to explain what was done. What the API provider did differently is documented in a machine-readable standard that can be used to automatically (AI/ML-based) handle these relatively minor differences. Why could Gen AI not be used to do that now? Is it a behavior chaos and semantics issue? I work with a startup trying to use LLM to generate code to read today's APIs. However, it needs good data (semantics issue), and a stream of current API use, to train a model. Not a lot of channels want to hand over an API trace so a startup can do what they do cheaper.

A few more fundamentals to think about:

- There is no travel industry-wide definition or standard relating to what an "offer" or an "order" contains or how it behaves. IATA has a unique definition that attempts to be compatible with the legacy PNR. That raises a question. I published elsewhere the "tube with seats" problem. The PNR today makes all products (hotel, car, cruise, insurance, etc.) look like a tube with seats to be compatible with existing PSS and GDS systems. Even if one has moved off the mainframe, the knock-on effects are still there. Then there is the OpenTravel order/offer definition for all verticals, but it does need some work. An offer/order must be agnostic to the product, price, and terms and conditions (Ts&Cs). This should be uniform in approach so providers of offer/order management solutions can handle anything and at scale. This is a way to be cost effective as bespoke requirements per travel provider would be costly. Providers can provide any product with any features at any price, and with any rules. This includes rules that may mean this offer is for a single person only (personalization).
- An understanding of a concept of an intelligent offer that should tell you the product, price, and Ts&Cs. It has *everything* a channel needs to market the product. Wherever the object goes across multiple channels or apps, anyone following the standard and working with it can find a customer and turn the offer into an order. Current offers/orders are not implemented this way, meaning the offer is not actionable as is. Multiple additional steps are needed and, as already explained, what those steps are differs from one "get offer" API to the next. This is why with most any other product you search for online, you see what you want, one click and you add it to the shopping cart. Not in travel. What you see may not actually be available and not actually at the displayed price and may not be suitable for your needs. Many more clicks are needed to sort it out. It is technically feasible to correct this and be like other products, but it takes cooperation.

Let me now get back to Chapter 1 questions. *How can travelers take greater control of their trips?* The cloud was designed around a shared architecture that is horizontally scalable. In a cloud native retail system, the only instance of an order with the full itinerary is in a traveler's smartphone wallet. Everyone else involved in the trip can only view their own information. In order to see more, incentives need to be provided to the traveler. As with other forms of retail today, providers of air travel services can provide more targeted offers, including trip-level solutions, depending on what the provider chooses to share. As such, a personalized offer can be made across all channels, not just a provider's app or website.

How can travelers get real-time information and meaningful options at different points in the end-to-end journey? Twisting the intent of this question slightly, uniform offers and orders allow travel retailing providers, including TMCs, to combine individual offers into a trip-level offer. A provider of, say, a BnB can add a rule to their offer to reduce 10% of the room stay if combined with ground transportation. Why? It is much more certain a traveler with transportation arrangements will show up. There are also personalization opportunities to say this offer is only for employees of company XYZ or attending a sponsored convention. There would be no limit to the opportunities to customize an offer to a particular traveler or persona.

Moving on to Chapter 7 and the pillars. For brevity I will focus only on the second pillar, ***understanding the real problem holding back collaboration***.

A little background on my more than four decades of experience in travel retail IT. I started in travel IT at Eastern Airlines in the 70s, about ten years before deregulation. This meant routes and fares were regulated. Airlines competed on service. The two mainframe providers, IBM and Unisys, provided not only an operating system designed for reservations, but the application as well. As such, all airlines as well as some hotels and car rental companies discarded their homegrown systems and consolidated on the two options. User groups were formed where all would meet and exchange not only ideas, but code! Everyone had the same issues, so it made sense and saved money to cooperate. This was an open-source community before there was open-source. Technically it was not open as ultimately the IP was owned by IBM or Unisys. However, everyone exchanged ideas and code and the vendors were ecstatic that the community was fairly self-sufficient. The key point here is sharing made sense as the reservation system was not a competitive advantage, just a cost of doing business. This gradually fell apart when deregulation happened. There was not a technical reason to stop sharing at the reservation system level; leadership decided not to work with competitors on common needs. Fast forward to Y2K when the industry was moving to XML off EDIFACT. This was a huge effort and the industry (air, car, hotel, rail, and more) came together. OpenTravel was created and XML was created to send messages at a shared cost, saving money.

The point of this diversion is that occasionally travel retail leadership understood the value of cooperation on noncompetitive efforts. In areas of IT where all faced a common problem, costs could be greatly reduced. However, in some cases there was a lack of will to cooperate. The situation now appears to be to move to contemporary systems for transmitting data in web applications and implanting offer/order in a cloud native way. There are still some product teams that still see value in proprietary APIs, even though they cause challenges for customers. Could it be that the proprietary APIs, with all their challenges, are a revenue source for some participants in the industry? This chaos to interoperate between providers and retail channels has spawned a number of service providers that pull in content from a number of proprietary APIs and send it back out over their own proprietary APIs with a transaction or booking fee. For air, in particular, there is a barrier to competition. In the late 50s, standards were established on how one airline could ticket for another. Keep in mind that the ticket itself had value. This system was automated in the late 60s and eventually became eTickets in the 90s, but some aspects of the process did not change. For example, there are restrictions on who can ticket. This may explain why the PNR, why filed fares, and why EMDs are so hard to change.

Finally, let me turn to the real problem(s) holding back collaboration. First and foremost, is the understanding that this is extremely complicated and no one participant, including vendors, can work the industry out of this situation. No one participant can move to a solution without a critical mass of other participants moving with them. Secondly, there is a large financial barrier to change, not just the cost of conversions, but the disruption of the ingrained travel retail revenue model. Not just the cost of the mentioned chaos, but the booking fee model as well. There is no magic bullet. A large part of the solution will be cooperation on noncompetitive efforts. This would mostly be by following open-source patterns that are already extremely successful elsewhere. A set of APIs can be created jointly at a shared cost for anyone to use. This will lead all to JavaScript Object Notation and Representational State Transfer (JSON/REST) at a lower cost. There are other areas of travel retail that are just a cost of doing business. Capital can be freed up for the high-value functions like offer and order management assuming that there is an agreement on how to make an offer a self-sufficient entity. Those delivering the best relevancy-based scoring shop function at scale will win. That is, there are a lot more profitable services to invest in than converting one proprietary API to another. As for the big issues for airlines stemming from the ticket and other choices that were made in the 60s and 70s, efforts like the NDC were made to address such issues. There are other initiatives that can be taken, such as open codes to deal with the standards silos to facilitate connections and interoperability. While there are a lot of opinions on what should have been done differently, one thought is that the way forward is an *industry-wide* agreement on how offers and orders should work and then define how PNRs and tickets can be accommodated until they are phased out.

In conclusion, it took the industry over 50 years to create the current situation. It will take a lot of effort to resolve the challenges. Keep in mind that the biggest steps for moving forward in the past happened during rare periods of cooperation. Real cooperation and openness will lead to results that *anyone* can adopt as a basis to build on. For another perspective, see *What's Game Theory got to do with Selling Travel?* (on opentravel.org).

Melbourne, Florida, USA

Foreword

Andrew Watterson

Chief Operating Officer, Southwest Airlines

When Southwest Co-Founder Herb Kelleher famously quipped that the airline industry was especially vulnerable to a 'change or die' reality, his wisdom foretold an environment through which commercial aviation continues to toil well into the 21st century. Consumers demand more for less, a seamless journey through an increasingly complex landscape of choice. For business leaders, Nawal Taneja provides something of a guidebook to navigate the multi-layered complexity to realize the incalculable value of forging true partnerships both among and within all levels of airline organizations. He applies best practices from other industries in a relatable way with much food for thought.

Dallas, Texas, USA

Foreword

Stewart Wingate

Chief Executive Officer, London Gatwick Airport

Clever thinking, technology, and investment

Ultimately, modern international airports aim to give their passengers the opportunity to travel effortlessly and seamlessly wherever they want in the world.

Increasingly, they must also strive to create stress-free environments, so that everyone's journey is an enjoyable and comfortable experience, regardless of the airline, destination or ticket price.

These are considerable challenges on a complex airport campus, with numerous operators, competing needs and limits on resource.

London Gatwick's transformation in this respect is in its second decade and is ongoing. One of the most pressing drivers of the airport's change is the need to meet growing future demand in a congested airport market.

Capacity constraints like this are a major challenge for airports that cannot relocate and build afresh. Innovative thinking – including adopting a manufacturing-line approach to airport throughput – can help constrained airports make better use of the infrastructure and resources they already have.

Analysing operations this way drives innovation and efficiency and can help deliver better passenger services, more competition and choice. These must however be backed by investment, both in the latest available technology and in improved facilities and infrastructure.

Airports across the world are already realising the benefits of automation and self-service. London Gatwick opened the world's largest self-service bag drop and this has seen us almost eliminate queues.

Technological innovation is an increasingly rapid process however and, if airports are to maximise the benefits they offer passengers, they must stay very close to emerging and immature IT advances – including AI – to deliver the required airport ecosystems of the future.

As Nawal Taneja points out throughout this book, today's passengers also expect high-quality service, and those of tomorrow will be even more demanding and vocal. Improved technology and efficiency will only go so far in this respect and must be implemented in parallel to regular investment in updated or new facilities, as well as in staff training to ensure high-quality service levels are delivered.

Passengers will also become more demanding about our industry's ability to deliver increasingly sustainable operations. Most already recognise the importance of doing the right thing for future generations, and to also earn the right to grow as businesses.

Doing sustainability properly can sometimes be expensive in the short term and so competes directly for resources and investment in new technology and improved infrastructure. However, for the medium and long term, as airports, we must strive to do it all, if we are to succeed and deliver the improved passenger experience of the future.

Horley, Gatwick, UK

Acknowledgments

I would like to express my appreciation for all those who contributed in different ways, especially Angela Taneja (my business research analyst), Peeter Kivestu (formerly with Teradata and now a Principal with Oplytix), Dietmar Kirchner (formerly an SVP at Lufthansa and now Senior Aviation Advisor and co-Chairman of the International Airline Symposium Planning Committee), Zhihang Chi (formerly the Vice President and General Manager of North America for Air China), and Eric Leopold (formerly with IATA and now with Threedot.io) for discussions on challenges and opportunities facing the global airline industry and related businesses.

The second group of individuals that I would like to recognize include, at:

AIXI—Cameron Byrd
All Nippon Airways—Nguyen Thi Thuy Linh
Amadeus—Jim Barlow
Amazon—Sean Smith
Amazon Web Services—Bob Kwik
American Airlines—Anthony Rader
BETA Technologies—Ryan Barta and Lexi Pace
Embraer Asia Pacific—Victor Viera Dos Santos and Adam Young
Emirates Airline—Anand Lakshminarayanan
Ferrovial Vertiports—Kevin Cox
Fulcrum Consulting—Eric Mahler
Links Rez—Brian Bell and Scott Brennan
London Gatwick Airport—Tim Norwood
Ohio State University (Center for Aviation Studies)—Blake Stringer
Protect Group—Nick Ashton
Solventum—Scott DeFoe
Split Rock Aviation—John Feren
Teradata—Frank Bush
Turkish Airlines—Hanife Hilal Demirtaş
Vietnam Airlines—Le Minh Tuan and Nguyen Quang Trung
Wells Fargo—Ali Faruqi

Third, there are several other people who provided significant help: at Routledge of the Taylor & Francis Group (Guy Loft, Senior Editor, Routledge Professional, Law, Transport, Health & Safety; Heather Doquiatan, Editorial Assistant, Routledge Professional, Law, Transport, Health & Safety; and Cathy Hurren, Senior Production Editor); and Suzanne Arnold, copy editor.

Finally, I would also like to thank my family for their support and patience.

1 Introduction

Different sectors of the travel industry are clearly trying to implement initiatives designed to improve traveler expectations and experience, reduce operating costs, improve profit margins, reduce the impact on the environment, and become much more adaptable, lean, and resilient. Relating to traveler expectations and experience, for example:

- Airlines are improving their websites and mobile apps to make them more user friendly, developing digital ID systems to pass through airports without showing physical documents, and fitting their fleet with high-grade inflight connectivity systems to offer fast and ubiquitous internet services as well as overhead bins to accommodate, for example, vertical loading of carry-on roller bags. Swiss International Air Lines introduced a new global travel "eSIM service" to provide its passengers mobile data connectivity during their travels, enabling "passengers to stay connected in over 150 countries without worrying about expensive data roaming fees."
- In the case of airports, some are broadening the appeal of their services. Hong Kong Airport Authority, for example, is helping its Hong Kong International Airport to shift from being a *City Airport* to becoming an *Airport City*—serving as a hub for the greater catchment area. Others are enabling travelers to make intermodal connections and improve traveler experience through the airport—for example, by reserving specific time windows to go through security. Singapore's Changi Airport has introduced its Changi App that enables the airport to offer travelers innovative and revolutionary "phygital experiences" in the rapidly evolving travel and retail space. In May 2024, Changi Airport also announced that it will introduce a fleet of four autonomous baggage-handling vehicles to perform operations at the airport.[1] Aeroporti di Roma launched "Airport in the City" at the Termini Station in central Rome where passengers, initially traveling on ITA Airways, can check in for their flight and drop off their luggage, with no additional costs.
- Aircraft manufacturers are pushing the R&D envelope to develop products that improve traveler experience—all the way from providing

DOI: 10.4324/9781003483960-1

nonstop services in ultra-long-haul markets to offering convenient and quiet services in ultra-short-haul markets. Relating to the first is Qantas' announced nonstop flights between Sydney and New York with the A350-1000, flying about 20 hours. Relating to the second, AutoFlight, a manufacturer of eVTOL (electric vertical take-off and landing aircraft) aircraft, made the world's first inter-city electric air-taxi demonstration flight between the southern Chinese cities of Shenzhen and Zhuhai on 27 February 2024.[2]

- Travel intermediaries are developing AI-embedded chatbots to understand the purpose and context of trips and provide relevant information on more environmentally friendly service options. Take, for example, Expedia's Romie, an AI-assistant that "roams" with travelers. It not only helps travelers with shopping and booking, but also with in-trip services. Engagements with Romie are progressive in the sense that the system learns more about a traveler over time to be able to provide more personalized recommendations.[3] Google is adding an itinerary-building capability on its Gemini Advanced generative AI chatbot through a simple prompt in easy-to-understand language.[4] Some online travel sites are even trying to crack down on fake reviews. And metasearch engines are about to introduce voice-based search.

And the need for adaptability and resiliency is evident based on the ongoing changes on the health, geopolitical, technology, and climate fronts. Change will continue but at an accelerating rate. Just think about the four trends identified at the recent World Economic Forum and their impact on businesses: the end of hyper-globalization, the politicization of the marketplace, the evolution of sustainability, and the rapid rise of artificial intelligence.[5] Within the aviation sectors, all stakeholders in the ecosystem are realigning their business models to (1) build adaptable, more resilient, and leaner businesses, (2) improve traveler experience, and (3) streamline operations while increasing productivity.

While innovations by different organizations relating to improvements in traveler expectations and experience have been adding value for travelers, the innovations being introduced have been transactional, fragmented, and incremental. From the perspective of innovative customer experience, there are still ongoing questions. For example:

- What is the definition of what comprises innovation?
- How can travelers get real-time information and meaningful options at different points in the end-to-end journey?
- How can airlines and airports engage better with customers?
- How can traveler experience be measured effectively?
- How can travelers take greater control of their trips?
- How can a more holistic approach be developed to bring about a streamlined customer service as well as a step change in traveler expectations and experience—stress-free end-to-end journeys?

Outside of the air travel industry, think about how recent advances in technology and business processes have allowed customers to have a mostly digital and seamless shopping experience when searching for and buying and then receiving a broad spectrum of products and services. In the case of travel, however, the shopping experience is disconnected. Even in the shopping process alone, the experience is disconnected, such as when a customer, on a conventional website of an airline, tries to buy different ancillaries (insurance, for example) or make a reservation not in a hotel linked with an airline, but in a particular brand of a hotel, desired by the traveler. Other business sectors have achieved such capabilities through the use of flexible digital platforms that can be embedded in websites. Then, once a journey starts in the air travel business, the traveler ends up moving from a digital to a physical environment in which the experience becomes disconnected, especially during delays or disruptions, not to mention in situations that require the use of multiple modes of transportation, or the use of multiple services at destinations, such as hotels, car rentals, theater shows, and sports events. The process needs to be frictionless. Think about parallels between air travel and the healthcare industry, parallels relating not only to challenges, but also to corresponding solutions. Both industries depend on complex ecosystems with partnerships collaborating in and around vital infrastructure hubs (airports and hospitals). See the points made by Scott DeFoe in his foreword and in a use case study at the end of Chapter 7. Furthermore, Bill Price and David Jaffe in their book *The Frictionless Organization* provide five excellent examples of how businesses can learn what their customers need and how to respond: "Airbnb's Video Epiphany; E.ON's Customer Insights for Development; Vodaphone's Fine-Tuning; Uber's Focus on Apps, Ratings, and Defect Rates; Red Hat's CX-360."[6] In the air travel sector, what is needed are open data ecosystems that can facilitate the exchange and control of data using, for example, open Application Programming Interfaces (APIs). However, these capabilities do not really exist in travel retail yet. For example, travel apps are needed that work at scale that can actually *book* all the content shown to the traveler.

There is no question that different stakeholders in the aviation industry have been collaborating to enable almost 9 billion passengers worldwide (in 2023) to travel safely and relatively smoothly. This collaboration has been among airlines, airports, ground-handling services, air traffic control systems, and other organizations. However, going forward, what is needed is a step change in proactive collaboration between airlines and airports and airlines and travel intermediaries, just to select three stakeholders in the air travel ecosystem, to co-create value, for travelers, in terms of experience, and for service providers to reduce costs and increase profit margins. Think about it from an airport's perspective. An improvement in traveler experience is important not only for airlines, but also for airports. Consider, for example, the desire of airports to increase their non-aeronautical revenue—that is, retail revenue. The ability to increase retail revenue is linked closely to the satisfaction of travelers. Poor traveler experience at airports can lead travelers to spend less time and less money in airport stores. How about some regional airports that can transform themselves with the use of small new electric aircraft, discussed in Chapter 5? As for travel intermediaries, a step improvement in collaboration between airlines and global distribution systems (GDSs), travel management companies (TMCs), online travel agencies (OTAs), New Distribution Capability (NDC) aggregators, and banks, for example, could enable airlines to access not only higher-fare travelers, but also higher-margin travelers, after taking into consideration all costs, not just marketing and sales, but also costs of delivery and fulfillment of services, promised or implied. Although business models of intermediaries have been changing, the change needs to be more structural in light of progressive changes coming in the distribution space.[7]

Think about the implications of American Express Global Business Travel (AmexGBT) acquiring CWT, keeping in mind that Expedia has a stake in AmexGBT and Booking.com (Expedia's rival) partners with CWT. Think also about the implications of Google adding an AI-based itinerary creation capability to its traditional search. This capability will enable shoppers to create itineraries based on prompts from users, and enriched information in Maps, relating to certain cities and places to visit.[8] Think, next, about the expansion of the partnership between Expedia and Amadeus. Expedia is incorporating further the use of the NDC into its operations, which will enable travelers to select from a broad list of offerings, such as seats. Similarly, Amadeus' systems will enable Expedia to offer more personalized services such as those available from airlines' websites—for example, early boarding, onboard Wi-Fi, and available meals.[9] Furthermore, consider the new arrangement between Chase and Southwest Airlines, enabling Chase cardholders to book Southwest flights on Chase Travel using points or cash.[10] Think also about the implications of Airbnb moving beyond its accommodation business to a multi-category business.

It is often said that it is very difficult to implement a step increase in traveler experience given the complexity of the air travel business; while it is true that the air travel business is complex, travelers should not be expected to deal with the complexity of the business. Instead, businesses need to deal with complexity behind the scenes and provide travelers with the availability, for example, of touchless curb-to-cabin biometric checks, followed by the use of digital passports to pass through border control facilities without stopping. Aircraft manufacturers and airlines have been collaborating since the beginning of the industry and now airports and airlines have begun to collaborate more, not only between themselves, but also with technology businesses to address travelers' frustrations. Take an example of how the Manchester Airports Group, Ryanair, and Amazon Web Services are using a near-real-time event platform to improve traveler experience on the day of travel. How about the incentives being provided by the Los Angeles International Airport to airlines to start new routes? How about Overair teaming up with Dallas Fort Worth Airport and the City of Arlington to bring eVTOL aircraft operations to Texas?[11] Besides the question relating to infrastructure, the airport and the manufacturer would also be looking, presumably, into the questions in other areas such as crew training and maintenance. While this is a beginning of a more holistic approach to meet travelers' current unmet needs (simplicity, convenience, and speed), different stakeholders also need to think about a wide spectrum of potential forthcoming desires of travelers, such as the desire to live in one city and work in another city, and the capability to resell their tickets.

Collaboration and coordination within major players in the travel ecosystem was insufficient even prior to COVID-19, when the aviation marketplace was somewhat linear, predictable, and rule-based. Going forward, the aviation marketplace is expected to become non-linear (growing or declining rapidly), become much more unpredictable (given the emergence of multiple new forces, not to mention their convergence and intersection), and become much more dynamic, requiring revolutionary leaps to collaborate. Take, for example, the non-linearity aspect. Prior to 2019, the structure of the aviation industry had been fairly stable. Airline traffic had been growing in a fairly linear manner compared to what happened after the appearance of COVID-19. As for traffic mix, the three major segments had been fairly stable—business, leisure, and VFR (visiting friends and relatives). Going forward, the structure of the aviation industry alone is likely to change significantly, with new players entering every business sector. For example, the capacity share of low-cost carriers (LCCs) is likely to increase, with the expected increase dependent on region of the world. There will also be a change in the mix of travel, with the bleisure segment (mixing business and leisure) becoming much larger. According to Grand View Research, the size of the bleisure segment was just over US$900 billion in 2022, and it is expected to grow at an annual rate of about 12 percent per year between 2023 and 2030.[12] This trend will call for noteworthy changes in connectivity initiatives as well as the re-bundling of travel options.

Similarly, the growth in the aviation sector in China and India had been following linear paths but on different paths. Going forward, these growth paths are likely to be non-linear, given the changing dynamics within the aviation space of both China and India. Not only has the population of India just passed that of China, but the potential in the growth of the air travel market is likely to be enormous. Consider the data discussed by InterGlobe Aviation Ltd in a recent company presentation. In the US, a developed aviation market, there are three seats per capita in the domestic market, compared to India with only 0.13 seats per capita. India is also well behind China, where the seats per capita is 0.49.[13]

How about Saudi Arabia, where different divisions of the government and the aviation community are trying to develop a tourism industry that is expected to bring in 100 million visitors by the year 2030?[14] Could a region of the Red Sea be transformed into a "playground for the adventurous"? Red Sea Global is opening its first destination and is planning to move from traditional sustainability to regeneration. "The focus on regeneration marks a shift in industry standards, with potential lessons on how tourism can more actively benefit local communities and environments."[15] Could the "New Silk Road," discussed in the next chapter, rebalance the economic activity globally?[16] All these changes in the marketplace will call for a deeper level of collaboration and coordination within the travel ecosystem.

Since the beginning of COVID-19 different organizations in the aviation businesses have clearly tried to introduce innovations to improve travelers' experience. Just think about five such initiatives introduced in 2022 and 2023 alone. In its Allegris initiative, Lufthansa is enabling a customer in the economy class on a long-haul flight to "possibly book a free seat next to the customer."[17] Berlin Brandenburg Airport launched its BER Runway option that allows travelers to reserve a specific time window for going through security. American Airlines began to work with smaller airports and the transportation company Landline to provide post-security shuttle services to connect small regional airports with major airports, as identified in Chapter 5. Expedia capitalized on the use of algorithms to provide better tips to shoppers on its website, including, for example, a price tracking feature. Kayak launched an image recognition tool to compare flight prices from a screenshot.[18] And Airbus, in partnership with Daher and Safran, developed EcoPulse, a distributed hybrid-propulsion demonstrator aircraft that made its first flight on 29 November 2023. This aircraft can leverage the benefits of distributed propulsion to improve aircraft performance (improved cruising, take-off, and landing performance, and reduced cabin noise, for example).

Why, despite these value-adding but fragmented initiatives, is there still no approach to a more holistic travel experience? Some examples of major challenges for a substantive change in collaboration include:

1. the ongoing high levels of complexity in the operations of airlines, airports, aircraft manufacturers, and travel intermediaries,
2. in the case of airlines and airports, the continued use not only of legacy systems but, more important, of legacy processes,
3. the difficulty in transitioning from the use of legacy systems to contemporary technology-based systems,
4. in the case of airlines, the risk involved in changing systems in view of the low-margin nature of the air travel business,
5. the reluctance of key organizations to share data (for example, airlines, airports, third parties operating at airports, and travel intermediaries),
6. the lack of trust (between organizations, with travelers, or both) and transparency,
7. the different interests of not only airlines, airports, and intermediaries, but also different subgroups within each of these three types of organizations—different segments of airlines (low-cost vs. full-service, for example), different customers of airports (airlines, travel concessionaires, and ground service providers), and different travel intermediaries (GDSs, OTAs, TMCs, travel-fare aggregators, metasearch engines, tour operators,

wholesalers, destination management businesses, and tourism boards, for example),
8 more focus on metrics (for example, costs and options offered) than on values (for example, improving the trip-planning process),
9 in the case of airports, ownership, governance, regulatory, and operating constraints relating to different groups working at airports, and
10 more interest in control than in content (explained below).

Think about the eighth point in the above list. The trip-planning process continues to be complex and overwhelming. In a recent survey conducted by Accenture, the data showed that during the last three months of 2023, 74 percent of shoppers walked away from a purchase because they felt overwhelmed by too many options. And despite the claim by travel businesses that they are customer-centric, 71 percent of shoppers see no improvement in their ability to make purchase decisions. Consumers want to make quick decisions, but they want to be in control. Could airlines finally use GenAI to anticipate shoppers' needs and then offer targeted content that is transparent?[19]

Think about the ninth point in the list above. On a worldwide basis, airports provide only a limited number of facilities. Many services are provided by others, such as governments, handling agents, concessionaires, not to mention airlines. And each organization looks after its own economics and performance. Besides the providers of these services, there are other shareholders to consider—"airport users, employees, local residents, environmental lobbyists, and governmental bodies." The situation makes it complex for an airport to develop its strategy when different groups have different perspectives and different interests. Despite this complexity, the extent of the services available at an airport will depend on the relationship between an airline and an airport.[20]

Think also about the last point in the list above, with respect to the interest in control. Airlines worldwide want to control the space they occupy in their terminals, particularly at their hub airports. This control by airlines makes it difficult for airports to manage the quality and quantity of services desired by travelers and communities—for example, the right mix of low-cost and full-service products as well as the right mix of services provided by independent airlines and airlines in the global alliances. However, carefully designed collaboration can create a win–win situation by trying to find common interests, without relinquishing control. Can such a level of collaboration take place between existing airports and airlines? Or would it have to wait until new airports and new airlines emerge? Consider, for example, the planned development of Riyadh's new King Salman International Airport and the new airline, Riyadh Air, and the potential for a new partnership between them. How about the further expansion of Dubai's Al Maktoum International Airport, which will be five times the size of the current Dubai International Airport?

But, perhaps most important, think about point number five in the above list: lack of commitment to sharing data. What if governments begin to require different stakeholders to share data on common platforms to protect the interests of consumers? Such requirements could easily develop based on the thinking of more pro-consumer countries such as Canada and some in Europe. Governments' involvement in the commercial side of airline and airport operations seems to be increasing. In the US, opposition to the adoption of facial recognition technology at airports in brewing. According to one report: "This technology poses significant threats to our privacy and civil liberties, and Congress should prohibit TSA's development and deployment of facial recognition tools until rigorous congressional oversight occurs."[21] In late April 2024, the US government came out with rules requiring airlines to make automatic refunds to passengers for flights cancelled or delayed significantly, or for significant changes to schedules. The point is that data-sharing initiatives, coupled with the use of data platforms, AI systems (to analyze complex data sets), and Data Clean Rooms (that offer a secure and privacy-compliant environment) can take collaboration to a much higher level without the involvement of governments. See the thought leadership piece by Bob Kwik in Chapter 8.

How about the relationship with travel intermediaries? Some airlines want to control the content provided to intermediaries, with the type and extent of control depending on the type of travel intermediary. Yet, as mentioned above, some intermediaries can provide access to high-margin travelers, after taking into consideration all costs. Revenue and profit margins of airlines could be enhanced through more effective upsell, cross-sell, and loyalty initiatives, not to mention higher conversion rates.

To repeat, the lack of a more holistic approach for a step change in traveler expectations and experience is the result of insufficient collaboration and cooperation within the interdependent travel chain. This is due to such factors as: high levels of complexity in the operations of different sectors of the air travel business; organizational rigidity and the reluctance of key organizations, even when they have access to data, to share data; different interests of and different constraints facing different groups; and focus on conventional view of performance. Relating to constraints, think about just one constraint facing some airports. While some governments want to see capacity reduced at their international hub airports (for example, in Amsterdam) for environmental considerations, other airports want to expand their operations (capacity and connections) not only to meet growing demand, but also to stop diversion of connecting traffic to other airports. In the case of Amsterdam, while Schiphol Airport did reduce the number of operations and slots, it then increased operations based on criticisms from airlines and a review by the government. Think also about how many years London Heathrow and London Gatwick Airports have been discussing the need for a third runway and a second runway, respectively. What about the challenges relating to the development of eVTOLs, discussed in Chapter 5?

As mentioned before, while the development of infrastructure is on the minds of operators, much more collaboration is needed between airlines, airports, and communities to enable passengers to board aircraft effortlessly and make connections seamlessly at major airports. And, while ultra-long-haul aircraft are being developed, a lot more thinking needs to go into the cabin configuration for greater comfort in the economy class sections. As for measuring performance, there needs also to be a balance between learning and experimenting while improving performance within the ecosystem.[22] The non-alignment in the objectives of different groups continues. Think about the desire of airlines to increase the share of direct distribution (by holding back some content) to save costs, given the thin margins of their operations, making it difficult for agents to access total content to fulfill the needs of shoppers.

Within the context of experience, the topic of personalization has been discussed for decades. While different organizations, such as airlines, have proven that they can provide personalized services to their very top-tier customers, there are three basic questions:

- how to provide the benefits of personalization in real time,
- how to scale personalization, and
- how to evaluate the economic value of personalization to organizations such as airlines to provide personalized services to customers, other than to those in the very top-tier status.

Think about the extent to which some airlines are going to offer personalized services besides cabin configurations, lounges, and processing through airports. Delta, for example, has made investments in Delta Private Jets to offer new travel solutions. However, what degree of personalization can be offered cost-effectively to passengers who only travel once or twice a year? And if these infrequent travelers were to be offered an exceptionally large number of bundled products and services, would they feel overwhelmed and confused? Would they be satisfied with just stress-free trips, from shopping to delivery? Think about a specific set of data from a Salesforce report that shows that "65 percent of customers expect companies to adapt to their changing needs/preferences, but 61 percent of customers say most companies treat them as a number."[23]

There is an urgency to move fast on collaboration initiatives. However, some managers feel that moving fast means sacrificing excellency. That does not need to be the case. There is sufficient evidence that it is possible to move fast while developing excellent solutions to problems. Frances Frei and Anne Morriss have written a book on this subject that has five insightful chapters: "Identify Your Real Problem, Solve for Trust, Make New Friends, Tell a Good Story, Go as Fast as You Can."[24] Relating to the content of the chapter on "Make New Friends," how about collaborating much more closely with government policy makers and communities? Again, think about the decades that London Heathrow has been asking for the authorization to move forward with the development of the third runway. Finally, it is also important to provoke commitment and to retain the necessary talent in the emerging age of work.[25]

And let us not overlook the need to listen to the voice of the customer. Although it is hardly a new concept in the airline industry, the challenge has been in its application. How can an airline analyze, interpret, and then respond to the input received from customers coming from different channels such as call centers, emails, social media, and customer-facing employees? There have been four basic challenges:

- capabilities needed to collect the relevant data from different sources (including sentiments) in a timely manner and classification of the data into different segments,
- the amount of data to be analyzed,
- the lack of structure in the data, and
- effective ways of receiving and using customers' feedback

Consider the first challenge in the list above. When conversations take place between customers and call centers, the verbal conversations need to be transcribed into text. There are issues relating not only to languages and accents, but also to the tone of conversations and their effective transcription.

Now GenAI can help in these areas, for example, in the transcription of phone conversations. GenAI can not only deal with multiple languages, but also the sentiments expressed in phone conversations and emails. Next-GenAI-based systems can handle very large quantities of structured and unstructured data and produce recommendations based on analyses. Theoretically, these systems can also take into consideration responses of employees in call centers, for example—not only actual responses, but also the tones. Systems can then respond with personalized recommendations and solutions.[26]

Air Travel Partnerships: How to Create Greater Value through Collaboration focuses on just four types of organizations within the air travel sector: airlines, airports, aircraft manufacturers, and travel intermediaries. And, while there has been some collaboration, for example, between airlines and airports on one side and airlines and travel intermediaries on the other side, the scope (depth and breadth) and pace of collaboration need to increase meticulously and intensively to offer a much more holistic travel experience. This calls for more effective management of the ongoing disruptions, fueled by such forces as extreme weather changes occurring more frequently, access to and costs of labor becoming a real challenge, and sustainability becoming a very high priority.

Air Travel Partnerships provides a framework, tools, and insights to enhance collaborations by design in an age of increasing uncertainty. The framework presented can help all four types of organizations to provide solutions to travelers' unmet needs and to take traveler expectations and experience to a new level, including through the provision of multimodal travel at airports and of advanced air mobility services within the catchment areas of airports, while helping to meet the goals of sustainability.

Chapter 2 updates two of the points raised in previous books in the series: airline retailing and sustainability. This chapter also discusses a few other ongoing and a few new trends and forces, including the New Silk Road (mentioned earlier) and the meta city. This part of the chapter discusses in some detail some ongoing needs of travelers, for example, end-to-end services, and their implications for partners in the travel ecosystem, for instance, the use of One Order and the provision of multimodal travel options.

Chapter 3 focuses on managing disruptions more effectively. The concepts of designing to fail and controlling turnaround operations are discussed, including insights from Formula 1 grand prix racing. Organizations (airlines, airports, and ground service providers, for example) need to use real-time data and technologies to collaborate to manage disruptions much more effectively to improve traveler experience and reduce operating costs.

Chapter 4 starts with the evolution of connected services that transitioned from conventional interlining to codeshared connections. Now, self-connecting and virtual interlining are examined as two alternatives to conventional interlining that can provide mutual value for travelers and for suppliers of services through a symphony of collaboration and coordination, not only among different categories of airlines and other modes of transportation, but particularly between airlines and airports.

Chapter 5 highlights four segments, Mobility-as-a-Service, eVTOLs, small electric airplanes for regional markets, and multimodal travel, as examples of segments of travel that have the potential to transform air travel in urban and regional markets. As for new segments of travel, there will be a critical need for collaboration and integration among different partners, operators of services, airports, and cities, for example.

Chapter 6 addresses, first, the continued existence of the challenges relating to data and its effective management. The second part focuses on adapting and evolving with transformative technologies, leveraging, for example, cloud-based technologies, and using GenAI responsibly. While airlines, airports, and travel intermediaries have an incredible amount of data, there is a clear need for collaboration and coordination relating to the quality of the data generated, sharing of the data, and protecting the privacy of the data.

Chapter 7 identifies four basic pillars for developing productive collaboration within the stakeholders in the travel ecosystem. The chapter also discusses how, besides achieving disruptive innovation through the use of technologies, it is also possible to achieve nondisruptive innovation through the use of existing and new data to co-create value for all stakeholders. This chapter ends with examples of business transformations through collaborative partnerships in five sectors: healthcare, automotive, telecommunications, financial, and athletic footwear and apparel.

Chapter 8 offers five thought leadership pieces that provide international perspectives relating to the theme of the book. These pieces are written by a diverse group of practitioners with extensive experience, both in the aviation domain and in other business sectors.

Some topics presented in this book have already been discussed in some previous books in this series. However, the content offered in this book represents the ongoing contemporary thinking (as presented in the next chapter) not only on the part of the author and the insights from the best practices in other businesses, but also in the thoughts of the writers of forewords and thought leadership pieces.

Notes

1 "CAG to Introduce New Autonomous Baggage Handling Fleet at SIN," *Airport Industry-News*, May 15, 2024. https://airportindustry-news.com/cag-to-introduce-new-autonomous-baggage-handling-fleet-at-sin
2 "Electric Air-taxi maker, AutoFlight, successfully performs world's first inter-city demonstration flight," *International Airport Review*, February 28, 2024. https://www.internationalairportreview.com/news/214920/electric-air-taxi-maker-autoflight-successfully-performs-worlds-first-inter-city-demonstration-flight/#:~:text=AutoFlight's%20eVTOL%20aircraft%20journey&text=This%20achievement%20marks%20the%20world's,cities%20of%20Shenzhen%20and%20Zhuhai.
3 "As Gorin Debuts as CEO, Expedia Group Launches New AI Assistant, Content Creator Shops," *Northstar*, May 14, 2024. https://www.phocuswire.com/expedia-explore-ariane-gorin-ai-romie?
4 "Google Takes Next Step in AI Trip Planning," *Skift*, May 14, 2024. https://skift.com/2024/05/14/google-takes-next-step-in-ai-trip-planning
5 Jo Taylor, "Resilience and adaptability are key to navigating today's world. Here's why," *World Economic Forum*, January 14, 2024.
6 Bill Price and David Jaffe, *The Frictionless Organization* (Oakland, CA: Berrett-Koehler, 2022), pp. 195–9.
7 Ben Vinod, *Mastering the Travel Intermediaries* (NY: Springer, 2024).
8 Justin Dawes, "Google's New Travel AI Tools Want to Plan Customer Trips," *Skift*, March 27, 2024. https://skift.com/2024/03/27/google-launches-new-ai-travel-tools-whats-new-in-search-and-maps
9 Dennis Schaal, "Expedia Wants New Features With Amadeus NDC Partnership," *Skift*, April 4, 2024. https://skift.com/2024/04/04/expedia-wants-new-features-with-amadeus-ndc-partnership
10 "Chase Travel Has What the Other Cards and Online Travel Agencies Don't — Southwest Flights," *Skift*, May 16, 2024. https://skift.com/2024/05/16/chase-travel-has-what-the-other-cards-and-online-travel-agencies-dont-southwest-flights
11 "Overair teams up with Dallas Fort Worth International Airport and City of Arlington to bring eVTOL aircraft operations to Texas,", eVTOL Insights, November 21, 2023. https://evtolinsights.com/2023/11/overair-teams-up-with-dallas-forth-international-airport-and-city-of-arlington-to-bring-evtol-aircraft-operations-to-texas
12 "Bleisure Travel Market Size & Trends," *Grand View Research*, n.d. https://www.grandviewresearch.com/industry-analysis/bleisure-travel-market-report
13 "Towards new heights and across new frontiers," A Company Presentation by *InterGlobe Aviation Ltd.*, March 2024. //www.bseindia.com/xml-data/corpfiling/AttachHis//1b8f3d29-8bde-4c7d-b9c3-368179791c7f.pdf

14 Deirdre Fulton, "Competition In The Middle East Intensifies As Saudi Arabia Works Toward Vision 2030," *OAG*, October 3, 2023.
15 "Red Sea Global CEO on Why The Red Sea Heralds a New Era in Global Tourism," *Red Sea Global + Skift Report*, December 11, 2023. https://skift.com/2023/12/11/red-sea-global-ceo-on-why-the-red-sea-heralds-a-new-era-in-global-tourism
16 Adel Alfalasi and Ben Simpfendorfer, "Why The New Silk Road Is A Dynamic Commercial Story: The route brings opportunity to Asia and the Middle East," *OliverWyman*, 2023. https://www.oliverwyman.com/our-expertise/insights/2023/jun/new-silk-road.html
17 "Lufthansa Allegris," Lufthansa. https://www.lufthansagroup.com/en/themes/lufthansa-allegris.html
18 "Kayak Launches Image Recognition Tool to Compare Flight Prices From a Screenshot," *Northstar*, March 5, 2024. https://www.phocuswire.com/Kayak-launches-suite-of-artificial-intelligence-powered-tools?
19 "The empowered consumer: The key to deeper consumer relationships, reducing the noise around decision-making," *Accenture Report*, 2024, pp. 2 and 6.
20 Anne Graham, *Managing Airports: An International Perspective*, Sixth Edition (London: Routledge, 2023), pp. 1–2.
21 "The Fight Over Airport Facial Recognition: Senators Clash With U.S. Travel," *Skift*, May 2, 2024. https://skift.com/2024/05/02/why-congress-may-stop-face-id-at-airport-screening/?utm_campaign=New%20Daily%20Newsletter&utm_medium=email&_hsenc=p2ANqtz-9ttOR4gPeppp7c2pMo3CIMiLgXHO50sTCfxjzlgwPBij1775Zg6dq_EwbzPBjFo32YBQsd9wpkt42sPG0HgwqmC8sGhg&_hsmi=305439460&utm_content=305436782&utm_source=hs_email
22 Eduardo Briceño, *The Performance Paradox: Turning the Power of Mindset into Action* (NY: Ballantine Books, 2023).
23 "State of the Connected Customer," Sixth Edition, *Salesforce*, 2023, p. 8.
24 Frances Frei and Anne Morriss, *Move Fast & Fix Things* (Boston, MA: Harvard Business Review Press, 2023).
25 Joe Mull, Employalty: *How to Ignite Commitment and Keep Top Talent in the New Age of Work* (Canada: Page Two, 2023).
26 Thomas H. Davenport, Jim Sterne, and Michael E. Thompson, "GenAI Can Help Companies Do More with Customer Feedback," *Harvard Business Review*, April 29, 2024.

2 New era for travelers and ecosystem partners

During the last three to four years, many executives began to ask, "when do we get back to normal?" Some analysts provided the following type of answer: "There is no getting back to normal. There is only a new normal—one that has been coming long before COVID-19."[1] Within this context, many businesses began to explore how to survive in a never normal world. The answer appears to be to (1) adapt rapidly, become resilient and lean, (2) look much more deeply into how the needs and demands of customers are changing, and (3) grow through innovation. One way all three goals can be achieved in a timely manner is to collaborate at a much deeper level with existing partners and to develop new collaborative partnerships, including with start-ups. Consider the second point. Customers are interested in, for example, making as much as possible of their purchases from one supplier, like Amazon. They want to see rich content, including through visual means. And they are being affected by new technologies, such as recommendations being developed by AI-supported systems. This chapter starts with a discussion on some examples on ongoing trends (discussed in previous books but with additional information) and some new trends. The second part of the chapter discusses in more detail some ongoing needs of travelers, such as end-to-end services, and their implications for partners in the travel ecosystem—for instance, the use of One Order and the provision of multimodal travel options.

Ongoing and new trends

A previous book in this series, *Airimagination*,[2] mentioned a number of trends that are bringing about social changes and the impact of these changes on people. That book and the one following it, *Strategic Airline Retailing and Solutions*,[3] attempted to describe the impact of these changes on the air travel business. This chapter updates two of the topics raised in the previous books (airline retailing and sustainability) and discusses a few other ongoing and a few new trends and forces. Here are some elaborations on the two major topics discussed previously.

DOI: 10.4324/9781003483960-2

1. *Airline retailing* continues to be transformed through digital transformation in such areas as presentation of rich content, revenue management, ancillaries, and payment systems. Rich content is being presented, for example, through images, videos, and tours of cabins. And now the thought is to use interactive videos to sell more by elaborating on content through storytelling. Revenue management—extending from pricing to inventory control—is transitioning from dynamic pricing to continuous pricing. This transition is being enabled by not only the intensive use of NDC and One Order, but also cutting-edge technologies such as artificial intelligence (AI). See the thought leadership piece by Hanife Hilal Demirtaş in Chapter 8. Continuous pricing, for example, calls for the use of real-time data and its analysis, enabling the optimization of capacity and a substantial improvement in the accuracy of forecasting. The next steps now are to realign business practices, integrate internal systems, and develop the relevant staff.

   In all of these areas, there is value in partnering and collaborating with innovative start-ups, eliminating the need to develop and maintain internal capabilities. Take, for example, visual presentation of rich content. Two start-ups are Routehappy (which was acquired by ATPCO), which offers its Premium Universal Product that can show images and videos, and 3D SeatMapVR that shows three-dimensional views of an aircraft's interior, seats, and services. Relating to revenue management, deeper incorporation of the NDC is an important part of taking revenue management to the next step, as it would enable airlines to offer more personalized, not to mention dynamic offers, including dynamic packaging. It is becoming important to partner and collaborate with not only existing stakeholders (such as GDSs and data providers), but also with leading start-ups, working in the area of NDC, an adversarial topic between some airlines and third-party distributors. Some airlines, for example, have been warning third-party distributors that if they want to access their full content, they need to be connected to their NDC technologies. These airlines had agreements with GDSs to distribute their NDC content. Keep in mind that it is the expanded adoption of this framework that will facilitate competitive pricing, dynamic pricing, and pricing of unbundled and re-bundled products.

   As for ancillaries, new initiatives are being explored that will provide benefits for travelers (enhanced experience by meeting different preferences) and for airlines (enhanced revenues). A number of developments are already leading to new ancillaries—calling for a shift in the mindset of both travelers and airlines, as well as the deployment of emerging technologies such as AI. This technology can not only help an airline to predict traveler behavior, but also enable them to offer a particular ancillary, or a customized bundle of ancillaries. The point is to offer the right ancillary at the right time, at the right touch point, with the right message, and through the right channel. For example, a Salesforce report shows that 71 percent of customers prefer different channels depending on context.[4] Airlines are now beginning to look at ancillary products and services through new markets and maximizing the revenue per passenger rather than the revenue per seat. Again, it would add value for airlines to work and collaborate with leading start-ups in this area.

As for payment systems, they can not only meet the changing needs of travelers (different payment options, frictionless transactions, and greater transparency), but also improve the bottom lines of airlines through the availability of new types of data and new partners, such as those from the financial sector. Airlines clearly see a benefit from the trend that is blending travel with fintech. Think of more innovative ways of "freezing prices" and offering subscription models that offer much more value for travelers and airlines, initiatives that would change the relationship between travelers and airlines.

2. *Sustainability* continues to be a controversial topic, not from the point of view of its need and urgency, but more from the point of view of the timing to meet the established goals and the costs involved. In November 2023, Virgin Atlantic flew a Boeing 787-9 (with Rolls-Royce Trent 1000 engines) from London to New York using sustainable aviation fuel (SAF). This is an example of the aviation industry's progress to net-zero carbon emissions. However, it is estimated that currently SAFs represent only about 3 percent of all the renewable fuel production. What would the percentage need to be to reach net-zero carbon by 2050? In any case, the meaning of "net zero" is still not clear. Does it mean net-zero carbon or net-zero impact of aviation on climate change?

   In the area of travel, ongoing debates relate to (1) what it will take to make sustainable travel a reality and (2) how to deal with the "say–do gap" between what travelers say they are willing to do and what they actually do. According to a report by Visa and Skift, there could be three reasons underlining the "say–do gap": (1) the high cost of sustainable travel, (2) lack of information about sustainable travel options, and (3) lack of credibility around sustainability claims.[5] In any case there is still the question about being able to measure the gap between what travelers say they are willing to do and what they actually do. To help shed some light on this ongoing debate, detailed data is now available from the *Visa Destination Insights* platform that is better than data coming from detached sources. According to this report, it is possible not only to "see where people are flying and track travel corridors," but also to get better insights into "where they go after they land and what their shopping preferences are" as well as "what travelers are doing, how they behave, and what's important to them."[6]

   Given the imperative to deal with sustainability now, what are some suggestions from outside of the aviation industry regarding the development and implementation of sustainable strategies? A new special report discusses four insightful areas: "Set Ambitious but Realistic Environmental

Goals; The Hidden Opportunity in Paradoxes; Get Ready for More Transparent Sustainability Reporting; Tackling AI's Climate Change Problem."[7] An intriguing one is described in a paper, "The Hidden Opportunity in Paradoxes," by Scott Anthony. He gives an example of paradoxical industries with "huge pressure to increase their output *and* reduce their impact on our planet."[8] Many industries, including airlines, face similar situations: how to grow in size and decrease their impact on the environment and how to automate and not reduce the size of the workforce. The answer may lie in thinking beyond the seeming constraints. While numerous positive steps have been, and are being, taken by governments, businesses, and the public to deal with the sustainability challenge, improvements continue to be relatively incremental to meet the net-zero goals, at least for the aviation sector. From one perspective, much larger investments need to be made in technology relating to electric propulsion and in not only SAFs, but also the needed facilities and infrastructure. From a broader perspective, the aviation industry needs to think about strategies to create value in the net-zero transition, despite the ongoing challenges, with vision and ambition.[9]

Here are some examples of topics that were discussed but will now be elaborated in greater detail in this book:

1. Operational challenges continue to exist in the airline industry worldwide, delivering poor customer experience and costing the industry billions of dollars. As discussed in the next chapter, although airlines are looking into major transformations in the areas of flight operations, ground operations, and maintenance to innovate their operations using advanced data and analytics, there is still a need to develop partnerships and collaborate much more deeply and proactively within the partnerships through better management of information. The starting point is a deeper analysis of the network from the perspective of not only financial performance, but also operational excellence. And there is also now a greater focus on minimizing turnaround times not just to improve utilization of aircraft and gates, but also to make progress in achieving operational excellence. This is clearly an area where there is a critical need for collaboration within an airline, among network, fleet, and schedule planning, and also passenger reservations, but also different aspects of flight operations, ground operations, and maintenance, for instance. Then there is the need to collaborate much more with airports. Both airlines and airports are beginning to create value through the use of cloud-based operational databases, as discussed in the next chapter.
2. Despite the hurdles involved, some passengers are already making self-connections and the number has been increasing. One estimate reported is that self-connecting flights "have grown fourfold within the past year."[10] Clearly there are challenges, such as the lack of information and then

claiming, re-checking, and re-claiming baggage when making a self-connection between two airlines. However, solution providers have begun to emerge. Not only are some airports willing to provide support services to self-connecting passengers, but there are also new businesses entering the marketplace. Airsider is one example of a start-up, offering its Airsider's Door-to-Gate service—a web-based travel platform for passengers' end-to-end journeys.[11] An entire chapter, number 4, is devoted to this subject, self-connecting or virtual interlining.

3. The urban mobility topic is becoming more important given the direction of climate change, changes in inflation, and the increasing challenges relating to the supply chain. Different countries are handling urban mobility at different rates. The Oliver Wyman Forum and the University of California, Berkeley, have produced a comprehensive report on the Urban Mobility Readiness Index that shows how 65 cities are dealing with urban mobility within the context of economic pressures, sustainable investments, supply-chain risks, and convenient mass transit systems.[12] Cities ranking high in the index include Helsinki and Amsterdam.

   Within the context of urban mobility, the development and operation of eVTOLs (electric vertical take-off and landing aircraft) are progressing at a fast pace. Here are just two examples. As mentioned in Chapter 5, an eVTOL developed by EHang, the EH216-S, has already been certified by the Civil Aviation Administration of China. And an aircraft has already been delivered to a Guangzhou-based operator, ETON, a technology business associated with the Guangzhou government.[13] In the US, NASA and Joby Aviation, an air-taxi developer, have been simulating the operations of up to 45 eVTOLs in the Dallas Fort Worth airspace. These simulations included up to 120 air taxi arrivals and departures per hour "alongside existing commercial airline traffic … using existing air traffic control (ATC) procedures."[14] These two developments represent real progress.

   For short-haul markets, think about the commuter services that Eviation's Alice electric aircraft could offer with a speed of almost 300 miles per hour, a range of about 275 miles, and a capacity of nine passengers. Similarly, BETA Technologies' CX300 (discussed in Chapter 5) has the potential to transform travel in thin short-haul markets. How many such markets are in the US? Think about the statistic that about a third of flights are less than 250 miles, a distance that is within range for electric planes. Another perspective is that commuter markets (under 90 minutes of flying time) in the US amounted to just under 30 percent in 2019.[15] When, not if, the challenges get resolved (government certification, charging facilities, runways at airports, etc.) these electric aircraft have the potential to transform the air transportation system in the US. Travelers flying to and from small cities could then be able to bypass major hubs that are congested.[16] A cargo version of Eviation's Alice is planned to be launched in 2024. Similarly, a cargo version of BETA Technologies' CX300 could be operating in 2025. The topics of urban mobility and air-taxi operations with small electric airplanes are discussed in Chapter 5.

4. Analysts are predicting that at the broader level AI could affect hundreds of millions of jobs and create trillions of dollars annually in new economic value throughout the world. Some are even saying that this explosion of AI will not only relate to the powerful technology businesses, but there will be a global race among nations for leadership in AI. Bhaskar Chakravorti, Ajay Bhalla, and Ravi Shankar Chaturvedi provide not only the drivers of this technology—innovation, capital, rules, and data—but also a score that ranks countries across the world.[17] There is, however, a trend and a discussion on the other side, namely, that while the opportunities for AI's deployment are expanding from businesses to academia to entertainment, new challenges are also beginning to emerge, such as AI's potential impact on climate change. Some analysts go further, by saying that the AI industry could be a significant contributor to carbon emissions.[18]

   Within the airline industry, although the benefits of generative AI (GenAI), at the present time, are limited in terms of, for example, receiving personalized recommendations, the potential is enormous in the coming years on both the commercial side and the operations side. The basic idea behind AI is that it not only can make use of larger and larger data sets, but also that it can apply intelligence to the data that is embedded in the systems. Moreover, AI-based systems adapt to the feedback received from users. In booking a flight, for example, a conversation can take place relating to a comparison of destinations. And, having booked a flight, the user can be asked if they want a hotel and, if yes, what kind of hotel, relating to location, price, and availability of selected facilities and services. The human-like conversation can make answering questions much easier, especially if the language barriers are removed. Moreover, the use of GenAI-based planning systems can help travelers who feel that they are overloaded with information by offering personalized recommendations. However, it is assumed that the GenAI-based systems have been trained with the use of personal information on travelers. This level of interaction, human-like conversations, and the availability of personal data, for example, will take a few years to become really useful. On the other hand, progress will be fast as improvements are likely to be on an exponential scale as opposed to a linear scale, especially as the tech-savvy younger generations become a larger segment of the travel market. These points are discussed in Chapter 6.

Each of the next four chapters (3–6) will elaborate on ongoing trends and their impact on different sectors of the aviation industry. However, there are some new trends that will also be examined. Here are just two examples.

a. According to some analysts, the New Silk Road is re-balancing economic activity globally. Governments and businesses in Asia and the

Middle East are enhancing their trade and investment links.[19] Moreover, whereas the Original Silk Road related primarily to the exchange of goods, the New Silk Road relates to the exchange of goods as well as talent, technology, and capital.[20] Clearly this expansion of the trade framework will affect businesses and would undoubtedly impact travel between the two regions. Some questions for the aviation community are: (1) what will now be the most important trade routes, (2) which will be the large, traded sectors, and (3) who will be the main trading partners within the global economy? Think about the Saudi Vision 2030 plan with its goals of diversification and improvement in competitiveness in general and within it the development of a major service and tourism-based sub-sector of the economy. This vision includes the development of new cities (such as NEOM, the city of the future), new airlines (for example, Riyadh Air and NEOM Air), new airports (one of the biggest in the region, the King Salman International Airport to be built in Riyadh), and luxury resorts in locations such as AlUla and the Red Sea. The plan is to develop a 300 million passenger market by 2030. Could this happen? Think about a statistic quoted in a recent report by OAG: "In 2000, the Middle East ranked globally as the seventh largest region with 70 million seats per annum. This year expectations are for 257 million seats, in touching distance of South Asia which is dominated by the Indian domestic market."[21] The approval of the Gulf Cooperation Council Zone Visa (similar to the Schengen visa in Europe) will facilitate this increase in travel.

b. Some analysts are suggesting the emergence of a new type of city, the meta city, that combines the physical clustering aspects with digital connectivity. According to the authors of an insightful recent article in the *Harvard Business Review*, a meta city "would be a web of cities that operate as a distinct unit and are attached to a major—often global—economic hub." The emergence of the meta cities could impact "where and how businesses locate their offices and compete for talent."[22] The authors of the article, "The Rise of the Meta City," provide not only examples of meta cities worldwide, but also their ranking in terms of global superstar hubs (London and New York), global talent hubs (Dubai, Bangaluru, Dublin, and four others), significant hubs (Chicago, Toronto, Barcelona, Seattle, and 13 others), and regional hubs (Houston, New Delhi, Dallas, Munich, and five others). The location and status of such cities would clearly impact travel to and from these cities. Two examples given in the article are: (1) a couple moved to Bristol from London, kept their jobs in London, worked remotely, and made a two-hour door-to-door commute for meetings two or three times per month; (2) an Egyptian businessman had his company based in Dubai that did significant business in Saudi Arabia. Since the pandemic, this businessman worked remotely from his home in Cairo, and commuted regularly to Dubai to connect with his business colleagues and to Riyadh to meet clients.

The New Silk Road and the meta city are only two examples of trends and forces that would have a significant impact on travel worldwide. To adapt to these forces effectively would require partnerships within the travel ecosystem and collaboration proactively and with innovation. These and other trends discussed in the previous books require managers in different sectors in the aviation business to forge strong partnerships, both within each organization, between marketing and operations, for example, and also within the travel ecosystem. The management aspects relating to these organizations are discussed in Chapter 7.

Impact on travelers and ecosystem partners

Going forward, the behavior and expectations of tomorrow's travelers could be different from the aspects discussed in previous books:

- how different generations of travelers are prioritizing travel,
- how they prefer to work,
- how they are influenced for travel,
- how they engage with social media,
- how they value loyalty programs,
- how they want to pay only for what they want,
- how they are driven by emotional values,
- how they lean toward co-creation of content and interaction,
- how they lean toward health and wellness,
- how they use technology (not just relating to travel, but in their lives),
- how they balance human touch and enabling technologies, and
- their expectations, priorities, and amenities desired from the travel service providers—advisors, airlines, airports, and destinations.

In general, travelers are not just becoming more demanding and more stressful, and a few are even becoming disruptive and unpleasant due in part to more stress, resulting from, for example, the need to navigate multiple websites and multiple times to select and make a booking, the need to arrive two to three hours before departure at major airports, longer times to check and collect bags, arguments about onboard luggage, and so forth. Stress for passengers is also resulting from the lack of information in real time on what is going on and what is going to happen (a lack of situational awareness). It could be helpful in simply knowing (with confidence) what time to arrive at the airport for a flight (considering queue lengths), how long it will take to check in and go through security, whether there will be sufficient time to make the connection if the incoming flight is delayed and then arrives in a different terminal, for example. Timely and reliable answers to these simple questions would reduce stress. On the other hand, airlines are under greater pressure to reduce costs while flight delays and wait times on the tarmac are increasing. Airports also see unhappy travelers (not just due to long wait times in lines in terminals, but also poor wayfinding systems and processes), and they face difficulty in managing congestion, not to mention pressure from communities for more routes on the one hand and control of the environment on the other hand. Ground service providers are continuing to work under increasingly divergent requirements (and standards) of airlines on one side and airports on the other side—requirements that also vary by situation.

As for travel intermediaries, much more collaboration is needed with airlines and airports if travelers are to be provided with end-to-end services consistently, seamlessly, and stress free, not just getting travelers from their points of origin (say their homes) to their points of destination (say their hotels), but also the availability of services at destinations. Travelers want end-to-end services starting not just from shopping to reservations, to check-in, to inflight, to baggage claim, but also, after arriving at hotels, from check-in, to accommodations, to dining, to entertainment, to check-out, to making payments. And, in the case of disruptions, travelers want to see total collaboration and coordination between airlines, other modes of transportation, and service providers at destinations. This level of service calls for extensive collaboration starting with the provision to agents by airlines of their full content that, in turn, assumes that airlines and agents have agreed on:

1 the costs of distribution—for example, the part to be covered by airlines and the part to be covered by travelers, and
2 the objective of airlines—for example, their desire to increase the reservations through the direct channel, to reduce distribution costs, or to be able to engage better with customers, or to sell more ancillaries directly, or through the bundling process.

On their part, distributors clearly need to acquire the latest capabilities, such as the NDC. On the other hand, could customer acquisition costs for airlines increase from the entry of new travel intermediaries in the distribution space—new technology businesses, new metasearch engines, new travel-fare aggregators, and new start-ups that provide new capabilities for airlines (in dynamic and continuous pricing, for example) and new value for travelers (better suggestions relating to shopping, for example)?

The starting point is clearly that travelers want shopping to become considerably easier. Think about just the following four areas.

1. The booking process needs to be considerably less complex.
2. Travelers should be able to provide their requirements much more easily, relating to trip purpose and context.
3. Travelers' inquiries need to be listened to, understood, and responded much more efficiently.
4. There needs to be much greater transparency between service providers and shoppers.

Think about the conclusions in a recent insightful report by OAG on how the flight booking experience can be elevated. The report points out that while, in the US, 92 percent of travelers now make use of online booking channels (indirect bookings through online travel agencies (OTAs) and direct bookings through websites of airlines), 43 percent of "US travelers find no pleasure in booking their travels." The report goes on to say that "Sectors like fashion, finance, and hospitality, like restaurants, outperform in terms of the online booking experience."[23] The question then is, why? Here are some reasons given.

- Travelers use their mobile devices with small screens to do the initial research on the flights (including glancing through the blogs in social media), but then move to the larger screens on laptops and desktops to make it easier to manage multiple tabs to compare different flights and options. Think about the following statistic quoted in the OAG report. "On average, travelers view 141 different pages of travel content—and as high as 277 pages for travelers in the U.S. before committing to a travel booking."[24]
- The process to make comparisons is difficult given the lack of transparency. And the lack of transparency becomes an even bigger challenge when travelers want to compare not only prices, but also other aspects of the trip such as schedules and cancellation policies. Insufficient transparency results in a large percentage of shoppers leaving the websites of airlines.

There is clearly a need to improve the booking process. Some suggestions are made in the last section of Chapter 6. While some suggestions relate to the use of technology (like using integrated booking platforms and AI/ML-based recommendations), there is also a need to rethink some critical processes, relating, for example, to the marketing of ancillaries. Again, there is a need for collaboration to improve the quality of the offerings and the delivery of the products and services offered and sold. Collaboration is not just with existing players, but also new players that could make a powerful entry. To start with, Google is already expanding its features in its search products—Maps, Flights, and Hotels. Now Google's search features can also help travelers choose sustainable options, for example, through a display of train schedules and prices to see viable alternatives. Google clearly continues to provide useful information and experience to shoppers for travel services. Going forward, Google may use AI to create content, improve quality rankings, and reduce spam.[25] Think also about the role Microsoft's Bing could play with its partnership with OpenAI. Next, think about the entry of JP Morgan Chase into the air travel distribution space. The financial giant estimates bookings will be US$15 billion in 2025, a level that could make it the third largest travel agency in the world, following Expedia and Booking.com.[26] There is no question about how banks and credit-card companies are getting involved in the air travel space.[27] Southwest has already moved into this space by enabling customers to book its flight on the Chase's Travel Port "to reach new potential customers, as well as meet current demand for existing customers by making it more convenient."[28]

As for other players, Southwest is extending its website to give users of Google Flights visibility into the airline's available flights and fares. The tradeoff is between higher distribution costs and access to new travelers.[29] As for Amazon, it is already in the aviation space with its operation of a fleet of cargo planes. Now Amazon is expanding its presence through services offered by Amazon Web Services that provide on-demand cloud-based applications and services to direct travel service providers (such as airlines and hotels) and travel intermediaries. These services and applications, deploying GenAI going forward, have the potential to improve traveler experience at truly personalized levels. Think about the voice chatbot that is now becoming incredibly human-like to provide answers and act as a translator. The capability is to understand not only multiple languages, but also slang and "non-verbal cues like exhalations and tone of voice." Next, think about influencers with large followers entering the travel distribution space using media channels (such as TikTok and Instagram) and some using evolving platforms to connect them (influencers) with clients (followers) to promote brands, products, and destinations. Tools are now becoming available to connect one influencer to many clients (unlike conventional travel agents, where the connection is between one agent and one client at a time).[30] As such, within the context of these developments, airlines clearly need to find strategic and tactical ways to collaborate with OTAs if one thinks about the growing role and power of OTAs in the hospitality sector. According to a recent report by Kalibri Labs, the market capitalization of Booking.com is now about equal to the market capitalization of Marriott, Hilton, and IHG, combined.[31] And let us not underestimate the movement in which some OTAs are trying to increase their engagements with their loyalty members to book via their apps.

How about the changing preferences of travelers relating to loyalty? Travelers want (1) a simplification of the rewards system, for both earning and redeeming benefits, (2) an extension of the benefits not only across the end-to-end journey, but also fitting the lifestyle of travelers, and (3) a common currency within the loyalty ecosystem. Consider the first point. Travelers should be able to go to the website or mobile app of an airline and see very clearly the benefits earned and the user-friendly options for receiving the benefits. Consider the second point. Travelers would prefer that the airlines expand their loyalty partnership networks to include not only travel service providers, but also different business sectors that fit the lifestyle of travelers. Consider the third point. Consumers are overloaded with loyalty programs, each one with its own rules for earning and redeeming benefits. What is desired is a common currency system to provide users with a choice of redemption options, focusing on simplicity, flexibility, consistency, transparency, and personalization, ultimately elevating the traveler user experience[32] (see Figure 2.1). Think about

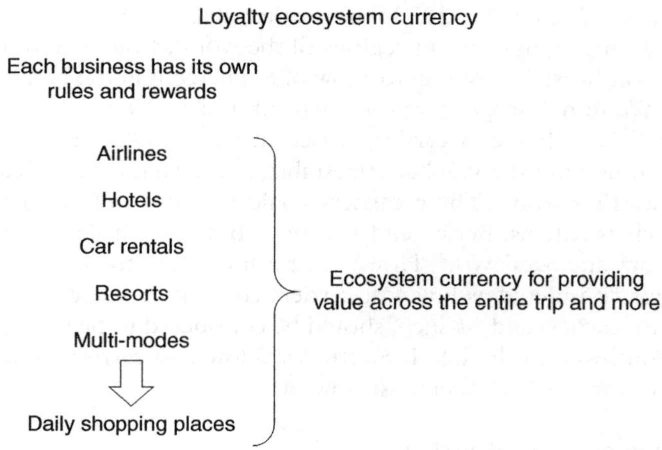

Figure 2.1 Simplifying the loyalty reward redemption experience

Avios, a global loyalty currency of the British Airways Executive Club and a number of other airline loyalty programs: "Beyond aviation, Avios is a loyalty currency collected and redeemed daily across a plethora of verticals from grocery shopping, fueling your car, hotel stays and much more."[33]

These changing desires of travelers relating to loyalty also present an opportunity for airlines to enhance revenues by creating an emotional connection with travelers that, in turn, would make them brand advocates. Optimizing revenue has become a challenge in an environment in which demand and loyalty are now more unpredictable, traveler expectations and needs are changing (personalization and flexibility, for example), and there are labor shortages. While managers recognize the value of digital transformation of offer management and flexible and integrated technology platforms to provide end-to-end journeys and solutions, three key questions arise:

1 where to start the transformation process and how,
2 how to manage orders (including the delivery aspects) and achieve scale, and
3 how to improve collaboration and cooperation between airlines and travel intermediaries throughout the entire journey?

How about the development of a personalized profile that is accessible to airlines, and OTAs? The challenge is not only the lack of sufficient collaboration, but also the dependence on legacy systems and channels to develop and offer rich content.

Next, the need for collaboration with travel intermediaries is increasing given, as mentioned earlier, the increase in the capacity offered by low-cost and hybrid carriers. According to the data published by the Statista Research Department on March 23, 2023, the market share of low-cost carriers in March 2022 ranged, in different regions of the world, from a high of 54 percent in the Southeast Asia region to a low of 8.6 percent in the Northeast Asia region. In Western Europe it was 45 percent and in North America it was 32 percent.[34] Now low-cost carriers, based in the Middle East, have begun to grow their networks. FlyDubai, Air Arabia, and Flynas have added services to new cities in Europe. These carriers could add not only larger cities in Europe (such as Athens, Berlin, and Brussels), but also smaller cities (such as Basel, Krakow, and Sarajevo).[35] However, it is important to keep in mind that some carriers considered as low-cost carriers could have some characteristics of full-service carriers and, as such, should be considered to be hybrid carriers. Consider Southwest in the US. Is Southwest a low-cost carrier if one assumes that low-cost carriers keep their costs low by

1 operating one type of aircraft,
2 operating aircraft with high-density seating,
3 flying to and from secondary airports,
4 distributing their products directly through their websites (bypassing distributors), and
5 not offering traditional services as part of the fare (baggage, food, and beverages, and so forth)?

Southwest does operate one type of aircraft but with different numbers of seats. Its cabin configuration has a higher level of seat pitch than some conventional low-cost carriers. It serves many large and congested airports, and it distributes its product through major GDSs. Its fare includes free transportation of two bags, and it does not charge for non-alcoholic drinks. Now Southwest is reported to be considering a transformational change to its single-class cabin that traditionally has not had assigned seats. Why? According to Southwest's CEO, "Customer preferences and expectations change over time," and "We are also studying the operational and financial benefits of any potential change."[36] Leaving aside the confusion of the classification of some low-cost carriers, the point remains that the rise of low-cost carriers is creating an interlining/connection issue. If low-cost carriers do not want to connect directly with full-service airlines, there is an opportunity for either airports and/or intermediaries to step in and offer relevant services to facilitate seamless and stress-free connections through collaboration, creating a win–win situation. See the discussion in Chapter 4.

Finally, an increasing number of travelers are getting interested in booking space in lower-price cabins, but then having ways (for example, effective and easily understandable bidding systems) to upgrade to higher-price cabins prior to departure. Bidding systems are clearly win–win situations for travelers (higher quality seats and services) and for airlines to earn additional revenues.

Travelers can use websites such as ExpertFlyer to get useful information, such as seat alerts.[37] Examples of currently available bidding systems are offered by companies such as Plusgrade[38] and SeatBoost.[39] There are two other trends taking shape—paying for flights on a subscription basis and price freeze options. While the subscription concept is not new, it seems to be coming in vogue again. In the US, Alaska and Frontier have launched subscription fares and in Japan, the airline Star Flyer launched a monthly flight subscription to allow remote workers to fly between the coastal city of Fukuoka and Tokyo as much as they wanted.[40] Relating to price freeze options, given the fluctuations of airfare prices, some companies are betting on being able to predict airline price fluctuations and offer guarantees to shoppers through their price guarantee programs. Google Flights and Kayak are examples of companies offering such price freeze options.[41]

In closing it might be helpful to discuss, now within the context of collaboration, a topic on which marketers frequently converse—the Gen Z travelers and their expectations. As summarized by Serenity Gibbons in her article on Forbes.com, the habits of Gen Z are disrupting the travel industry in three ways:

1. "They Prefer Uncharted Territory.
2. They Want a Unique and Elevated Experience.
3. They Take Advantage of Technology."[42]

Preference for uncharted territories will certainly have value for airline network planners and intermediaries. Seeking a unique and elevated experience as well as taking advantage of technology will have implications for airlines, airports, and distributors, discussed in this book. Again, the focus now is not only on the holistic nature of the travel experience, but on its creation by design through collaboration, based on dialogue with real travelers and engagement with key stakeholders.

There are also significant insights from a recent podcast by McKinsey and Company in which the authors surveyed more than 5,000 travelers from China, Germany, the United Arab Emirates, the UK, and the US.[43] Here are just a few highlights of the insights.

- The podcast identified the following clusters of travelers that seem to share the same attitudes and motivations toward travel:
    - sun-and-beach travelers
    - culture-and-authenticity seekers
    - strategic spenders
    - trend-conscious travelers
    - premium travelers
    - adventure seekers.
- Travel has become a top priority for Gen Zers and their top consideration for selecting a destination is "experiencing something new."

- Younger generations' choice of destinations is influenced by lower costs (offered by low-cost carriers whose services are expanding), mobile connectivity, and social media (for example, posts).
- For older generations, the top travel motivator is "friends and family"—either to visit them or to travel with them.
- Baby Boomers spend three times more on travel than Gen Zers to make travel easy and convenient. However, Gen Zers spend a much higher percent of their disposable income on travel. Moreover, while Gen Zers may spend less on some components of travel (air fares, hotel accommodations, etc.), they are willing to spend much more on experiences, for example, "spend $500 entrance fee to go gorilla tracking and have that experience."
- Older generations feel that "if you're not a digital native, the steps of traveling have become quite challenging."

Finally, relating to business travelers, the importance of employee experience became a high priority in the past three years, for example, due to the increase in hybrid work, facilitated by technology, requiring a redesign of the workplace, work styles, and needs of hybrid workers traveling on business. This aspect, in turn, is having an impact on business travel, including the choice of a traveler's booking channel. This development is increasing costs, due, for example, to the inability to get discounted rates from travel suppliers, and the lack of compliance with corporate policies. When business travelers start booking outside of the corporate travel platform to meet their own needs and satisfaction, businesses not only see an increase in costs, but also a loss in control relating to, for example, add-ons and upgrades booked by travelers.

For all segments of travelers, disruptions are becoming an important element of concern. While airline disruptions have always been a challenge, the situation is getting significantly worse. As discussed in the next chapter, the key to managing disruptions effectively is through collaboration and better management of information that is in real time, integrated, transparent, easily accessible, shareable, and made actionable using emerging technologies.

Notes

1 Joseph Coughlin, " Get Over It!—Why There Is No Going Back to Normal After COVID-19," *MIT Center for Transportation & Logistics*, May 29, 2020. https://ctl.mit.edu/news/get-over-it-why-there-no-going-back-normal-after-covid-19

2 Nawal K. Taneja, *Airimagination: Extending the Airline Business Boundaries* (London, UK; Routledge, 2023), pp. 1–2.

3 Nawal K. Taneja, *Strategic Airline Retailing and Solutions: From Offers to Fulfillment to Loyalty* (London, UK; Routledge, 2024).

4 "State of the Connected Customer," Sixth Edition, *Salesforce*, 2023, p.14.

5 "New Report: Accelerating Sustainability in Travel and Tourism," *Visa + Skift*, December 12, 2023. https://skift.com/2023/12/12/new-report-accelerating-sustainability-in-travel-and-tourism
6 *Discover Visa Destinations Insights*. https://usa.visa.com/products/visa-destination-insights.html
7 "Sustainable Strategy: Rightsizing Goals and Assessing Impact," *MIT Sloan Management Review*, Winter 2024.
8 Scott D. Anthony, "The Hidden Opportunity in Paradoxes," in "Sustainable Strategy: Rightsizing Goals and Assessing Impact," *MIT Sloan Management Review*, Winter 2024.
9 Laura Corb, Anna Granskog, Tomas Nauclér, and Daniel Pacthod, "Full throttle on net zero: Creating value in the face of uncertainty," *McKinsey & Company*, September 2023.
10 "How airports can change the game for self-connecting passengers," *Airsiders*, June 5, 2023. https://airsiders.com/how-airports-can-change-the-game-for-self-connecting-passengers
11 *LinkedIn* post, Airsiders, summer 2023. https://www.linkedin.com/posts/airsiders_innovation-passengerexperience-activity-7071491902566506498-WfS-
12 "Urban Mobility Readiness Index," Oliver Wyman Forum and University of California, Berkeley, 2023 Report. https://www.oliverwymanforum.com/mobility/urban-mobility-readiness-index.html
13 Greg Waldron, "Guangzhou eVTOL delivery sets state for EHang tourist flights," *FlightGlobal*, December 21, 2023. https://www.flightglobal.com/aerospace/guangzhou-evtol-delivery-sets-state-for-ehang-tourist-flights
14 Howard Hardee, "NASA and Joby simulate up to 45 eVTOLs in Dallas Fort-Worth airspace," *FlightGlobal*, December 20, 2023. https://www.flightglobal.com/airframers/nasa-and-joby-simulate-up-to-45-evtols-in-dallas-fort-worth-airspace
15 Jesse Klein, "The first frontier for electric aviation: Short-haul flights," *GreenBiz*, October 31, 2023. https://www.greenbiz.com/article/first-frontier-electric-aviation-short-haul-flights
16 Justin Gerdes, "Opinion: Electric planes will revolutionise regional travel," *Energy Monitor*, July 5, 2023. https://www.energymonitor.ai/sectors/transport/opinion-electric-planes-will-revolutionise-regional-travel/?
17 Bhaskar Chakravorti, Ajay Bhalla, and Ravi Shankar Chaturvedi, "Charting the Emerging Geography of AI," *Harvard Business Review*, December 12, 2023. https://hbr.org/2023/12/charting-the-emerging-geography-of-ai?
18 Niklas Sundberg, "Tackling AI's Climate Change Problem," *Sloan Management Review*, December 12, 2023. https://sloanreview.mit.edu/article/tackling-ais-climate-change-problem.
19 "Make Change Your Ally In 2024," *OliverWyman Forum*, December 2023.
20 Adel Alfalasi and Ben Simpfendorfer, "Why The New Silk Road Is A Dynamic Commercial Story: The route brings opportunity to Asia and the Middle East," *OliverWyman*, 2023.
https://www.oliverwyman.com/our-expertise/insights/2023/jun/new-silk-road.html
21 "Middle East Aviation: Transformation, Growth and Future Challenges," *OAG*, May 6, 2024.

22 Richard Florida, Vladislav Boutenko, Antoine Vetrano, and Sara Saloo, "The Rise of the Meta City," *Harvard Business Review*, November 29, 2023, updated December 1, 2023. https://hbr.org/2023/11/the-rise-of-the-meta-city
23 "Unlocking Full Potential: Elevating the Flight Booking Experience," *OAG*, March 13, 2024, pp. 4 and 5.
24 "Unlocking Full Potential: Elevating the Flight Booking Experience," *OAG*, March 13, 2024, p. 6.
25 Morgan Hines, "Travel Companies Navigate Changes to Google's Search Function," *PhocusWire*, April 18, 2024. https://www.phocuswire.com/google-seo-search-travel-blogger-ota-core-update-march and https://blog.google/products/search/google-search-update-march-2024
26 Paul Stevens, "JP Morgan Chase to offer full service travel agency," *Marketing and Distribution News*, August 10, 2022. https://shorttermrentalz.com/news/jp-morgan-chase-travel-agency
27 "Banks vs. OTAs: How Credits Cards Took Over Travel," *Skift*, May 17, 2024. https://skift.com/2024/05/17/banks-vs-otas-how-credits-cards-took-over-travel
28 Chris Dong, "Booking a Southwest Flight Just Got Easier for Chase Cardholders," *TRAVEL + LEISURE*, March 20, 2024. https://www.travelandleisure.com/chase-travel-southwest-airlines-booking-portal-8611809
29 "Southwest Fares Are Appearing on Google Flights," *Skift*, May 22, 2024. https://skift.com/2024/05/22/southwest-fares-are-appearing-on-google-flights
30 Betsy Mulé, "Influencers are a New Class of Travel Agents—But Lack the Right Tools," *PhocusWire*, August 7, 2023. https://www.phocuswire.com/Influencers-new-class-of-travel-agents?
31 Cindy Estis Green, Mark V. Lomanno, and Dave Roberts, "Demystifying the Digital Market & Guide to Commercial Strategy," *Kalibri Labs*, 2023, p. 8.
32 "Reimagining Loyalty to Engage Today's Consumers: How Brands Can Forge Deeper Connections in a World of Choice Overload," *Skift + IAG Loyalty*, 2024. https://skift.com/insight/new-report-reimagining-loyalty-to-engage-todays-consumers
33 "What is the Avios currency?" IAG Loyalty, n.d. https://www.iagloyalty.com/what-is-the-avios-currency#:
34 "Market share of low cost carriers worldwide in March 2022, by region," *Statista*, April 16, 2024. https://www.statista.com/statistics/1088686/low-cost-carrier-market-share-region
35 Deirdre Fulton, "Middle East LCCs Focus East to Expand European Networks," *OAG*, April 9, 2024. https://www.oag.com/blog/middle-east-lccs-focus-east-to-expand-european-networks
36 Howard Hardee, "Southwest considering 'transformational' changes to single-class cabin: CEO," *FlightGlobal*, April 25, 2024.
37 Expertflyer.com
38 Plusgrade.com
39 Seatboost.com
40 Alex Ledsom, "Will You Pay A Monthly Subscription For Your Next Flight?" *Forbes.com*, February 25, 2023. https://www.forbes.com/sites/alexledsom/2023/02/25/will-you-pay-a-monthly-subscription-for-your-next-flight

41 Elaine Glusac, "Looking for the Best Deal on Airfares? Consider a Price Freeze," *The New York Times*, April 19, 2023. https://www.nytimes.com/2023/04/19/travel/price-guarantees-google-flights.html
42 Serenity Gibbons, "Gen Z Habits Disrupting The Travel Industry," *Forbes.com*, December 20, 2022. https://www.forbes.com/sites/serenitygibbons/2022/12/20/gen-z-habits-disrupting-the-travel-industry
43 Kurt Strovink, Margaux Constantin, Jasperina de Vries, and Roberta Fusaro, "A new itinerary for the tourism industry," *A McKinsey and Company Podcast*, June 14, 2024. https://www.mckinsey.com/industries/travel-logistics-and-infrastructure/our-insights/a-new-itinerary-for-the-tourism-industry?

3 Managing operational turbulence

Although airline disruptions have always been a challenge, the situation is getting significantly worse. For example, according to research conducted by Amadeus about 52 percent of airports around the world are experiencing more disruptions than before the COVID-19 pandemic.[1] While disruptions continue to be related to weather, mechanical failures, problems related to computer failures, capacity restrictions, congested airspace, high load factors, and more recently to staff shortages and supply-chain challenges, operational thinking, data, practices, and systems need to be redesigned within a collaborative framework to cope with disruptions. Some businesses use the term "design to fail," meaning that a system is capable of recovering and maintaining service when one or more components fail. Managing disruption within this framework will not only improve customer experience, but also reduce costs. Similarly, reductions in times to turn the aircraft around at gates will not only improve customer experience and increase aircraft utilization, but also reduce aircraft delays. Think about the recent CrowdStrike outage that took place on July 19, 2024 that forced the cancellation of thousands of flights worldwide. And lower aircraft turnaround times will contribute to environmental sustainability. There will be lower emissions due, for example, to the lower amount of the use of Auxiliary Power Units (APUs). While some operational groups within airlines have tried to learn from the operations of Formula 1, as highlighted at the end of this chapter, there are now some new insights that can be used by the teams responsible for aircraft turnarounds.

Managing disruptions more effectively

Despite different approaches on the part of different organizations (airlines, airports, airport ground service providers, and so forth) for managing disruptions, the number of disruptions has been increasing as highlighted in the above example. Airline disruptions lead to poor traveler experience, poor image of the brand (airline and airport), and higher operating costs. So, the question is how disruptions can be managed much more effectively? Although there is no simple answer to this question, the solution appears to

DOI: 10.4324/9781003483960-3

relate to the better management of information that is in real time, integrated, transparent, easily accessible, shareable, and made actionable using advanced technologies. From this perspective the remedy would be for each organization in the travel ecosystem, especially airlines and airports, to take a data-driven approach. Airlines, of course, have been using a variety of strategies to manage disruptions, including proactive and data-driven strategies. They have been doing so in the areas of aircraft, crew, and maintenance scheduling and planning. Predictive maintenance, for example, is an example of both a proactive and a data-driven strategy. The object is, of course, to predict when a part will fail. Data sources include sensors, pilot and maintenance write-ups, and flight data recorders. There is even the thought of using algorithmic planning that can provide informed information on the optimal way to reassign crews and accommodate passengers resulting from a disruption.[2] Improvements have already begun to be considered. For example, a new source of information is satellite tracking, which provides accurate and real-time information on the location of all aircraft. The availability and the use of real-time aircraft positional information can now be factored into delay predictions.[3] Think about Western Sydney International Airport, which is operating a Category III3B runway that allows aircraft to land with near-zero visibility, during fog, for example. This capability coupled with the deployment of cloud-based systems will reduce disruptions that affect passengers, airlines, and airports.[4]

Although travelers' complaints about airline performance have been increasing in such areas as flight cancellations and delays, baggage handling, and involuntary bumping, the problems took on a new level in some parts of the world, for example, in the US during 2022 and 2023. At some airports there was a meltdown when thousands of flights were cancelled. As a result, besides using more data that is actionable, the next step now being explored is how inter-organizational work practices in airlines, airports, and travel intermediaries can be redesigned within the context of new technology to help the air travel system become much more resilient to delays and disruptions to lessen the systematic impact of the disruption, with a faster recovery time. Although processes are being changed, they need to be changed much more within a collaborative framework. Could distributors emerge who can help stranded travelers get reaccommodated even if reservations were made by an airline or a different travel intermediatory? However, such scenarios require not only the need for and value of collaboration, but also different methods of collaboration and coordination. How will a distributor, who did not make the reservation, find the information on the reservation of a stranded passenger at a minute's notice? From this perspective, better disruption management could even be a revenue opportunity. Some travelers would pay for auto-rebooking in the event of a delay (similar to travel insurance).

While the conventional approach for airlines has been to build in more slack in their systems, the question has always been, by how much and where. And now it appears that extreme weather events will not occur in isolation—one-time events—but other occurrences will also emerge simultaneously, such as pilot shortages, critical workers going on strike, supply-chain problems, ATC shortages, ground handler shortages, as well as shortages of aircraft and parts. One airport, Changi Airport in Singapore, is breaking new ground in the area of handling baggage. The airport has started working with a fleet of autonomous baggage-handling vehicles that would not only deal with the shortage of ground staff, but also make airport operations more reliable.[5] There are additional constraints at airports, too. Amsterdam's Schiphol Airport, for example, has discussed the possibility of a reduction in the annual number of operations to deal with operational challenges, including the need to limit noise.

Airlines have begun to look at new technologies that integrate data on aircraft, crews (availability and connectivity), connecting passengers, airport resources (gates, ground service providers, and so forth), to minimize irregular operations. However, problems are mammoth at airports where airlines operate large hubs—Atlanta and Heathrow, for example. There are major decisions to be made: delay flights or cancel them, and which ones. American has been working with a system known as Hub Efficiency Analytics Tool (HEAT) that can help with the decision on which flights to delay and which to cancel.[6] However, the problem can become much more complex based on a given situation—for example, which has higher priority, crew considerations or passenger considerations. While new systems have been adding value, they have a way to go to deal with the multitude of constraints and priorities, and all in real time. For example, it is not just the number of connecting passengers, but the personal needs of each and every connecting passenger. And even if technology is now available to handle such large and multiple problems, data is not available on the need of each and every origination and destination (O&D) passenger and every connecting traveler.

Travelers want real-time information at every touch point based on their needs and channel preferences. Moreover, customers want the capability not just to get the information without being put on hold, but also to be able to interact with suppliers throughout their journeys. Currently, there are significant differences in responses provided, for example, relating to channels of communications. Going forward, effective management of disruptions needs to include what and how information is communicated to travelers, what advice is given to travelers, and how travelers are empowered to find effective solutions to their disrupted trips. As such, how different airlines and different airports respond to disruptions and the affected travelers will affect their own brands and the loyalties of travelers relating to their choice of both airlines and airports. Consequently, while disruptions are becoming more frequent and more severe, viable opportunities now do exist for both airlines and airports to respond to these new challenges. For example, technology is now available to monitor disruptions and to try to prevent, or at least reduce, disruptions, but also to interact proactively with each and every customer.

Going forward, it is now possible to work with each and every traveler to meet their needs during disruptions, including providing them with sophisticated forms and options for self-service that can be personalized. Let us not forget that passengers want to be empowered and feel that they are in control. And the power of social media cannot be underestimated during disruptions and the need for transparency to gain travelers' trust. Consider that there are estimates that an average person spends more than two hours a day on social media. Think about the negative impact of travelers expressing their dissatisfaction with an airline or an airport. Think about the potential of a negative message going viral. The power of social media cannot be underestimated as many people now read online reviews before making a purchase. Moreover, an increasing number of passengers are contacting airlines via a social media channel, such as X, formerly Twitter.

Technology can even help airlines and airports stay engaged with customers to determine their needs even before customers realize their needs. Where is the information on such needs? Data is not just located within Passenger Name Records (PNRs); it also resides in many locations, within airlines and third parties. Queues need to be cut, in physical locations (in terminals) and on phone lines. Incentives need to be offered: reaccommodations without additional costs, vouchers, hotel accommodations, and alternate modes of transportation. And in some cases, human intervention needs to kick in. The design process calls for not only the use of advanced technologies, but also the use of comprehensive mapping of customer journeys. Since time is critical during disruptions, the use of messaging apps (such as Facebook Messenger, WhatsApp, and WeChat) becomes important. How about the use of super-apps (multi-purpose apps) to enable customers to perform comprehensive searches, make bookings, make payments, work with multiple travel organizations (airlines, hotels, car rentals), or communicate with live agents to manage the entire trip?

Super-apps allow users to accomplish a number of different tasks, even if they are not related. One example of a super-app is Rappi, which was created in Latin America to connect small businesses or stores in a neighborhood. Within the airline industry, AirAsia is known for developing and using a super-app. Super-apps are a good way of keeping travelers engaged and provide exceptional customer experience, as well as earning ancillary revenues through the use of dynamic pricing. Super-apps will be the next big thing in air travel.

It is estimated that two-thirds of delays and cancellations are within the control of airlines.[7] For managing disruptions effectively, there are eight major challenges.

1. It is necessary to close the gaps between the data that is being generated, the data that is being stored in real time, and the data that is being analyzed.
2. It is necessary to analyze the data effectively, using, for example, predictive analytics.
3. It is necessary to develop not just automated communications, but seamless communications with updates at every touch point throughout

the journey and through the channels of communications preferred by passengers, not airlines.

4. It is necessary to show empathy given that passengers during disruptions are likely to be stressed. In fact, not only messages can be sent via multiple channels to ensure reach, but they can also be followed up with calls. Complex situations may require the use of technology as well as human beings.
5. While preventing delays is not always possible, empowering travelers (by providing personalized self-service options) needs to be a strategy.
6. Transparency is also important to offer self-service options, like changing reservations, getting refunds, and getting meal vouchers when an airline does not have all the information to solve a problem. Oddly enough, the number of options (car rental and choice of hotels, etc.) needs to be limited so as not to overwhelm customers. Fewer but meaningful and timely options need to be offered.
7. Two-way notifications to confirm itinerary changes and to track refunds and reimbursement need to be employed.
8. Timing is important given that governments are beginning to develop regulations for airlines relating to travelers affected by disruptions. From this perspective, it would be helpful to have a clear mindset with a willingness to collaborate and to coordinate to empower employees and systems to improve customer experience during disruptions and to keep policy makers away from developing stringent regulations to deal with disruptions.

As mentioned earlier, a number of technologies can help airlines and airports to manage disruptions much more efficiently and effectively. The goal would be to plan proactively for uncertainty through scenario simulations; this, in turn, calls for asking a few hypothetical questions and working with digital-twin models to simulate complex events. Given that a digital twin is a digital representation of a physical process, depicted in a digital form of its environment, it should enable an airline to simulate real operational disruptive situations with their outcomes. Similarly, a digital twin of an airport infrastructure and processes should simulate disruptive situations. Theoretically, an airline's digital twin and an airport's digital twin could be integrated to fine-tune the management of operational disruptions. In the area of maintenance, airlines have already begun to use artificial intelligence (AI) in prescriptive and predictive maintenance. However, as Cameron Byrd and Barry Lott point out in their thought leadership piece in Chapter 8, the key is to know your data. The data needs to be clean, timely, and available when needed.

Sensors embedded in aircraft engines are already providing critical data for proactive maintenance to reduce flight delays. Machine learning models that have been trained to recognize patterns in the existing information are already being used. The recommendations coming from these models, trained on the incredible amount of data coming from sensors embedded in engines, can be used by maintenance staff to investigate certain areas to be able to foresee potential problems. Now, similar sensors are being considered in other parts of the aircraft, such as seats and galley equipment to perform proactive maintenance. In addition, AI and machine learning technology can be used to predict the arrival time of an aircraft at a runway and at a gate, taking into consideration numerous factors such as weather, the location of aircraft, type of aircraft, and so forth.

While airlines have used different strategies to manage disruptions, such as proactive planning and contingency planning, more recently the interest appears to be in predictive maintenance (as opposed to reactive maintenance), and algorithmic planning. The use of predictive maintenance, using numerous sources of data, computer simulations, and more recently AI and machine learning do show a good potential to predict when certain parts may fail, leading to flight delays and possibly cancellations. Algorithmic planning is being considered, first, as a good way to reaccommodate passengers, taking into consideration the number of seats available, the number of passengers to be reaccommodated, and the costs. Second, this data-driven approach can also be used to deal with scheduling crews and aircraft, having taken into consideration regulations relating to both crew times and maintenance schedules.

GenAI, which has advanced rapidly in airlines' commercial space (call centers, trip planning, pricing, etc.), is now showing real opportunities in operations, particularly in the area of maintenance, given, on the one hand, the availability of huge amounts of data through multiple sources (manuals, write-ups by flight crew, work orders, maintenance performed, not to mention sensors) and, on the other hand, the need to organize and interpret that data to minimize the time an aircraft is out of service. A recent report by McKinsey & Company goes into detail on the use of AI in different areas of maintenance—for example, how AI-based systems can:

- help aircraft technicians spend less time troubleshooting problems by enabling mechanics to have "conversations" with digital assistants about specific problems and potential solutions,
- help reliability engineers to go through huge amounts of unstructured maintenance records (maintenance logs) to examine very quickly failure patterns and set up automatically planned maintenance tasks,
- help technicians, having found and repaired the problem, do administrative work, like document the activity and fill in reports,
- monitor maintenance work performed "to create targeted feedback on a potential problem," and
- help supply-chain managers analyze "disparate communication and delivery patterns to automatically identify early-warning signs of supply and delivery problems."[8]

However, these maintenance initiatives will require not only the availability of large quantities of data that is of high quality, the needed technologies and skilled personnel, and a willingness to change to digitalized processes with an integrated IT design, but also collaboration among different functions and stakeholders. The collaboration part is necessary not only to achieve efficiencies but, much more important, to preserve safety and regulatory compliance.

Designing to fail

Given that disruptions are inevitable, could designing to fail be a paradigm shift for managing disruptions? Designing for failure means that disruption management teams look into systems and processes to understand when the system might fail and to have as much control as possible in managing the failure, fast recovery, and also to develop and implement self-healing processes. The design to fail concept is more than a disaster recovery plan. Various components need to be designed to adapt to failure and self-recovery to the extent possible. One way to start the design to fail process is to imagine a disaster and analyze what happened. Which parts failed? Which parts were interdependent? What was the impact on different stakeholders, inside (for example, crews) and outside (for example, airports), and, of course, travelers? This requires a different mindset—for example, not only the ability to visualize different components in real time, but also to see the whole system. It is the visualization framework that makes it possible to "see" the system and all the parts in real time and, most important, the interdependencies. Visualization will also identify what data is required, how and where redundancies should be built in, and where are the weaker links that can make the system collapse.

All stakeholders need to be part of the design to fail system, not only internal (scheduling, reservations, crew planning, maintenance, ground ops), but also external (airports and ground service providers). There are five critical success factors:

- effective collaboration and coordination,
- comprehensive, high-quality, and relevant data to train the systems,
- visualization of the planning stages and flows,
- transparency and mutual understanding among departments, and
- provision of feedback.

Within airlines, disruptions are usually managed by airline control centers that reassign resources (aircraft and crews) and accommodate stranded passengers by minimizing costs, keeping in mind customer and employee experiences. While disruption management within control centers is not a new problem, it has become a much more serious problem requiring not only different ways of functional planning (say, scheduling), but also airline recovery. An important point is that whereas airline planning focuses on finding optimal solutions, airline recovery focuses on feasible solutions in real time, solutions that may only be sub-optimal, depending on the type of disruption and its severity. While the design to fail concept will be helpful, it will require a large paradigm shift for proactively managing disruptions with a focus on both traveler experience and employee experience. Obviously, it is difficult to anticipate every area of failure regarding a disruption, but building in failure scenarios will help.

Let's start with the assumption that flight disruption can be separated into two categories: (1) relating to aircraft and its crew, for example, a maintenance problem or the absence of a crew member for any number of reasons; (2) an external event relating to, for example, weather, or ATC, or an airport closure. In both cases the delay can produce a downline impact on the network. Airlines operate larger Integrated Operations Control Centers that work 24/7 and every day of the year to minimize the downline impact by taking short-term actions, such as swapping aircraft and crew, deadheading crews, ferrying aircraft, and reaccommodating passengers. Usually, the aircraft recovery process follows the process to recover crews and then the recovery of passengers. Large airlines, such as American, can have up to 15,000 staff in such centers, usually divided into three segments, one managing aircraft, a second managing crews, and a third managing passengers. However, the paradigm shift is in the development and implementation of integrated recoveries—aircraft, crews, passengers (their connections and their baggage), and in some cases, cargo, too. The need for an integrated solution is based on the fact that the three recoveries, aircraft, crews, and passengers (and sometimes cargo also) are interrelated and, as such, the ideal solution is to solve the three aspects simultaneously—aircraft, crews, and passengers. And these scenarios need to be factored into the design to fail systems.

Just like airlines, airports also have their operations control centers, and operations control centers at both airlines and airports have been going through significant changes. Both are not only complex, but they are also multilayered. In recent times, another consideration has become important: minimization of emissions, requiring even more collaboration. As such, the new areas of development are the use of advanced technologies to integrate data in real time, data coming from multiple sources and systems to make informed decisions. Both airlines and airports have been getting very good at using early warnings of upcoming problems, like bad weather. Now more is being done using advanced analytics not only to analyze historical data but also to predict future situations. Then there is potential use of prescriptive analytics as to what actions should be taken based on the results of what could happen. Now think about the value of collaboration. An airline needs to optimize its own resources (aircraft, crew, and passengers) while an airport needs to do the same thing (aircraft departures, aircraft pushback flows, taxiway congestion, aircraft holding times). Collaboration is clearly needed in three areas: data accessibility and integration, functional coordination, and communications.

AI and smart analytics can predict potential disruptions and failures of equipment and assist in the deployment of autonomous ground vehicles (for example, to transport baggage). The availability of 5G networks can help in the handling of very large amounts of data and providing more reliable channels of communications (ground to air and ground to ground). Another opportunity is the usage of the cloud for pulling in the data for analysis using AI. The data relates to locations and availability of aircraft and crews (compliance with government regulations), status of maintenance on each aircraft, weather (existing and forecast), airspace restrictions, availability of gates, and information on impacted passengers (their locations, origins, destinations, and connections). In these cases, AI systems can make meaningful recommendations without biases if the systems have been trained with carefully selected data and if the system making the recommendations is able to connect up with multiple sources where additional and needed data is located. The key benefit of these new systems is that they can take into consideration many more variables and help make decisions fast. These attributes are normally beyond the capabilities of humans (the depth and breadth of the variables to be considered, the ability to collect and integrate data from multiple sources, and the speed with which analyses are performed). The end result is a much higher level of customer experience, and lower costs of disruptions. Information coming in can be even more detailed, like if the aircraft being considered is owned by the airline or leased (relating to costs) and if the aircraft is new or old (affecting the level of CO_2). With the capability to use enormous amounts of data and analyze many more options, it is even possible to look at the availability of aircraft from partners, such as within the Lufthansa group or within the IAG group.

Operations control centers (OCC) can *now* be truly the nerve centers of airlines and airports where real-time data is used to monitor real-time operations and make real-time decisions in case of disruptions to provide numerous real-time options for recovering aircraft, crews, and passengers. Let's not forget that besides data and technologies, there are also human factors relating to how decisions are made, and how they are communicated, not just between different parts of airlines and different parts of airports, but also between airlines and airports, given that reducing aircraft delays calls for a multifaceted approach. And, of course, it is the human factor element that relates to teamwork.

Table 3.1 lists some barriers to better disruption management. Big challenges continue to be the existence of poorly integrated systems, getting control of the siloed data, and finding effective ways to make tradeoffs—for example, balancing customer experience and operating costs when making decisions on which flights to delay and which to cancel. While operations control people think that they know which flights are critical, there is a need for a single source of truth relating not only to data, but also to assumptions relating to the criticality of flights, relating to not just aircraft and crews, but also passengers. For example, it is not just about the predictions of delays for crews, but also the connections of crews. In terms of passengers, it is not just about their connections, but also the costs relating to their food and their hotel accommodations. Consequently, the OCC group needs to find ways to solve problems urgently, through an analytical assessment of different scenarios.
Now with the availability of more data, smart analytics, and AI, the operations control center groups have the capability to see new ways of looking at the

Table 3.1 Top barriers to better disruption management according to airline leaders

Inability to cascade information within the airline	44 percent
Fragmented operational systems within our airline	40 percent
Inability to understand the impact of decisions on onward plans of passengers	34 percent
Lack of common technology platform with stakeholders at the airport	26 percent
Lack of computerized/automated planning for rebuilding flight schedules	26 percent

Source: "Better together: rethinking how to manage disruption in aviation," *Amadeus Insights*, 2023, p. 15.

problems (customer and employee experience as well as operating costs and new ways to collaborate and cooperate to find a balance among these inputs). But there is still the challenge of creativity (relating to communications, for example) and the role of empathy relating to both customers and employees. Remember 80 percent of all flights being on time still means that 20 percent of all flights are delayed! And aircraft delays not only cost airlines, but also cost passengers in terms of missed connections, hotel stays, and meals. Now everything can be looked at much more carefully, within a collective framework, and much more proactively—maintenance and inventories of spare parts, for instance. More sophisticated systems are already being considered to monitor the health of aircraft in real time (using sensors and data) and the sharing of data. Even more important now is the need for much more data-driven scheduling of flights that takes into consideration, not just the maximization of aircraft utilization, but also the minimization of delays, as well as the need for flexibility to adjust schedules based on operational considerations (for example, management of crews) and demand considerations. The goal is keeping customers informed and giving them personalized options based on information that is integrated as it comes from different sources. Passengers need to be enabled to manage their onward journeys. Websites and apps need to be upgraded to handle the needs of a much broader group of travelers, from those interested in managing their vacations to those managing their businesses.

If travelers are to be assisted no matter how their reservations were made, directly though airlines or through third parties, then emerging systems need to be used to figure out the information on travelers (their itineraries and their preferences). Travelers can now be communicated with through their native languages and through multiple channels, including direct calls. It is now possible to find a balance between humans and technology based on the complexity of the situation and the need for empathy. After all, even though technology offers speed, it cannot replace social interaction and empathy. To some extent, hyper-personalization can be scaled, giving each and every passenger the information they are looking for and as many self-service options

Table 3.2 Top reasons airlines are investing in disruption management capabilities

Improve our image	70 percent
Improve the passenger experience	66 percent
Differentiate	58 percent
Improve staff morale	44 percent
Reduce costs	34 percent

Source: "Better together: rethinking how to manage disruption in aviation," *Amadeus Insights*, 2023, p. 11.

as possible. But hyper-personalization will require the availability of data at a granular level and the capability to integrate different databases (reservations, CRM, and operations, just to name three groups).

Airlines are clearly making large investments to reduce disruptions. Some reasons are listed in Table 3.2. Notice the ranking of the brand image compared to costs.

In the airline industry an increase in delays and cancellations is causing financial problems for airlines, not to mention financial burdens and stress for travelers. Given the importance of customer satisfaction, disruptions are clearly having a negative impact on the brands of airlines. Leading airlines have, of course, begun to manage their communications with travelers on a much more proactive basis, relating to not only timely information (through emails, apps, and SMSs) with transparency and honesty, but also optional arrangements to reaccommodate travelers, not just through the use of technologies, but also with human interventions to prioritize and resolve complex problems. However, there are challenges, such as overbooked flights and insufficient staff, not to mention the lack of staff empowerment to resolve travelers' problems effectively and in a timely manner, within the context of empathy.

Controlling turnaround operations

The key to controlling turnaround operations is to collaborate to optimize the turnaround process. Delays discussed in this section are those functions that are performed at the gate, not by the ATC asking for gate holds. Major delays at gates relate to the docking of the aircraft, unloading passengers and baggage, fueling, catering, pilots going through their pre-flight routines, and push back. Can you believe that Southwest Airlines started by turning aircraft around in as little as 10 minutes? Even now, with additional constraints, the airline tries to turn around the aircraft in 30 minutes. Going forward, the new concept that can be examined is the careful and methodical monitoring of each function and each organization performing various functions. Improving turnaround times will improve customer experience, increase utilization (of aircraft, crews, and gates), and reduce aircraft delays. As mentioned earlier, the solution calls for not only the deployment of leading-edge technologies, but also changes in processes that improve collaboration and coordination, given the involvement of multiple organizations performing multiple functions. Think about just the main functions that take place at the gate:

- connecting the jetway and ground power,
- loading and unloading of passengers, baggage, and cargo,
- cleaning,
- catering,
- fueling,
- maintenance,
- connecting the pushback vehicle, and
- de-icing at some locations.

Now think about the multiple organizations involved depending on aircraft types, capacities, points of origin and destination, and type of flights (point-to-point vs. connections). Think, just for a moment, about the optimum time for connecting the pushback unit. Early connections mean inefficient use of resources. Late connections mean delays. Next, there is the sequencing of some tasks, catering and fueling, for instance. Some of these decisions cannot be made in advance as the timing of the tasks may depend on particular situations such as the late arrival of an aircraft and the amount of fuel needed. The key is to recognize that many tasks that need to be performed are interdependent.

There is a need to develop metrics for each function. Now, data, AI, and computer vision can be used to compile a much more comprehensive picture of turnaround operations to make decisions not on a minute-by-minute basis but on a second-by-second basis. This calls for a need to have the right resources (equipment), and the right people (maintenance) at the right time and at the right place. These decisions need to be made in real time, depending on the situation, and not based on averages. Better predictions can obviously reduce taxi times for inbound and outbound flights. Undoubtedly, there will always be unforeseen events such as aircraft damage from ground vehicles and missing passengers. These situations call for understanding, monitoring, analyzing, and communicating much more effectively on what is happening in real time. And technology has begun to play a major role in each of these areas, particularly in the area of monitoring through the use of AI and computer vision to improve the coordination between airlines, airports, and the ground service providers to provide mutual benefit. Airlines can use their aircraft more efficiently. Airports can increase capacity without having to build more stands. However, even if coordination is improved not only within different parts of an airline and also with external parties such as airports, and ground handlers, there are yet more parties involved, such as air traffic controllers and government control authorities, such as immigration and customs. For a much higher level of coordination, besides flexibility among different players, there is a need for transparency. Think about the role of schedule planners who try to optimize connectivity in the hub-and-spoke systems. Flexibility needs to be built in, leveraging advanced data and technologies to better deal with when things go wrong or when additional services are required at the very last minute, like de-icing of the aircraft. As discussed below, the use of AI and computer vision can be extremely valuable for predicting delays in situations where de-icing is required.

Multiple leading-edge technologies are available and can be utilized behind the processes to reduce turnaround times—AI, cloud-based systems, platforms, and computer vision. AI can not only handle enormously large quantities of data but also make sense of the data and predict outcomes, based on weather forecasts, for example. Platforms can help connect with people in different organizations in real time. These technologies are not replacing humans responsible for control of operations, but they are supporting their collaborative decision-making processes through better collaboration and coordination with an examination of the smallest detail. Keep in mind that computer vision, an interdisciplinary field within the framework of AI, can enable computers to obtain information from digital images and videos to identify objects and people.

Before airlines and airports started using cloud-based systems, data was stored in computers located on premises. These systems had limitations such as:

- data was not updated in real time, but updated on an hourly basis, at best,
- data was not integrated as it was located in different systems,
- storage space was limited given the increase in the amounts of data available and data needed, and
- concurrent queries could not be handled efficiently.

Moving data to the cloud is helping airlines and airports not only in the availability of integrated data that is in real time, but also the use of analytics, not to mention the handling simultaneously of multiple queries from multiple groups—flight operations, reservations, check-in groups. Moreover, different users can now access and interact with the data using platforms. The main point is that data-driven coordination can bring a step-change improvement in operations—not only relating to on-time departures, but also to lower turnaround times. Moreover, with data available in real time on passengers' connections, the system can better match arriving aircraft and gates, an example of digital transformation, leading to collaborative decision-making based on the availability of a "single source of truth" relating to data. It is now possible to track how far an aircraft is in its turnaround process by integrating data from different sources and different channels, such as cameras installed in aircraft stands and using algorithms to analyze data. Turnaround dashboards can display the information in real time, information that can be used by all partners—airlines, airports, ground service providers and so forth.

Schiphol Airport in Amsterdam developed an AI- and camera-based technology to strengthen collaboration to improve turnaround predictability. The project was known as Deep Turnaround. The goal was to use AI to translate images coming from two cameras at each ramp and make the information actionable for all users. The images were captured from more than two dozen processes, such as fueling, cleaning, and catering, and transmitted to the cloud every five seconds. The information generated, when combined with other information, such as flight data, enabled the prediction of when an aircraft turnaround could be completed. The information generated was accessible via an API and could be integrated in the airport's management system.[9] This information, combined with historical data, can now be used to identify the causes of turnaround delays.

Artificial intelligence, machine learning, and cloud-based technologies are also being looked at for use in reducing aircraft turnaround times. Think about situations in which a departing aircraft is waiting for a crew coming from another flight. While airlines are pretty good at making decisions to swap aircraft and crews, the process can be made much more efficient with the use of better data (more data and connecting data that is scattered) and AI and machine learning technologies.

How about the assignment of ground handlers to service aircraft that are coming in early or late at gates? New technology is already being used to handle such situations. Take, for example, American Airlines' development and implementation of "Smart Gating" technology to reduce aircraft taxiing times and turnaround times. The AI-based system uses (a) multiple data sources simultaneously (weather, aircraft types, status of flights, runway assignments and taxiways, availability of gates and airport staff as well as connections of passengers and their bags), and (b) platforms to make data available in real time to all relevant staff (airport operations, ground service providers, crews). The system has improved aircraft turnaround times, and on-time performance, while balancing operational performance and traveler experience.[10]

Insights from the Formula 1 grand prix

For many years leading airlines have thought about applying the strategies and tactics used by Formula 1 teams, given the parallels between the two sectors. The goal for an airline is to optimize its operations at an airport—making the right operational decisions at the right time and using technology to support the decision-making process. In the case of motor racing, data has been used to develop a bigger picture, running thousands of simulations. However, the capabilities developed by Formula 1 require not only the use of data and technologies, but also a high-performance culture and a willingness to change processes. Think about the insights that can be gained by airlines from the experience of Formula 1 to analyze and improve aircraft turnarounds. Think about the value of reducing the turnaround time by 10 minutes for a short-haul carrier like Southwest or Ryanair. Assuming four to five trips per day means a saving of 40–50 minutes a day. But it would require working at a microscopic level of detail for a short-haul operator. In US domestic operations, airlines typically take between 45 and 75 minutes to turn around an aircraft, depending on the airline, the aircraft, the airport, and congestion. However, let's not forget that while some factors are under the control of an airline (and/or an airport), others are not, as in the case of weather and ATC operations at a given time. On the other hand, think about "a pit-stop" during a grand prix, where a group of people come together to make sure that a specific job gets done as safely and as quickly as possible regardless of the occurrences that are under the control of the group or not. Now focus on the choreography needed to produce a perfect outcome. Consider some parallels:

- managing limited resources,
- planning for unexpected events and developments,
- the critical nature of teamwork to achieve the final goal,
- the importance of effective communications and trust within the team members,
- using simulations and predictive analytics (to test different scenarios) to optimize the strategy, and
- making decisions in real time and within a team framework using real-time data (car performance and tire wear, for example).

In the final analysis, organizations (airlines and airports, for example) and practitioners (operations control centers, for example), need to be clear on what they are trying to achieve—high utilization of equipment and crews, reduction in operating costs, or maximization of customer and employee experience. Poor on-time performance will not only be reported to government agencies (the FAA in the US) but will also show up in social media and word-of-mouth, influencing travelers on the airlines they choose to fly. Force-fitting different goals into a single approach will lead to confusion in time-critical situations relating to the management of disruptions. The goal can be to work with emerging technologies and carefully designed-to-fail systems to tap into the experience trend—customers and employees. Carefully designed-to-fail systems can address some challenges beforehand, such as over-booking policies, supply-chain issues, and adequate empowerment of relevant categories of staff at gates and in call centers, for example. However, since for travelers there are not only financial implications, but also stress, the key to reducing stress for travelers lies in (1) preemptive and proactive communications with travelers and proactive, adaptable, and transparent reaccommodation options to meet their travel needs. Next, there is a need for feedback from travelers and staff not only from a learning perspective, but also from an improvement perspective. The commercial air travel business is highly dynamic and overly complex, and disruptions are inevitable. As such, it is during disruptions that seamless and proactive collaboration among multiple stakeholders as well as the availability of self-healing systems are needed the most. Each stakeholder needs to have access to not only the right information, at the right time, but also collaborative technologies. As for self-healing systems, two examples are self-connections and virtual interlining, discussed in the next chapter.

Notes

1 Elena Avila, "How can information sharing help airports overcome disruptions?" *Amadeus*, December 19, 2023. https://blog.aci.aero/how-can-information-sharing-help-airports-overcome-disruptions

2 Vinod K Vijayan, "Airline Disruption Management," *LinkedIn* article, March 8, 2023. https://www.linkedin.com/pulse/airline-disruption-management-vinod-k-vijayan

3 Rachel Humphries, "More flight disruptions? Or shall we automate airline operations?" *Cirium: Aviation Analytics*, October 6, 2023. https://www.cirium.com/thoughtcloud/flight-disruption-or-automate-airline-airport-operations

4 "Better together: rethinking how to manage disruption in aviation," *Amadeus Insights*, 2023, p. 19.

5 "CAG to Introduce New Autonomous Baggage Handling Fleet at SIN", *Airport Industry-News*, May 15, 2024. https://airportindustry-news.com/cag-to-introduce-new-autonomous-baggage-handling-fleet-at-sin

6 Gary Leff, "How American Airlines Decides Which Flights To Delay And Cancel During Bad Weather," *View from the Wing*, February 21, 2023. https://viewfromthewing.com/how-american-airlines-decides-which-flights-to-delay-and-cancel-during-bad-weather and Gary Leff, "New American Airlines Technology Has Prevented 1,000 Flights From Cancelling," *View from the Wing*, July 6, 2023. https://viewfromthewing.com/new-american-airlines-technology-has-prevented-1000-flights-from-cancelling

7 "Navigating Through Operational Turbulence: Applying Data and Analytics to Improve Efficiency," *Frost & Sullivan*, 2020, p. 24. https://www.frost.com/wp-content/uploads/2020/01/White-Paper-Navigating-through-operational-turbulence.pdf

8 Christian Langer, Daniel Leblanc, Dave Marcontell, Joe Nutter, Eric Porter, and Joel Thibert, "The generative AI opportunity in airline maintenance," *A McKinsey & Company Report*, April 8, 2024.

9 "Using AI to improve turnarounds and collaboration," Case study, Amsterdam Airport Schiphol, *Schiphol Aviation Solutions*. https://www.schiphol.nl/en/aviation-solutions/page/case-study-amsterdam-airport-schiphol

10 "Smart Gating Helps American Airlines Reduce Taxi Times," *AviationPros*, April 9, 2024. https://www.aviationpros.com/airlines/article/53098912/smart-gating-helps-american-airlines-reduce-taxi-times

4 Embracing self-connections and virtual interlining

Self-connections and virtual interlining have already proven that they can clearly provide more options to travelers and more benefits for airlines. For airlines, think about the benefits resulting from extensions of their networks, improvements in load factors, and improvements in operational efficiency. The latter comes from reducing the complexity inherent in the use of conventional interlining and codesharing. And enhancing customer options can add value in the area of branding. However, the development and implementation of virtual interlining processes has challenges for passengers and airlines, not to mention airports. Before starting to make a case for self-connections and virtual interlining, it might be useful to highlight some aspects of conventional interlining and codesharing.

Conventional connections

Airlines began offering connected services decades ago, first through the use of conventional interlining processes and then through codesharing, to expand route networks and enhance connectivity. And although both processes have involved significant complexity, airlines have been trying to offer streamlined and connected experiences through both processes—a single ticket, a single check-in for the traveler and bags, not to mention a rebooking capability in case of a disruption. The booking processes have been managed by GDSs and Passenger Service Systems (PSSs).

Interline agreements gradually became quite complex, going well beyond the connection of flights and handling of baggage, when other factors came into play, such as ticketing, and expenses, such as GDS fees and IATA agency commissions. Then came the codesharing process as airlines became partners in alliances. Within alliances, some airlines began to develop new strategic partnerships, joint ventures, enabling them to coordinate schedules and flight connections. Airline alliances have been clearly successful given that now almost 50 percent of all scheduled airline seats are flown by members of these alliances, enabling passengers to fly worldwide with a high level of connectivity. And now a number of independent airlines could decide to join one of

DOI: 10.4324/9781003483960-4

the three global alliances for at least two reasons. First, an important concern for these independent airlines is the growing presence of low-cost carriers. Second, some airlines in alliances have begun to codeshare with airlines outside of their alliances. Two clear examples are Turkish Airlines (a member of Star Alliance) and Qantas (a member of oneworld). This development would provide an increase in connectivity for travelers. Moreover, some full-service airlines are beginning to codeshare with LCCs to develop mutual benefits. Think about the announced codeshare partnership between Malaysia Airlines and IndiGo, the large Indian LCC. This codeshare will clearly benefit Malaysia Airlines, which is planning to expand into the Indian market, and benefit IndiGo, which is planning to expand its international network.

But, while codesharing processes in alliances have been offering value for partners and travelers, what is their future going forward given the changes in the marketplace? According to the data available from OAG, the overall capacity offered by the three global alliances (Star, SkyTeam, and oneworld) is about 45 percent. The share of global capacity offered by the LCCs is about 30 percent. The non-aligned carriers offer the remaining 25 percent of the total capacity. And just as the full-service airlines have their alliances, some low-cost carriers now are also in their own alliances, such as Value Alliance and U-Fly. If codesharing is working, why is its future questionable? First, as mentioned above, some full-service carriers in alliances have now begun to codeshare with carriers outside of their alliances. Second, the connectivity process has improved with the emergence of technology businesses that facilitate self-made connections and virtual interlining. Third, codesharing processes do provide some concerns on the part of some travelers—for example, insufficient clarity and transparency on some rules (relating to check-in, baggage handling, and rebooking in the event of a disruption, and refunds) as well the inability to access benefits for premium loyalty members such as services during a flight. The rules can also apply to the aircraft of one airline carrying the code of another airline over the airspace of a particular country.

The main benefit for members in the global alliances was to expand their global networks (inter-airline codeshare connections) without increasing the size of their fleets, serving new markets as well as underserved markets. Without alliances many airlines could not have expanded their international networks due to the constraints of ownership and control. As a result of global alliances, members in each of the three global alliances were able to serve about 1,000 destinations. This is a major benefit for a non-aligned airline to increase its network coverage by joining one of the global alliances and offering codeshared flights. Another major benefit of codesharing was in the display of flights in the GDSs: online connections of an airline were shown with a higher priority than interline connections, involving different airlines. This provided a clear benefit when two different airlines appeared to be the same airline within the codeshare framework. Codesharing processes do provide some concerns for travelers, though, as outlined above. Moreover, connectivity depends on the degree of alignment in schedules and capacity among the partners. It is this alignment that provides travelers more frequency and departure time options. But, in alliances not all members are equal. There is a much greater unity among airlines within an alliance that are in joint ventures, in some cases even involving equity.

From the perspective of travelers, besides having access to a greater number of destinations (ability to fly from any city to any other city worldwide on a single ticket) and some flexibility, there is also the value of using the loyalty points on any of the members in an alliance. And there is a certain amount of alignment in the passenger processes. However, while it is relatively easy to measure the benefits relating to the expansion of networks, benefits in the other two areas are difficult to measure. On the other hand, there is no question that benefits could increase in each of the three areas if collaboration and coordination could increase. Many members in each of the three alliances have already begun to codeshare with airlines outside of their alliances. Now, with virtual interlining it may be possible to work with LCCs. However, the process is complicated. For example, each carrier in an alliance needs to participate in industry groups such as the IATA's Billing and Settlement Plan and the Airlines Reporting Corporation to coordinate travel for passengers on multi-legs and for the two types of carriers (marketing and operating) to settle the ticketing and processing of the fare. Other players in the process are travel agents and GDSs as well as systems such as PSSs.

Basically, the construction of an itinerary and its pricing is performed by a GDS that receives information from businesses such as OAG (for schedules) and ATPCO (for fares) and inventory (from airlines) and sends the information to the validating airline. Then the operating airline bills the validating airline. The process for generating a Passenger Name Record (PNR), ticketing (after the payment for an itinerary, a single ticket for the multi-segment travel), and settlement (for the funds between the marketing and the operating airline(s)) is the responsibility of the validating airline.

Think about just a few aspects of the complexity. A passenger requests an itinerary, say from an agent. The GDS puts together flights from the schedules published by airlines and made available through such businesses as OAG, keeping in mind such factors as Minimum Connect Times (MCTs). This is just the beginning of the complexity. Now add the complexity introduced by codeshares that operate over and above interline agreements. The codesharing process involves a passenger buying a ticket on one airline and flying on a different airline that is using the name of the airline selling the ticket. In other words, an airline markets seats flown by a partner.

The complexity is high for administering and offering interline flights. The complexity just starts when airlines want to have the interline capability that requires the need to enter into the Multilateral Interline Traffic Agreement and the IATA Clearing House. Then there is the need to negotiate bilateral agreements that include an agreement on general business rules, such as special prorate agreements. And the complexity keeps increasing—for example, having to deal with e-ticketing, fees to distributors, and the establishment of Electronic Miscellaneous Documents (EMDs). Another challenge in interlining is that when the interlining activities get constructed by third parties, such as a GDS, airlines do not have access to the data, especially in real time. On top of that there can be issues relating to the involvement of multiple currencies, delays between payments, and the leakage of revenue. How about the revenues coming from ancillary sources?

Self-connections

There are at least two alternatives to conventional interlining: self-connecting and virtual interlining. Self-connecting involves virtually no complexity as the connecting flights are searched for by the passenger and separate tickets are purchased by the passenger. The concept has been practiced for some time in Europe. A survey, conducted by OAG between December 2015 and January 2016, showed that 40 percent of the respondents would self-connect if they could save at least \$100, another 34 percent for a saving of at least \$200, and another 15 percent for a saving of at least \$300. The survey also revealed that the largest percentage of travelers willing to self-connect was individuals who were traveling in domestic markets.[1] A more recent OAG report estimates that the number of self-connecting passengers has increased from 55 million travelers in 2017 to 179 million in 2022.[2] And going forward the number of self-connecting passengers could increase well over 10 percent.

Self-connections offer many benefits, such as opportunities for,

(a) traveling in markets that do not have connecting services, or at least, services that are convenient,
(b) lower fares, and
(c) flexibility relating to the choice of destinations, airports of origin and destination, and the ability to have a lengthy layover at selected destinations.

Relating to the second point above, namely lower fares, one estimate is that virtual interlining can save about "25% to 30% on average, depending on whether it's international or domestic."[3] However, there are some challenges facing passengers.

1. The search may take a long time and may not result in either the lowest fare or the best combination of price and value. Extra time can be required to create complex itineraries due to the need to navigate multiple websites of multiple airlines to align the itineraries.
2. For some travelers the self-connection process could be confusing, given the number of airlines (including alliance partners) and their hubs, and the complexity of the search process.
3. Passengers would be responsible for transferring their bags from the inbound flight to the outbound connecting flight.
4. Passengers would need to deal on their own with any delays or cancellations.

5. There is also a consideration involving trust, relating to for example, not only baggage transfer and rebooking, but lack of access to mobile apps that enable passengers to manage their itineraries (with access to multiple airlines) on the day of travel.

However, as commented in a previous book, players such as kiwi.com and Dohop have entered the marketplace to assist travelers making self-connections by reducing the risk of missing connecting flights due to delays and cancellations, problems relating to rebooking flights and getting bags transferred (an intensifying problem due to the labor shortages at airlines). They are making available different types of insurance plans to reduce the risk. Since the booking behaviors and processes of different segments vary, for example by generation and the number of people in a group, there are a broad spectrum of new players to assist different segments with their varying needs. Think about individual travelers who are only traveling with carry-on baggage.

As for airlines, as self-connections increase, some will feel competition as different airlines will vie for this segment. A few are already considering self-connections in the development of their schedules and implementing improvements in the day of travel experience. Passengers willing to self-connect want to pay lower fares by having access to flights of LCCs. From this perspective, some full-service airlines are beginning to look for routes where there are no direct flights, traditional connecting options are limited, or the schedules are poor, such as the day or time of travel.

Think about Worldwide by easyJet, a platform that enables passengers to book connections that give them more choices to travel. Passengers can make connections on easyJet and a selected number of partners as well as Deutsche Bahn rail, creating self-connected journeys to the destinations of their choice.[4] Passengers are required to collect their bags from the first flight and re-check them in for the connecting flight. Self-connected itineraries give passengers the option to choose the way they want to travel. EasyJet plans for connection times for passengers to have a reasonable amount of time to make connections, including the connection of the bags. EasyJet provides a connection protection service that is included in the price of the booking. The connection service is facilitated by Dohop, where a dedicated, multilingual team is available through multiple channels—telephone, email, and chat.

Recognizing some revenue opportunities, especially if passengers end up spending more time at airports, a few airports have also begun to step forward to redesign their terminal layouts and services to facilitate processes for self-connecting passengers. These airports are focusing on the situations involving passengers missing connecting flights and needing assistance with claiming and re-checking bags, not to mention on-site assistance to advance the process of self-connections. London Gatwick and Hamburg Airports are just two examples. Some airports and airlines also have begun to work with ground service providers to offer multimodal transportation—connected journeys involving different modes of transportation—airlines, trains, long-distance buses, urban mobility services. In Italy and Germany, trains operated by railway companies (Trenitalia and Deutsche Bahn) have already begun to facilitate multimodal connections at airports. Deutsche Bahn has even joined the Star Alliance group that also includes the linkage of loyalty programs.

One critical success factor is the collaboration and coordination between service providers, key technology players, and data integrators (with data coming from not only multiple sources, but also in different formats). A second success factor is the ability to use data and analytics to evaluate the risk of connections. A third one is the availability of innovative mobile apps that offer not only reliable and timely information at any touch point, but also a customer-centric management of trips across different modes of transportation during the day of travel.

A few airports have even developed specific platforms to help travelers make self-connections. Two examples are ViaMilano in Malpensa and GatwickConnects in London Gatwick, where specific processes have been established to facilitate passenger transfers that avoid the need for controlled areas and enable passengers to manage their baggage directly. Kiwi.com partnered with Budapest Airport to help passengers navigate through the airport with a new service called bud:connects, a self-connecting transfer service to help passengers minimize the time to make connections. The airport developed bud:connects transfer desks, staffed with trained agents to help passengers make transfers. The facility can also print boarding passes and provide fast-track security vouchers for passengers with short connecting times. Similarly, kiwi.com partnered with Marseille Provence Airport to launch self-connect service in 2022.[5] Kiwi.com enables passengers to book flights on airlines that do not have codeshare agreements and have a smooth transfer experience.

However, airports need to go further to deal with the greatest risks (uncertainty) facing travelers, relating to dealing with misconnections of flights and loss of baggage. This represents an opportunity for a new generation of third-party distributors and for insurance businesses to work with airlines and airports. While some airports have begun to work with LCCs to develop and promote self-connect services and systems, the process has been slow due to:

1. Most city pairs are already served by interline and codeshare connections.
2. Some LCCs have begun to serve major airports.
3. Some airports are not willing to provide dedicated areas for baggage transfer service and facilities for the management of missed connections, ViaMilano, GatwickConnect, and bud:connects being the three exceptions.
4. For airports, as mentioned above, there is a need to work with airlines on the one side and travel businesses like Dohop and kiwi.com and their platforms, on the other side.
5. Self-connectivity is mostly viable within domestic markets and many intra-European markets, particularly within Europe's Schengen area.

The decision by travelers to self-connect comes down to savings and flexibility, convenience of airports, and cities of destination. It is a balance between these factors and the risks. Could some passengers pay a premium for eliminating the risks relating to baggage transfer and rebooking? The future looks good because, in addition to new players to assist travelers, some airports are beginning to play a more active role—for example, by providing multimodal transportation services. The partnerships are being facilitated by new technology. In the final analysis, travelers want convenience and self-control. Self-connections are clearly part of the self-control desire.

Virtual interlining

If conventional interlining (involving the most complexity) is at one end and self-connections (involving the least complexity) is at the other end, then virtual interlining is somewhere in the middle. The concept is fairly simple. A traveler goes to the website of an airline and looks for a specific destination. If the airline does not offer service to that destination, the shopper leaves the website. What if an organization offering virtual interlining were to step in and help the shopper find another airline that serves that destination? It would then be a win–win situation, for the shopper and both airlines. The concept was brought to the marketplace by kiwi.com, in 2012, in Brno, Czech Republic. Formerly it was known as skypicker.com. It is reported that now this online travel agency has begun to use AI-based algorithms to make connections with airlines and ground service providers and offer coverage for disruptions. There are some newer generations of providers of virtual interlining services, such as Dohop, Air Black Box, and TripStack. Their platforms can interact with airlines' systems through the use of APIs. These systems avoid the complexity involved in setting up multiple agreements, mentioned above. Passengers can purchase multi-leg itineraries through a single reservation. Emirates, for example, has partnered with BLADE and GO7 (a travel platform) to enable its passengers to travel seamlessly between Dubai and Monaco/Nice, completing their trips with a single Emirates interline ticket.[6] Other features being developed are the use of AI-based algorithms to construct flight connections, disruption-protection services, and coordination with airports to facilitate transfers. Of course, existing OTAs, such as Expedia, and metasearch engines, such as Skyscanner, also offer virtual interlining services.

Virtual interlining is simply a process to create an itinerary by combining the services offered by multiple airlines. The airlines involved do not need to have a partnership with specific agreements. Providers of virtual interlining services work with sophisticated platforms to handle the creating of an itinerary and a seamless connected experience. It is a more flexible and a more cost-effective option, for example, by combining the services offered by a much broader spectrum of airlines. Consider, for example, the agreement between Jetstar and IndiGo to offer virtual interline connections to provide more opportunities.[7] Think about passengers traveling on the two low-fare airlines between

India and Southeast Asia, making connections, for example, at Singapore's Changi Airport. Think about the value created by Jetstar Connect. Jetstar already had experience with the virtual interlining process, having arranged, in 2019, with Tigerair Taiwan.[8] Jetstar had already developed an interlining platform (Jetstar Connect) that is embedded in its website. Jetstar Connect is reported to be similar to easyJet's interlining platform and both platforms are facilitated by Dohop.[9]

As virtual interlining is quite different from conventional interlining and codesharing, it requires the development and implementation of internal strategies to achieve technology enabled virtual interlining as well as strategies for collaboration and coordination. Initially, the new entrants (kiwi.com and Dohop) purchased single segments from GDSs and then recreated complex itineraries for customers and added services such as hotel accommodation, in case of missed flights, and arrangements to take alternate flights. Then some airlines started thinking seriously about the concept. Think about Worldwide by easyJet, mentioned above.

One challenge was not being able to use the customs-free transit areas. The benefit, however, is clear: cheaper itineraries, since at least one carrier is a low-cost carrier. Examples of airlines beginning to use virtual interlining include Jetstar, Indigo, Thai VietJet, Jazeera Airways, Aegean Airlines, and AirAsia. Flexibility and lower costs could be important in a consumer-driven world, not to mention, younger generations like millennials whose behaviors are changing, driven by innovative technologies. Virtual interlining is clearly an opportunity for the new players to increase the value of their platforms. However, while there are opportunities, there are also some challenges.

First is not only to work closely with passengers on the one side and travel service providers (airlines, ground transportation services, airports, and hotels) on the other side, but also intermediaries such as GDSs and metasearch engines. The metasearch engines can, in fact, be a source of a new partnership as they also aggregate different flight options. On the other hand, travel metasearch companies used to be among the high-ranking businesses in travel since they enabled travelers to compare flight and hotel prices from different vendors at a glance. As such, many online travel agencies decided to take an equity stake in the metasearch engines—Priceline Group in Kayak, Expedia in Trivago, and Trip.com in Skyscanner. However, with the emergence of the likes of Google Hotels, YouTube, and TikTok, the role played by the metasearch engines may be declining.[10] On the other hand, the use of GenAI can develop a user-centric approach that creates the right solution for the right traveler that would "require globalization with the right amount of localization."[11]

Second, they can enhance their platforms to enable NDC connections, enhancing ways for airlines to sell their inventories. Keep in mind that many full-service carriers will be implementing IATA's One Order, which presumably will merge three documents into one record, PNR, eTicket, and EMD, enabling an increase in the sale of ancillaries. Keep also in mind the objective of control, on the part of the full-service airlines, of the booking relating to not just the prices and ancillaries, but also their distribution strategies.

Third, the search rules in the booking engine need to be extremely customer-centric, enabling a reasonable degree of personalization as well as working with dynamic pricing schemes that change prices based on variation in demand and competition as well as seasonality, day of the week and time of the day.

Fourth are the challenges and opportunities relating to commissions—not just the basis, flat vs. adjustable, but also the source of traffic (for example, metasearch engines) and time and destinations relating to individual bookings, not to mention the extent of customer services.

Fifth, there needs to be an extensive database on customers to build and develop their trust and eventually loyalty. This database will also allow the business to understand customer segments and eventually individual customers within each segment, and target them with better offers, build trust, and eventually loyalty. The goal is not just to offer customized itineraries (hopefully at lower prices), but also to provide a unique customer experience. Since the coverage offered by large OTAs (such as Expedia) is deep and wide, it might be helpful to start with services in niche markets, regions, and demographics.

Sixth, the use of analytics is vital to improve the customer conversion rate.

Seventh, while the segment that wants to self-connect appears to be large, more information is needed on the size of the segment and the key behaviors of this segment. How much money could this segment save through the self-connection process?

Eighth, how can airlines, airports, and distributors seize this opportunity by simplifying the process through collaboration and coordination? There is clearly value for all partners. Some airports, for example, can add incremental traffic and revenues by capitalizing on these opportunities by implementing products and services that meet the needs of this segment. How much an airport can benefit will depend on the strengths and weaknesses of an individual airport. And the additional revenues will come from both the aeronautical sources and non-aeronautical sources. The question is the increase in the revenue base compared to the required investments.

Moving forward

Since the management of inventory is one of the top priorities of airlines, virtual interlining can play an important role for airlines that have already moved forward from conventional interlining to codesharing. Now they can transition to virtual interlining that provides more options to travelers and can help airlines improve the management of their inventories. The new generation of virtual interlining can provide mutual benefits for travelers and for partners (airlines and airports). However, it will require not only collaboration between airlines, airports, and distributors, but also an increase in digital transformation on their part. PSSs are being upgraded leveraging new technologies to develop new interfaces and new applications. PSSs with older-generation technology prevented airlines from offering shoppers rich content, some degree of personalization, different payment systems, not to mention mobile access. Despite these limitations, the legacy systems have been dependable. On the other hand, they have been inflexible (in terms of customer-centric applications and user friendliness) and fairly expensive to maintain. The plan is now to upgrade the three key modules of the PSSs with the objective of improving internal communication within the systems—the Airline Reservation System, the Departure Control System, and the Inventory Control System. The integration of these three modules will help managers take revenue management to the next level, not only transitioning from dynamic pricing to continuous pricing, but also leveraging the NDC framework, encompassing Offers and Orders.

Next, improved APIs can provide better links for airlines and different data sources to enable travelers to book their multi-leg trips through a single reservation. And, going forward, AI-based algorithms can not only enable travelers to create complex itineraries, but also acquire protection policies (insurance) to deal with disruptions—delays and cancellations. And, as mentioned above, forward-looking airlines are already looking at effective ways to adapt the NDC structure given the potential of having access to real-time data in a single place. The goal should be not only to make offers that can be delivered, but also to deliver on the offers that have been made.

The conventional concepts of interlining and codesharing flights are already changing for a number of reasons, some of which were mentioned above.

- While alliances have provided benefits to both airlines and travelers, some challenges are emerging too—for example, individual airlines have had to work with their own brands as well as the alliance brand.
- Some airlines are changing their membership in alliances—for example, SAS will be leaving Star Alliance and joining SkyTeam.
- Some airlines have formed a strategy to offer their lowest fares only through their own digital channels (websites and apps) and the NDC-driven channels.[12]
- Airlines within alliances are codesharing with airlines outside of alliances (Turkish and Qantas are two examples mentioned above).
- PSSs are transitioning from the use of conventional technology to the use of modern technology with improved use of APIs as discussed above.
- LCCs are expanding—for example, since 2017, they have accounted for about one-third of the global air travel industry.[13]
- Some travelers are beginning to look at travel from very different perspectives, relating to destinations and activities, with the rise, for example, of "anywhere travelers," a segment that has a strong passion for experiences that takes them to less obvious destinations.[14]
- New distributors are now gaining ground: the likes of kiwi.com, Dohop, and Air Black Box.

- New businesses are entering the marketplace to offer multimodal transportation. For example, BlaBlaCar, headquartered in Paris, now operates in 21 countries. It was reported that "Last year, 80 million travelers booked a bus or carpool ride on BlaBlaCar, a 23% jump from 2022."[15]
- New technology is emerging, for example GenAI software, for airlines to understand how travelers are using their websites and apps to identify opportunities for improvement. Think about this development. Airlines spent an incredible amount of time understanding how shoppers were using their websites and apps by studying "actions, such as keystrokes, clicks and pages viewed." Now, new technology service providers, such as Quantum Metric, are launching new GenAI-intelligence-powered session systems that can summarize users' actions in seconds, a process that took hours in the past.[16]
- Similarly, GenAI technology can also enable travelers to create contemporary itineraries easily even when the itineraries are complex.

For all airlines, full-service and low-cost, virtual interlining offers an opportunity to expand their networks, to expand their customer bases by providing shoppers more options on their websites, and to sell not only their basic products, but also a broad spectrum of ancillaries, conventional and new. Even though full-service carriers have already made investments to deal with the complexity relating to conventional interlining and codesharing, virtual interlining will not increase complexity if low-cost carriers begin to interline with full-service carriers.

While most travelers talk about their frustrations in many areas, such as onboard services—(food and beverages, inflight entertainment, seat comfort, and so forth), and baggage handling, the top problem appears to be disruptions. While airlines and airports have been trying to find ways to measure the pain caused by disruptions and viable solutions to minimize disruptions, as discussed in the previous chapter, now passengers can also try to find some solutions to disruptions by making self-connections and taking advantage of virtual interlining. Virtual interlining is a major transformation to help passengers deal with disruptions and to expand their itinerary options with the availability of multimodal travel. However, while the IATA framework for conventional interlining worked really well for full-service airlines, it could not accommodate the operations of low-cost carriers and providers of multimodal transportation. This is where virtual interlining comes in, requiring a symphony of collaboration and coordination between airlines and airports, not only among different categories of airlines, but also for new segments of travel, discussed in the next chapter.

Notes

1 "Self-Connection: The Rise and Roadblocks to a Growing Travel Booking Strategy," *OAG*, 2016.

2 "Reshaping Airline Journeys: The Unfolding Saga Of Virtual Interlining," *OAG*, July 6, 2023.

3 Linda Fox, "TripStack Onboards NokAir for Virtual Interlining Technology," *PhocusWire*, October 19, 2023. https://www.phocuswire.com/tripstack-virtual-interlining-nokair
4 "Worldwide by easyJet", *easyJet*, n.d. https://www.easyjet.com/en/help/extra-services/worldwide#:
5 "Marseille Provence Airport launches self-service for passengers," *International Airport Review*, April 13, 2022. https://www.internationalairportreview.com/news/175916/marseille-provence-airport-launches-self-service-for-passengers
6 "Emirates partners with BLADE and GO7 to provide a personalised, streamlined travel experience," *Future Travel Experience*, May 2024. https://www.futuretravelexperience.com/2024/05/emirates-partners-with-blade-and-go7-to-provide-a-personalised-streamlined-travel-experience
7 "Jetstar and IndiGo announce virtual interline partnership," *Jetstar*, April 8, 2022. https://newsroom.jetstar.com/jetstar-and-indigo-announce-virtual-interline-partnership
8 "No compromise needed. How Jetstar Connect offers a customer experience close to traditional interline without the associated costs and complexities," *Dohop*, May 30, 2023. https://www.dohop.com/press-media/jetstar-connect
9 "Reshaping Airline Journeys: The Unfolding Saga Of Virtual Interlining," *OAG*, July 6, 2023.
10 Dennis Schaal, "How Travel Metasearch Lost Its Mojo," *Skift Research*, April 1, 2024. https://skift.com/2024/04/01/how-travel-metasearch-lost-its-mojo
11 Linda Fox, "Trip.Com Group on Growth Strategies, Experience and Generative AI," *PhocusWire*, April 2, 2024. https://www.phocuswire.com/schubert-lou-trip-com-group
12 Linda Fox, "The Impact of American Airlines' Distribution Changes One Year On," *PhocusWire*, April 3, 2024. https://www.phocuswire.com/american-airlines-distribution-ndc-surcharges?
13 "Low-cost carrier market worldwide – statistics & facts," *Statista*, December 18, 2023. https://www.statista.com/topics/6024/low-cost-carrier-market-worldwide/#topicOverview
14 "The Biggest Travel Trends to Expect in 2024," Condé Nast Traveller, December 30, 2023. https://www.cntraveler.com/story/travel-trends-2024 and "The Anywhere Traveler Puts New Destinations on the Map," *Skift*, January 10, 2023. https://skift.com/2023/01/10/the-anywhere-traveler-puts-new-destinations-on-the-map
15 Morgan Hines, "BlaBlaCar Receives €100M To Bolster Multimodal Growth," *PhocusWire*, April 3, 2024. https://www.phocuswire.com/blablacar-funding-growth-rideshare
16 Mitra Sorrells, "New Tool Uses Generative AI to Help Travel Brands Understand Online Activity," *PhocusWire*, April 4, 2024. https://www.phocuswire.com/generative-ai-help-travel-brands-understand-online-activity

5 Introducing new segments of air travel

New segments of travel can have a transformative impact on air travel in urban and regional markets. Four such segments are discussed in this chapter: Mobility-as-a-Service (MaaS), electric vertical take-off and landing aircraft (eVTOLs), small electric airplanes for regional markets, and multi-modal travel. Although some of these concepts have been discussed in previous books in this series, the information presented in this chapter is updated and expanded.

Mobility-as-a-Service (MaaS)

Mobility-as-a-Service (MaaS) is usually a demand-based transportation system in which individuals do not drive their own vehicles. The concept has value in dense urban areas where it is not cost-effective to provide public parking space for privately owned cars. The concept began to be explored when some people began to consider the idea of moving away from personally owned modes of transportation (cars, scooters, etc.) and use the services of public and private transportation service providers. The goal of many major cities has been to provide reliable and affordable transportation to large numbers of people using, for example, a holistic mobility platform and MaaS apps that offer users a single interface to find and use different public transport systems, including shared mobility services. The platform can provide users seamless access to a region's mobility, with information on where to start trips, where users can park their vehicles, and how to transfer between different modes of public transportation services and shared mobility services.

Within the context of air travel, the MaaS concept tends to be associated with getting to and from the airport (from home, hotel, office, etc.). However, the concept can be broadened so that airports, airlines, and OTAs could offer seamless and cost-effective airport connectivity while improving the overall travel experience. In some ways, it is already available, for example, through the use of limo services. But it tends to be expensive. Going forward, think about how collaboration could operationalize and expand the MaaS concept to meet the personalized needs of travelers cost-effectively. The MaaS

DOI: 10.4324/9781003483960-5

concept can then enable travelers to plan, book, and pay for a broad spectrum of mobility services. Service providers and distributors can then offer travelers solutions based on their personal needs. And, going forward, interest in MaaS would increase significantly as a result of

1. adding more transportation services by buses, trains, and airlines,
2. enabling travelers to make choices based on costs, convenience, flexibility, and environmental considerations,
3. using innovative end-user mobile apps to make bookings and make contactless payments,
4. the emergence of autonomous vehicles and electric vehicles,
5. the emergence of on-demand car services, including shared cars, and
6. the emergence of eVTOLs and vertiports (discussed in the next section).

In some ways, from an air travel perspective, the deployment of electric aircraft to provide air-taxi services is part of the MaaS concept. And let us not overlook an extremely important benefit of MaaS. Increasing the depth and breadth of its operations would allow the collection of relevant and timely data to enable service providers to offer personalized services and track travelers' experiences. This data could also be used to determine the viability of services to be provided in other travel segments discussed below.

From a broader perspective, one could consider Advanced Air Mobility (AAM) a part of MaaS. In the US, AAM is often discussed by the aerospace industry as well as by the National Aeronautics and Space Administration (NASA), and the Federal Aviation Administration (FAA). In addition, Urban Air Mobility (UAM) can be thought of as a subset of AAM, that would have operations on lower altitudes within urban and suburban areas. The US government is obviously interested in looking into effective ways to integrate AAM concepts into the existing National Airspace Systems (NAS). The FAA has already been looking into modernizing its air traffic infrastructure through its Next Generation Air Transportation System (NextGen). Many attributes of NextGen are needed to support the development and implementation of the systems required for AAM to transport people and goods within cities, within communities, and in rural areas. The application of AAM could be an air-taxi operation or delivery of goods or inter-regional operations.

Electric vertical take-off and landing aircraft

eVTOLs fall within the category of AAM aircraft. They are powered by batteries, expected to operate up to 4,000 feet above ground, and can have a range of up to about 150 miles. They would be operated from vertiports that would be more than simple helipads, designed to support eVTOL operations—for example, with charging facilities to accommodate a high volume of operations. Some analysts believe that some vertiports could be simple stopping places (including the tops of buildings) that can be at simple helipads. However, a vertiport would need to be more than a simple place on top of a building to accommodate an eVTOL. Even a simple vertiport on top of an existing building or on top of an existing parking garage will require some additional engineering and reinforcement to accommodate the eVTOLs. New structures, on the other hand, can have the necessary elements designed in from the start. Then there are analysts who believe that large vertiports should offer multiple services, such as food and beverages and some amount of shopping. While some larger vertiports will have some additional amenities (like simple food and beverages to go), they are likely to be limited, with no retail facilities. Whereas there is often significant down time at conventional airports, eVTOLs largely involve moving passengers as quickly as possible with as little dwell time as possible—for example, 10 to 15 minutes from arrival at a vertiport to departure of an eVTOL from the vertiport. The fast turnaround of an eVTOL, combined with the high land costs in most urban locations, will most likely cause infrastructure providers to limit or even eliminate retail activity.

Experiments to develop an autonomous air-taxi service can be traced back to 2017 in Dubai and in Germany where Lilium, a German company, flight tested its unmanned first flight of the two-seat Eagle full-size prototype.[1] After that, progress in the development of technology was slow for a couple of years based on the considerations of regulatory certification and public acceptance. However, interest and investments in eVTOL technology began to increase significantly starting around 2019. Now, fast forward to October 2023, when China's Guangzhou-based urban mobility company, EHang, actually received certification for its EH216-S eVTOL. It's a pilotless vehicle, powered by batteries, and can carry two passengers. Early in 2024, EHang carried out a demonstration flight in Costa Rica to show its potential in Latin America. The initial version of the aircraft has a payload capacity of just under 500 pounds, and a range of just under 20 miles.[2]

In a different region, California-based Joby Aviation and Dubai's Roads and Transport Authority (RTA) started to work with the UAE's General Civil Aviation Authority to develop and operate air-taxi services, using aircraft developed by Joby Aviation. The planned network is shown in Figure 5.1. The four vertiports shown will be developed by Skyports.[3] This particular partnership is expected to be successful, given that there is a specific network, a plan to develop the necessary infrastructure, and the availability of an aircraft with an appropriate capacity (say, up to four passengers), a range (say, around 100 miles), and a speed that could be up to 150 miles per hour. Operations are planned to be launched in 2026.

Opportunities in the UAE are being sought out not just by Joby, but also by Archer, which is developing a partnership with Falcon Aviation Services to start operations from Dubai's Atlantis The Palm resort to the Marina Mall in Abu Dhabi's Corniche district with Archer's four-seater eVTOL, Midnight; and BETA Technologies, which has secured a Minimum Viable License (MVL) from the UAE Regulations Lab to conduct for-hire cargo missions

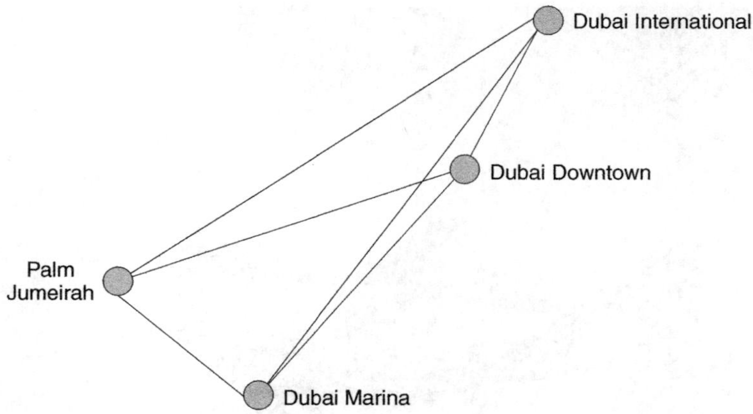

Figure 5.1 An overview of the planned Dubai air-taxi network

Source: Based on an image created by Joby Aviation, 2024[28]

with UPS. As mentioned above, operations could start as soon as 2026. The trip is expected to use existing heliports and take 30 minutes compared to about a two-hour drive during peak traffic. The arrangement between Archer and Falcon is reported to be backed by the Abu Dhabi Investment Office.[4] The US Federal Aviation Administration has already issued its final airworthiness criteria for Archer's piloted four-passenger Midnight eVTOL aircraft. The development means that Archer can look forward to achieving a type certification for Midnight. Joby has received such a regulatory approval.[5]

Why the interest in the UAE when there are huge opportunities in highly congested cities in Asia, such as Bangkok, and not only congestion in Manila and Jakarta, but also archipelagos in the Philippines and Indonesia? One answer may be not only the availability of funds to get the vehicles developed and certified quickly, but also the potential for the needed infrastructure to be developed at a fast pace to start operations.

BETA Technologies, the developer of A250, is taking a different design approach. Instead of tilting propellers, the A250 has four dedicated lift propellers and one pusher propeller, employing a Lift + Cruise mechanism. The VTOL propellers lift the plane vertically and then the single pusher propeller takes over, allowing the pilot to stow the VTOL propellers for wingborne flight. Such a design is relatively simple to reduce failures and lead to a faster certification process. Since the two types of propellers have different functions (four for the lift and one for the cruise), the design of the vehicle can be optimized without concern over making compromises, which would be the case for tilting propellers (see Figure 5.2). The A250 has a capacity of six (five passengers and a pilot), is being engineered for a range up to 250 miles and a speed approaching 155mph. This eVTOL aircraft achieved its first crewed

Figure 5.2 BETA Technologies A250

Source: Printed with permission of BETA Technologies

transition flights (core capabilities of vertical lift and horizontal cruise, in combination) in April 2024 at Plattsburgh International Airport in New York. While other eVTOL aircraft developers have also achieved transition flights with their models, those flights were with pilots in a remotely piloted position. Since beginning its flight test regime in 2018, BETA has tested its full-scale flights with pilots on board. The A250 is expected to receive FAA type certification in 2026.

In addition to the A250, BETA is developing another plane, the CX300, an electric conventional take-off and landing (eCTOL) aircraft that will use largely the same airframe and the same propulsion system as the A250 (see Figure 5.3). The CX300 could play an important role in short-haul passenger and cargo markets, given the expected operating costs. BETA Technologies has reported that it could cost US$17 in electricity to fly its A250 a distance of 150 miles, compared to US$700 in jet fuel for a turbine plane flying the same distance.[6] The CX300 is expected to receive FAA type certification in 2025. BETA's customer base, across both the A250 and the CX300, includes UPS, Air New Zealand, Blade, Bristow, United Therapeutics, Helijet and LCI. The company has also contracted with partnerships with the US Air Force and the US Army.

Airlines throughout the world have shown interest in eVTOLs. The low-cost operator Gol, based in Brazil, is planning to incorporate eVTOLs in its

Figure 5.3 BETA Technologies CX300

Source: Printed with permission of BETA Technologies

network, given the level of congestion in São Paulo. The idea would be to provide air-taxi services connecting different parts of the city to the two airports in the city, Guarulhos International Airport and Congonhas Airport, and services between the two airports. Gol is reported to be partnering with Grupo Comporte, a large transport company in Brazil. Beyond São Paulo, using Vertical Aerospace's VX4 (accommodating up to four passengers and a pilot), services could be expanded to other cities in Brazil, such as Rio de Janeiro. Services are reported to begin in 2026.[7] Lilium, the German manufacturer of eVTOLs, is planning to sell a large number of its aircraft to Saudia, as well as Azul Airlines and NetJets. In the US, United and Archer are planning to work with numerous partners (for example, the City of Chicago, Chicago Department of Aviation, World Business Chicago, the State of Illinois, and Vertiport Chicago) to develop the needed infrastructure to support the integration of eVTOL aircraft operations into Chicago's transportation ecosystem in 2025.[8] In Asia, not only are there opportunities for the introduction of eVTOL services, but there are also opportunities for businesses to work with manufacturers of eVTOLs based in Europe and North America.[9] India's InterGlobe Enterprises is reported to have signed an agreement with Archer to purchase up to 200 Midnights that would be used for commercial flights in such cities as Delhi, Mumbai, and Bengaluru.[10]

Manufacturers of eVTOLs talk about the convenience and experience of air taxis. Take, for example, Joby Aviation, which has not only acquired Uber's Elevate division, but Uber has also strengthened its partnership with Joby that will integrate its "aerial ridesharing service into the Uber app, and vice versa, across all U.S. launch markets."[11] Joby plans to start its commercial taxi service by 2025.

However, a number of questions are being raised about the technology and the operations. A report by McKinsey, for example, raises the following key questions:

1. Would there be sufficient frequency to match the flexibility of a car?
2. Would there be a large number of vertiports, located at convenient locations to minimize the total trip time and maximize the ground-to-air connectivity?
3. Would passengers travel to the vertiports in their own vehicles or would there by multi-ride systems and processes?
4. Would operators of air-taxi services provide such services and facilities as onboard Wi-Fi and small trays on seatbacks for laptops? Vertiports, their numbers and locations, as well as facilities, will play an important role in terms of not only reducing the total trip time but also processing, such as check-in and security.[12]

Another main question is how airlines would integrate the air-taxi operations into their networks, beyond transporting passengers to and from congested cities and airports. For example: Could there be services for point-to-point travel?

1. What would be the source of pilots, assuming that the aircraft will not be operated without pilots in the near future? Would they be attracted from existing helicopter and fixed-wing commuter operators with the opportunity to join the mainline services? Would they be trained mostly on flight simulation devices? Would this approach be acceptable to government regulators in charge of the certification process for complex urban surroundings with single-pilot operations? What would be the cost of these devices?
2. In addition to the number and location of vertiports in city centers, where will their locations be at airports?
3. As mentioned above, what is the feasibility of performing check-in and security clearance at the vertiports at the beginning of trips, assuming its acceptability to government regulators, a feature that would require a fundamental change in the size and design of vertiports?
4. Would there be sufficient space for baggage (especially for passengers connecting to long-haul overseas flights), keeping in mind the weight–range constraints?

5. How about the operating costs? One analysis by ARK Invest shows that a trip from Manhattan to John F. Kennedy Airport, which is likely to be \$500 with a traditional helicopter, could be \$430 with an electric vehicle. However, as the technology scales in the coming decade, the total cost of an electric air-taxi ride could be as low as \$180. This amount split among three to four passengers could mean about \$50 to \$60 per passenger.[13]

These questions are not to raise doubts on the value of eVTOLs, but simply to point out that a number of challenges still need to be addressed. Just one example would be not only batteries that have higher densities and faster charging times, but also longer life cycles. Another would be regulatory hurdles—for example, if there might be a need for "4D highways in the sky." However, this regulatory hurdle may not exist in the near term as, initially, eVTOLs will fly only in Visual Flight Rules (VFR) conditions. In congested metropolitan areas, they are likely to follow existing helicopter routes. Consequently, at the beginning, there will not be a need to overhaul the airspace system and provide for enhanced 4D operations. At some point, when eVTOLs operate under Instrument Flight Rules (IFR) conditions and when there is a need to overhaul the airspace, it may involve enhanced 4D operations. With the exception of BETA Technologies' A250, which is an IFR platform, other eVTOLs will fly in VFR conditions. While airspace is an important consideration in the site selection for a vertiport, in the foreseeable future, operations will not be treated differently than conventional aircraft utilizing VFR conditions.

Leaving aside the challenges, what about the opportunities? Think about the value that autonomous drones have begun to add in some areas of airline maintenance—to inspect aircraft, for example, after a wide-body aircraft lands, having gone through lightning strikes. Drones can take photos that technicians, on the ground, can then examine in detail. The starting point is, clearly, to use drones to inspect non-safety work. How about drones to transport people? People are willing to get into electric cars, but would they be equally comfortable in boarding electric planes without pilots? Although for urban travel the operating costs of autonomous vehicles would be lower (no costs of crews), the question then would relate to public acceptance of the pilotless transportation. How would regulators develop the certification standards and regulations for autonomous vehicles for passenger transportation? Although the technology for air-taxi services with eVTOL vehicles is almost here and even if we assume that their operations will receive regulatory approval, there is still the question of public acceptance and engagement with local communities, relating, for example, to the development of a huge number of vertiports. Will the local communities see the benefits? In an Oliver Wyman Forum, South by Southwest (SXSW) panel discussion on urban mobility, it became clear that "Urban Mobility Needs Tech, Guardrails, and a Human Touch."[14]

Figure 5.4 A tentative Ferrovial Vertiport design under consideration involving a new parking structure that can be utilized by a city

Source: Printed with permission of Ferrovial Vertiports

Ferrovial Vertiports, a leading developer of the infrastructure for eVTOL operations, is paying a lot of attention to the public acceptance and community engagement aspects. It is designing vertiport networks "as gateways that will connect communities with employment, education, medical care, recreation, and travel opportunities that would otherwise be inconvenient, time-consuming, or simply inaccessible without advanced air mobility."[15] Ferrovial is using different kinds of data (for example, actual phone and app data) and non-conventional modeling techniques to estimate demand relating to the movements of people and vehicles relating to any two points on the map, with consideration of first- and last-mile routes. The analyses make use of heat maps that are then utilized to pinpoint optimal locations of vertiports. The object is to maximize demand and minimize travel time across different catchment areas.

Figures 5.4 and 5.5 show two images of two different concepts for vertiports. Figure 5.4 shows a tentative Ferrovial Vertiport design under consideration involving a new parking structure to be utilized by a city, with the top floor utilized as a vertiport containing two FATOs (Final Approach and Take-off Area) and six aircraft parking stands. Figure 5.5 shows a tentative Ferrovial Vertiport design under consideration involving land adjacent to a waterway where both a park and a vertiport could co-exist by elevating the airfield onto a platform, thereby ensuring operations are separated from activities of the park.

Figure 5.5 A tentative Ferrovial Vertiport design under consideration involving land adjacent to a waterway

Source: Printed with permission of Ferrovial Vertiports

Small electric airplanes for regional markets

All-electric, zero-emission, airplanes show the potential to totally transform air travel in regional markets. The economics of the existing aircraft have forced airlines to connect passengers in regional markets through congested mega-hubs. Now electric aircraft can totally transform the short-haul market, less than 500 miles. In the US, start-up Eviation flight tested a nine-seat, all-electric plane, the Alice, in September 2022. According to the media, Eviation's order book is already valued at more than US$4 billion.[16] Its aircraft could carry a payload of 2,500 pounds and provide a range of almost 500 miles. Operations could start in 2027. And, besides the envisioned economics of all-electric aircraft, think about the reduction in noise, pollution, and carbon footprints.

Regional markets represent a real opportunity for transformation with the availability of small, all-electric aircraft. There are some estimates that about one-third of the flights within the US are less than 250 miles (sometimes still referred to as commuter flights), which shows the potential for small electric airplanes. Think also about this statistic: "About 90 percent of people in the United States live within a 30-minute drive of a regional airport. Only 60 percent live within the same distance of a large commercial airport."[17] Regional airports (more convenient for travelers) can create dedicated facilities for these airplanes. Not only are they closer, but security will be less of a hassle. And now noise will also not be an issue for these regional airports.

Travel in short-haul markets has been provided mostly by LCCs. Large, full-service carriers seem to be moving toward the use of large aircraft for a variety of reasons, the shortage of pilots being one. Public support for travel in regional markets has been decreasing, relating, for example, to the Essential Air Service Subsidies in the US and Public Service Obligation Routes in Europe. There are also the concerns for noise. On the other hand, numerous regional airports exist that are underutilized. As mentioned earlier, while 90 percent of the population lives within 30 minutes' drive from regional airports in the US, in Europe it is still only 50 percent of the population that lives within a 30-minute drive from regional airports.[18]

Total trip time in regional and short-haul markets (between 100 and 500 miles) by ground transportation has, for the most part, been less than using the air mode. Short-haul travel in the US and in Europe has been mostly by car, more in the US than in Europe, due to the availability of superior rail services. And now the pilot shortage is contributing to the reduction in services at regional airports. The reduction in flights to and from regional airports could also lead to fewer choices of departure and arrival times. However, the situation is likely to change for a number of reasons:[19]

- advances in technology,
- a greater focus on sustainability,
- increasing frustration with road congestion and congestion at major airports,
- the emergence of viable MaaS, discussed above, and
- potential savings in maintenance and overhaul for operators, not to mention the simplicity in some areas of maintenance.

Based on the potential benefits of small electric aircraft, airlines have already begun to order these aircraft. United and Air Canada have already been investing in Heart Aerospace, a Swedish maker of electric and hybrid airplanes for regional markets. This aircraft is not only suitable for regional markets, but it is also a green aircraft. While some manufacturers are making existing airplanes hybrid (for example, ZeroAvia and Cranfield Aerospace Solutions), Heart Aerospace is designing its ES-30 hybrid as a new-generation aircraft, encompassing new technology. The manufacturer had already developed and tested the all-electric E-19, which was fitted with an electric motor and a lithium battery pack that could fly longer distances. This aircraft not only had a low carbon footprint, but also had the potential for lower maintenance costs compared to traditional turboprops. Then the manufacturer of the hybrid ES-30 had two options, an all-electric airplane with a smaller range (up to 125 miles) or a smaller-capacity airplane with a longer range, possibly up to 500 miles. The US Dallas-based carrier JSX has already ordered a significant number of hybrid ES-30s. The aircraft is expected to enter the market in 2028. Heart Aerospace's ES-30 will be a four-propeller battery-powered aircraft. The company claims a 30-minute fast-charge turnaround time.

Commercial activity is clearly focused on major hubs that are congested and electric vehicles have the potential to develop regional airports that would reduce congestion at major hubs. As mentioned above, Eviation already has orders for its electric aircraft for US$4 billion. One customer is Air New Zealand, and the shipping company DHL could be another.[20] JSX has shown interest in acquiring up to 300 different types of hybrid-electric planes to serve smaller communities that are underserved. As mentioned above, services are expected to begin 2028. JSX is a Part 135 and Part 380 Public Charter carrier.[21] JSX plans to serve numerous regional airports where not only connectivity would be improved, but economies of the region would also be boosted. Some of these airports lost commercial flights during the COVID-19 pandemic.

However, even though a large percentage of people in the US and Europe live within a 30-minute drive from a regional airport, there are some major challenges for more services to and from regional airports.

Here are some examples of challenges:

1. There is not enough traffic for airlines to offer reasonable capacity. Point-to-point transportation in regional markets needs to be identified, quantified, and marketed effectively by all partners, airlines, airports, distributors, and communities. From where and how do airlines and airports get reliable and relevant data on how people travel? Could the use of cell phones be one viable source of such data? Then there is the challenge of estimating operating costs and fares. Relating to costs, for example, battery density is expected to increase, but at what prices? Relating to fares, how would travelers evaluate the savings in time against additional costs and lack of flexibility?
2. Right now, there is not sufficient infrastructure to start and maintain operations. Just as in the case of eVTOLS, some new infrastructure needs to be developed—charging facilities and the extension of the electric grids. And on the part of the regional airports, they cannot invest the needed funds for infrastructure (operational and digital) given insufficient demand.
3. There are some concerns about the safety standards. Presumably, one reason the batteries are heavy is because of the built-in safety standards to prevent thermal runaway (overheating). The weight vs. energy density will have an impact on the range and payload of these aircraft. There is also the question of the reliability of the technology.
4. Although there has been a dramatic improvement in the power and range of electric cars, the story is a little different in the case of electric aircraft—for example, the weight of batteries relative to the energy produced to propel the aircraft.
5. While electric airplanes will be environmentally desirable, their range may be limited. The batteries need to be not only high density (powerful relative to their weight), but also durable and not subject to bursting into

flames under some circumstances. And let us not overlook the possibility of an aircraft having to circle the airport for as much as 30 minutes or fly to an alternate airport that could be 50 miles away.

6. How would the air traffic management systems and processes accommodate the larger volume of new aircraft in crowded airspaces?
7. Technology has been moving faster than regulators (who look for safety aspects and reliability requirements) can keep up with. An electric engine is not equivalent to a conventional propulsion system. In any case, different elements of the software and electronic control systems need to be fully integrated.
8. Consumer behavior changes may also represent a challenge. Would they be willing to travel in small airplanes even if it meant services would be direct as opposed to with connections through major airports? How about distribution issues, for example accessibility? How will service operators provide an end-to-end experience that is seamless, keeping in mind the need for convenience, flexibility, and accessibility (mobile apps)?

The answer may be in the convergence of a number of developments—for example, the development of small regional aircraft that are cost-effective for operators and for travelers relating to the fare–convenience–flexibility tradeoffs. Digital technologies can be used to provide customer experiences similar to those available at large airports, but without the hassles, and to make operations more efficient. Think about fitting electric aircraft with advanced avionics. Next, think about the use of 5G wireless technologies to improve mobile applications, significantly. Then, there are cloud-based technologies to provide solutions for airports, airlines, and passengers, relating to, for example, check-ins and boardings. It is the cloud-based technologies (discussed in Chapter 6) that can enable small regional airports to have similar capabilities to larger airports. Think about the use of advanced booking and tracking platforms. And, through the willingness to collaborate and coordinate, goals of partners can be aligned. For example, the rationale for an increase in investments by airports can be supported by the expectation that greater travel activity through regional airports will improve connectivity with other communities with regional airports (located between 100 and 500 miles), and improve the economies of the regions surrounding regional airports, not to mention relieve some of the capacity pressures felt by the larger airports.

Technology can transform US regional airports into the first choice for passengers. And, the technology is here, starting with the hybrid airplanes that can be a viable solution as the time for design-to-certification for clean-sheet electric aircraft can be exceptionally long. In the hybrid aircraft all that is being done is the retrofitting of the propulsion systems. Archer Aviation and NASA have even begun to collaborate to test some Advanced Air Mobility (AAM) concepts—for example, "examine the safety, energy and power performance capabilities of the cylindrical battery cells."[22] This would be another step forward for Archer achieve its plans to enter its Midnight aircraft into service in 2025. And as mentioned above, BETA Technologies' CX300 could easily provide viable services in thin short-haul markets, either on a scheduled or on-demand basis. Moreover, given the eCTOL design aspects, the capacity of the CX300 could relatively easily be increased to nine passengers. Think also about another area of technology, relating, for example, to advanced navigation systems and precision GPS approaches.

While the technology for ultra-short-haul flights (as in the case of four- to five-seat eVTOLs) or regional flights (with 10–30 seats) is becoming available, the question for their viability will also depend on the customer experience that can be offered. For short-haul travel, for example, while transportation by air would take less time and could even be more predictable, travel by car offers much more flexibility and avoids the need to change travel modes. It is an on-demand option instead of being dependent on pre-determined schedules of airlines. And there is no reason to be concerned about the first part and the last part of the trip for door-to-door service. True, ground transportation can also be subject to congestion on the road (predicted and unpredicted), but the same concerns relate to air transportation. In addition, the price would generally be lower for ground transportation, especially for a larger number of people in a car. Consequently, while the current demand for air travel in short-haul markets—especially ultra-short-haul markets—is relatively small, think about the potential for growth coming from such sources as diversion from ground vehicles and stimulation from much more customer-centric operations and services. The amount of diversion from ground transportation and stimulation would, in turn, depend on numerous factors such as prices and trip times as well as convenience, flexibility, and environmental benefits of the services offered. To repeat, small electric airplanes not only have the potential to transform the transportation in regional markets, but also reduce the amount of travel in cars and buses, which, in turn, would be good for the environment.

Four thoughts for looking into the future.

- First, it is possible to have a hybrid aircraft, for example, Electra's hybrid-electric short take-off and landing (eSTOL) vehicle. The US-based manufacturer Electra is developing such an airplane that can take off from runways as short as 150ft and reach speeds of about 200 miles per hour. The final design can have capacity for two pilots and nine passengers. An Australian air-taxi infrastructure developer, Skyportz, has set up a subsidiary, Wilbur Air, that plans to acquire 100 such aircraft to be operated by partners across Australia (which has assorted geography), using short airstrips in both urban and remote areas.[23]
- Second, ZeroAvia, based in the US and the UK, is focusing on developing, by 2025, hydrogen-electric propulsion for vehicles with a capacity between nine and 19 passengers and a range of 300 miles. By 2027, the capacity could be increased to between 40 and 80 seats and a range up to 700 miles. ZeroAvia has already obtained experimental certificates for prototype aircraft from the UK CAA and the US FAA. The company has

also developed partnerships with aircraft OEMs to produce aircraft by 2025. Alaska Airlines contributed one of its Bombardier Q400 regional turboprop to ZeroAvia to be retrofitted with a hydrogen-electric propulsion system to determine the applicability of zero emissions flight technology.[24] Airbus, under its ZEROe program, has partnered with some airports in North America and Delta Air Lines to determine the feasibility of airports developing the infrastructure to support the distribution of hydrogen fuel for commercial passenger aircraft. Such an aircraft could be ready by 2035. There is value in exploring the use of hydrogen power to reduce carbon emissions, as there are at least two significant challenges to using sustainable aviation fuel—costs and short supply. On the other hand, there are challenges relating to the use of liquid hydrogen to power commercial aircraft. For a unit of energy, the hydrogen-powered aircraft may end up carrying up to four times the volume compared with fossil-based jet fuel, for the same range. In addition, there is the challenge of storing hydrogen at extremely low temperatures (around minus 253°C).[25]

- Third, Wright Electric, a company based in Los Angeles, is reportedly developing an electric 186-seater aircraft with a range of 800 miles to be available in 2030. According to Wright Electric the starting point for an all-electric aircraft could be to offer one-hour flights in dense markets such as London–Paris, New York–Boston, and Los Angeles–San Francisco. If successful, the viability of this achievement could then be a turning point in short-haul air transportation.
- Fourth, instead of using batteries, while solar-powered airplanes may show an opportunity in the long term, they are not likely to be viable in the near future.

Multimodal travel

Multimodal travel is becoming more attractive to travelers, given its flexibility and cost-effectiveness, not to mention it being a more sustainable transportation option. There are, however, numerous challenges facing multimodal travel:

1. insufficient reliability due to lack of sufficient collaboration and coordination among different service providers,
2. high costs of the infrastructure needed for customer-centric and seamless end-to-end journeys, and
3. complexities of multimodal transportation, relating to shopping and delivery of services promised.

Consider the last challenge. Think about the challenge for making a booking and changes at the same time for all modes of transportation options, resulting from the lack of sufficient collaboration between transportation service providers (airlines, rail, ground transportation, including ride-sharing services) and airports for infrastructure needed for operations.

On a limited scale, some airlines have begun to work with airports and transportation companies (such as Landline in the US), to provide post-security shuttle services to connect at local airports. For example, American can now connect passengers from small airports, such as Allentown Airport in Philadelphia (ABE) and Atlantic City Airport in New Jersey (ACY), to the transit area at the larger airport, Philadelphia Airport (PHL). Passengers arriving at the smaller airports can check their bags and clear security before boarding the Landline buses and arrive on the airside at the major airport and then enter the *post-security* area in the terminal and go directly to the lounge or the connecting aircraft. Landline's buses have a capacity of up to 35 passengers and offer complimentary Wi-Fi and power at every seat. Travelers can even earn loyalty credit on both the airline and the bus service provider, in this case, Landline.[26]

Think about the third challenge again, requiring travelers to use multiple booking platforms and apps, a process that is time-consuming and frustrating. However, advances in technology can now enable travelers to book multiple modes of transportation on a single platform, mega apps. How about the payment options? Could they be, for example, pay-as-you-go or subscriptions, for instance, monthly, depending on the modes of transportation included? However, leaving aside the availability of customer-centric mega booking apps, effective multimodal transportation requires operational collaboration, including at the government level. For example, one assumes that the Transportation Security Administration would have been involved in the American Airlines' *post-secure* bus service, discussed above, to keep the bus operationally "sterile."

On the positive side, collaboration between high-speed rail and air travel at intermodal transportation hubs is becoming evident. One only needs to see operations at Frankfurt and Amsterdam airports. Further improvements in seamless transitions between trains and airplanes can encourage passengers to complete part of their journeys on rail (rather than on connecting flights), which will not only reduce the carbon footprint but also reduce congestion at airports. Again, think about Frankfurt Airport, where a train can easily take connecting passengers from long-haul flights to not only many destinations within Germany, but also in Belgium, France, the Netherlands, and Switzerland. Connecting services on trains would also add much value during disruptions in airline operations.

Now, being a member of the Star Alliance, Deutsche Bahn can offer AirRail services with dedicated flight numbers relating not only to Lufthansa flights, but also to the flights of other members of the Star Alliance, operating to and from Frankfurt. Similarly, from Amsterdam's Schiphol Airport, a high-speed train provides convenient AirRail services in cooperation with KLM and its SkyTeam partners, using shared flight numbers. In China, there is a major intermodal hub at the Shanghai Hongqiao International Airport that is connected to one of the largest railway stations in Asia and has been providing high-speed rail links to numerous cities in China. And the new Beijing Daxing Airport was designed from the beginning to have an intermodal hub to provide enhanced high-speed rail connections. Two key features of an effective intermodal hub are (1) to offer stress-free and seamless connections to travelers from the airport terminal to the rail station and (2) to offer dedicated flight numbers between the two modes of transportation to make available end-to-end tickets. Both aspects require a deep collaboration among airlines, airports, rail service providers, and communities.

From the collaboration perspective, airports would need to integrate various modes of transport and transport-related services into wide-ranging, on-demand mobility service platforms that could be used by travel intermediaries and ultimate users. In addition, airports would need to develop and operate multimodal terminals with a focus on not just efficiency, but also on seamless traveler experience.

Even if one considers multimodal transportation within the narrow context—different modes of ground transportation—bus, car, rail, and taxi—to and from an airport, there is a need for a convenient and seamless accessibility and connectivity, based on the preferences of different segments of passengers. Insights from these preferences can be obtained from not just the use of existing data and performance indicators, but also on the potential information coming from surveys, interviews, and social media. This means not only a need for an airport to develop a strategy for multimodal transportation and multimodal facilities, but also for the creation of effective collaboration with not only the service providers, but also the community. And equally important, after an airport develops an effective strategy and implementation plans, effective indicators need to be developed to track performance and user satisfaction.

The concept is simple: integrate seamlessly different modes of transportation to ensure that people reach their final destinations efficiently, conveniently, and comfortably. Think of the vast network of roads that provide travelers unmatched accessibility and flexibility, travel from virtually anywhere to anywhere at any time. Then, in some parts of the world, for example, in Europe, widespread rail networks enable passengers to travel widely and efficiently, not to mention considering their sustainability aspect. Next, there is air transportation, offering a vast network that offers speed and efficiency. Last, there is extensive public transportation. The challenge has been and continues to be the ability to combine all modes of transportation to provide travelers flexibility, convenience, speed, and *reach*. It can be done. Look at the delivery services provided by Amazon to offer same-day or two-day deliveries by combining different modes of transportation. The critical success factors include:

1 understanding the patterns of travel and ridership using high-quality and reliable data,

2 evaluating the sufficiency of the existing multimodal infrastructure,
3 planning for smooth transitions between modes,
4 using integrated platforms to enable seamless communications (among service providers and users) to provide transparency, real-time updates, and solutions in case of disruptions, regardless of how they happened,
5 offering the capability of single reservations and self-service options to make changes, on the go,
6 having a capability to track travelers, regardless of the mode of usage,
7 assessing user behavior relating to the acceptance of multimodal services and providing the capability for users to provide feedback for improvements, and
8 establishing interoperability and standardization of the systems and services to ensure interaction and cross-functionality.

Relating to the last point, interoperability relates to the capabilities of different systems to communicate and exchange data effectively. Standardization relates to the adoption of common rules and formats for data, as well as communications between the partners. Consideration of these points will reduce the complexities of using multiple modes of transportation and provide flexibility.

Ground transportation modes can add much value to the air mode in enabling passengers to make end-to-end trips, while supporting the sustainability movement. But, as mentioned above, there are challenges. The fragmented nature of different modes not only makes the booking process complex for end-to-end trips but makes it difficult for service providers to offer seamless experiences. Both challenges can be addressed through (1) improvement in collaboration and coordination, and (2) innovation. As mentioned in the previous chapter and in this chapter, trains in Europe have already begun to collaborate with airlines and airports. Now a GDS could easily introduce a sufficient innovation to help in the booking process for end-to-end trips through an effective interface among all the modes of transportation. Multimodal transportation has the potential to be a game-changer in today's travel sector. In all four cases discussed in this chapter, the common links include (1) the development and implementation of a powerful customer-centric platform, (2) an effective ecosystem for service providers to work together, and (3) delivering a positive customer experience. All three points will either make or break the four new segments of travel discussed in this chapter.

MaaS, which integrates various transportation services, has the potential to transform the way people move in urban areas. The concept, both on-demand-based and subscription-based, using a single platform and partnerships, is ready for significant growth in different parts of the world. The future of eVTOLs, flying taxis, carrying up to six passengers, is extremely bright. As for Advanced Air Mobility vehicles, companies such as Archer Aviation, BETA Technologies, Joby Aviation, Lilium, Volocopter, and Wisk are designing vehicles that would not only be cost-effective, but they will produce less noise pollution.[27] As for the progress in small electric aircraft, as mentioned above, Eviation Aircraft already launched its nine-seat Alice in September 2022, which flew from Moses Lake, Washington for eight minutes at 3,500 feet. And BETA Technologies' CX300 could easily be modified to transport nine passengers. As for multimodal travel, as cities keep growing and the urbanization trend expands around the globe, there will be a critical need to integrate different modes of transportation seamlessly. And let us not overlook that eVTOLs can provide first- and last-mile connectivity that is cost-effective and timely. The new segments of air travel discussed in this chapter will call for a significant level of adaption that can be facilitated by data and technology, discussed in the next chapter.

Notes

1 Rob Hodgetts, "Successful test flight brings Lilium electric air taxis closer to reality," *CNN Travel*, April 25, 2017. https://www.cnn.com/travel/article/lilium-electric-vtol-jet/index.html
2 Greg Waldron, "EHang EH216-S in Costa Rican demonstration foray," *FlightGlobal*, March 19, 2024. https://www.flightglobal.com/aerospace/ehang-eh216-s-in-costa-rican-demonstration-foray/157420.article
3 Gordon Smith, "Flying Taxis in Dubai by 2026? Latest Plans Revealed," *Skift*, February 12, 2024. https://skift.com/2024/02/12/flying-taxis-in-dubai-by-2026-latest-plans-revealed
4 Charles Alcock, "Falcon and Archer Launch Abu Dhabi - Dubai eVTOL Flights," *AINalerts*, March 11, 2024. https://www.ainonline.com/aviation-news/futureflight/2024-03-11/falcon-and-archer-launch-abu-dhabi-dubai-evtol-flights
5 "FAA issues final airworthiness criteria for Archer Midnight eVTOL," *Vertical Mag*, May 24, 2024. https://verticalmag.com/news/faa-issues-final-airworthiness-criteria-for-archer-midnight-evtol
6 "Beta Technologies ALIA-250," *Electric VTOL News*, n.d. https://evtol.news/beta-technologies-alia
7 Tony Harrington, "How airlines may deploy eVTOLs," *FlightGlobal*, March 15, 2023. https://www.flightglobal.com/airlines/how-airlines-may-deploy-evtols/152334.article
8 "United Airlines and Archer Announce First Commercial Electric Air Taxi Route in Chicago," *Archer*, March 23, 2023. https://investors.archer.com/news/news-details/2023/United-Airlines-and-Archer-Announce-First-Commercial-Electric-Air-Taxi-Route-in-Chicago
9 Alfred Chua, "Asia-Pacific to be key market for AAM, despite few manufacturers of scale: panel," *FlightGlobal*, September 28, 2023.
10 Charles Alcock, "Falcon and Archer Launch Abu Dhabi - Dubai eVTOL Flights," *AINalerts*, March 11, 2024. https://www.ainonline.com/aviation-news/futureflight/2024-03-11/falcon-and-archer-launch-abu-dhabi-dubai-evtol-flights
11 "Start-up of the Week: Joby Aviation aims to be the Uber of skies," *International Finance*, July 12, 2023. https://internationalfinance.com/aviation/start-week-joby-aviation-aims-uber-skies

12 Ramya Mahalingam, Adam Mitchell, and Robin Riedel, "How customer experience will make or break advanced air mobility," *McKinsey & Company*, March 7, 2023. https://www.mckinsey.com/industries/aerospace-and-defense/our-insights/future-air-mobility-blog/how-customer-experience-will-make-or-break-advanced-air-mobility

13 Sam Korus, "Unit Economics Suggest That The Cost Of Traveling By Electric Air Taxi Should Drop Precipitously," *ARK Invest*, August 9, 2023. https://ark-invest.com/articles/analyst-research/electric-air-taxi-cost-drop

14 *Oliver Wyman Forum*, "Urban Mobility Needs Tech, Guardrails, And A Human Touch," April 17, 2024. https://www.oliverwymanforum.com/mobility/2024/apr/urban-mobility-needs-tech--guardrails--and-a-human-touch.html

15 Based on a conference call with Ferrovial Vertiports group on June 12, 2024.

16 Justin Gerdes, "Electric planes will revolutionise regional travel," *Energy Monitor*, July 5, 2023. https://www.energymonitor.ai/sectors/transport/opinion-electric-planes-will-revolutionise-regional-travel

17 Jesse Klein, "The first frontier for electric aviation: Short-haul flights," *GreenBiz*, October 31, 2023. https://www.greenbiz.com/article/first-frontier-electric-aviation-short-haul-flights

18 Lukas Brink, Ryan Brown, Sarina Carter, Axel Esqué, Benjamin Meigs, and Robin Riedel, "Short-haul flying redefined: The promise of regional air mobility," *McKinsey & Company*, May 31, 2023. https://www.mckinsey.com/industries/aerospace-and-defense/our-insights/short-haul-flying-redefined-the-promise-of-regional-air-mobility

19 Lukas Brink, Ryan Brown, Sarina Carter, Axel Esqué, Benjamin Meigs, and Robin Riedel, "Short-haul flying redefined: The promise of regional air mobility," *McKinsey & Company*, May 31, 2023. https://www.mckinsey.com/industries/aerospace-and-defense/our-insights/short-haul-flying-redefined-the-promise-of-regional-air-mobility

20 Jesse Klein, "The first frontier for electric aviation: Short-haul flights," *GreenBiz*, October 31, 2023. https://www.greenbiz.com/article/first-frontier-electric-aviation-short-haul-flights

21 Stephanie Allmon, "Texas company lines up hundred electric-hybrid planes for takeoff," *Houston Energy Transition Initiative*, December 26, 2023. https://energycapitalhtx.com/jsx-electric-hybrid-planes

22 Dominic Perry, "Archer and NASA collaborate on battery testing to 'push AAM industry forward'" *FlightGlobal*, 22 January 2024. https://www.flightglobal.com/aerospace/archer-and-nasa-collaborate-on-battery-testing-to-push-aam-industry-forward

23 Howard Hardee, "Australian electric aviation start-up Wilbur Air eyes 100 Electra aircraft," *FlightGlobal*, April 12, 2024. https://www.flightglobal.com/aerospace/australian-electric-aviation-start-up-wilbur-air-eyes-100-electra-aircraft

24 "Alaska Airlines and ZeroAvia developing world's largest zero-emission aircraft," News Provided by *ZeroAvia* and reported by *PR Newswire*, May 1, 2023. https://www.prnewswire.com/news-releases/alaska-airlines-and-zeroavia-developing-worlds-largest-zero-emission-aircraft-301812349

25 Jon Hemmerdinger, "Airbus to begin hydrogen fuel feasibility studies with North American airports," *FlightGlobal*, May 21, 2024. https://www.flightglobal.com/airframers/airbus-to-begin-hydrogen-fuel-feasibility-studies-with-north-american-airports/158371.article

26 Jonathan E. Hendry, "American Airlines Uses Secure Airside Bus Services To Connect Local Airports," *Simpleflying.com*, April 7, 2023. https://simpleflying.com/american-airlines-secure-local-airport-transfer-bus
27 "5 eVTOL Companies Shaping the Future of Air Mobility," *MRL*, September 28, 2023. https://www.mrlcg.com/resources/blog/5-evtol-companies-shaping-the-future-of-air-mobility
28 "Flying Taxis in Dubai by 2026? Latest Plans Revealed," *Skift*, February 12, 2024. https://skift.com/2024/02/12/flying-taxis-in-dubai-by-2026-latest-plans-revealed.

6 Adapting and evolving with transformative technologies

Most businesses have been transforming their decision-making processes with data while advances in technology have been making it easier to collect data, gain insights from data, make predictions with data, and share data. Two examples of data-gathering-and-analysis technologies are cloud computing and GenAI. Within the context of the theme of this book, data and these two technologies are vital for developing game-changing collaboration strategies within each organization and among partnerships. While airlines, airports, and travel intermediaries have an incredible amount of data, three challenges continue to exist.

1. How to derive the most value from the data that organizations do have?
2. Where to get new data and how to access it?
3. How to share data from the perspective of business strategies, keeping in mind the concerns over data privacy and security, not to mention competitors?

Businesses have already begun to use cloud-based technologies to integrate multi-dimensional data and GenAI is already being used to understand and learn from the data. These technologies have already started to help different organizations in the aviation industry to realign their internal management systems within their own organizations and to develop responsible GenAI strategies for internal operation and collaboration with partners. But, while early experimentation with GenAI promises compelling benefits, businesses face considerable challenges such as the management of potential risks and the need to reskill some segments of the workforce, not to mention the need to rethink business processes. Soon, however, new technologies will enable management not only to make more accurate decisions, but also to make decisions in a much shorter time.

DOI: 10.4324/9781003483960-6

Managing data effectively

Different approaches have been tried by different organizations to manage data successfully. For example, different divisions within an organization, like airlines and airports, have created their own data sets and then used different technologies to analyze their unique situations. In the case of an airline, examples of two major divisions would be sales and marketing, and operations. Within each of these divisions there are subdivisions that have even more of their own data sets—for example, loyalty within sales and marketing, and crew scheduling within operations. The problem with such an approach to managing data has been that it not only leads to duplication of efforts (and additional costs), but also the management and maintenance of a vast number of data sets and the associated technologies to work with the data. At the other end of the spectrum, some organizations have experimented with developing single central data groups to support the needs of different divisions and subdivisions. While such an approach can reduce costs by avoiding duplications, it does not provide customized data for each end user, for example, operations, let alone subdivisions within operations, such as crew scheduling and rostering, or maintenance.

Now two relatively innovative approaches have been suggested to manage data to maximize its value. One approach is to use GenAI (discussed below) to bring about a substantial improvement in the "internal knowledge management system,"[1] The second approach suggested is to manage data as if it was a product (physical or digital)—in other words, packaging data the way an organization would package its products.[2] The creators of this concept explain it in the way an automobile manufacturer manages its products. There is a basic car (built on a given chassis) to which each customer can add the features desired by the customer to fit the lifestyle of the customer.

The other challenge relating to the management of data is not only to access data with ease to develop and implement strategies, but also to take into consideration concerns over data privacy and security. Clearly, there are issues relating to the sharing of data—for example, what data to share, who owns the data to be shared, and how airlines, airports, and travel intermediaries need to change and align their work practices to share data that can then be used to predict outcomes. On the other hand, in order to develop collaboration at the holistic level, there is a need to:

1. have data on travelers—for example, the preferences of different travelers going through an airport,
2. build relational databases, including access to third-party databases, and
3. use analytics to drive insights from the data and to innovate at scale.

These challenges relating to data accessibility for different users and the sharing aspects could be resolved with the best practices concept presented above—"managing data like a product."

One starting point would be to think about some standard data-related questions about travelers and their common concerns. Think about some basic but up-to-date information on travelers that is needed by airlines to develop relevant products and services (as well as the associated content), and by travel intermediaries to support travelers during their shopping processes and their actual journeys.

1. What are the key subsegments in each of the major segments of travelers and their priorities? Amadeus has produced a report in which they describe such subsegments as "excited experimentalists, memory makers, travel tech-influencers, and pioneering pathfinders."[3]
2. While airlines know that leisure travelers tend to be much more price conscious than business travelers, what is the price elasticity of different subsegments within each segment? How much more time does each subsegment of the leisure segment spend on searching (shopping) before making bookings?
3. What are the needs and priorities of not only the bleisure segment, but also sub-subsegments within that segment, such as the subsegment that works offsite?
4. While the millennials and the Gen Z travelers are often the topic of discussion, what does the travel industry really know about them, other than the size of these segments and their economic status? Do we assume, for example, that they will prefer self-service and touchless options, including the use of digital IDs, sophisticated biometrics, and mobile platforms?
5. What about travelers at the other end of the age group, the seniors who are likely to have a greater share of the disposable income, but may want more assistance at various touch points? Should airlines, airports, and travel intermediaries have dedicated teams to handle the needs of senior travelers?
6. Travelers continue to claim that they want personalization, but (a) are they willing to provide the needed data, (b) how much are different segments willing to pay for such products and services in different situations, and (c) are airlines and airports able to scale the adoption of such needs?
7. Travelers imply that they want seamless journeys, referring, for example, to intermodal travel, and travel booked and managed through a single platform. How much are different segments of travelers willing to pay for such an experience for service providers to develop the infrastructure to offer and manage such products and services?
8. While most travelers are concerned about the impact of their journeys on the environment, how much of a premium over the ticket price are they willing to pay for sustainability? How does this vary between different segments of travelers, business vs. leisure, vs. visiting friends and relatives? And, how can the "say–do gap" be identified?

These are just a few simple and basic questions that need to be answered with some accuracy using not only an airline's tech stack, but also multiple other sources, such as partners in the travel ecosystem. For example, travel intermediaries play not only an important role in engaging with travelers to identify and meet their travel needs, but they are also in a unique position to gather vital information on the needs and priorities of different segments and different subsegments within each segment. Leaving aside the need for information on the priorities of different segments of travelers, think about the inability to answer, to some degree of definitiveness, some simple questions raised by travelers during their everyday journeys.

1. Why is the travel booking process so complex? Why is it difficult for travel intermediaries to effectively manage travelers' inquiries? Why can I not have more control over my itinerary during disruptions? Why can I not check in at the airport, with my bags, at the counter of any airline in an alliance partnership?
2. Why are airlines not offering the capability to book comprehensive intermodal travel (or green modes of travel) on their websites?
3. Why can the airport not use better technology to predict how many security lines should be open at a given time based on the number of total people, including those holding pre-clearance checks?
4. Why do some airlines, working within alliance partnerships, not know where precisely a traveler's bag is?
5. Why does the airport/airline not have a gate available if the flight arrives ten minutes early, when both the airport and the airline know an hour before the arrival time of the plane?
6. Why is a new jet bridge operator being trained at a peak time, delaying connecting passengers in deplaning the aircraft? Could the training of a gate agent to use jet bridges not be done late at night when an aircraft is parked at a gate for the night?
7. Why do travel service providers (airlines, airports, distributors, etc.) not collaborate and coordinate to execute a service disruption and recovery quickly and that is more customer-focused?

Of course, airlines and airports know the answers to these typical questions (perhaps not in real time) that infrequent travelers have. But do suppliers of services (airlines, airports, and distributors) need not just more data, but information in real time and how can that information be relayed effectively to travelers, especially infrequent travelers? Even internally, the lack of relevant and timely data is also leading to the creation of operational and commercial problems. Think about the discussion in Chapter 3. An aircraft's pull-back from the gate is delayed due to the late arrival of connecting passengers. How long should the departing aircraft wait? Is there enough data to know quickly if the connecting passengers have checked bags that would need to be loaded on the departing aircraft? At which gate would the aircraft with the connecting passengers arrive? Would there be any connecting passengers who need wheelchairs? Would there be sufficient wheelchairs and baggage handlers to take care of the logistics as soon as the aircraft is connected to the gate? Although the needed data does exist:

- is it easily accessible?
- are diverse groups within an organization (an airline or an airport) willing to coordinate the data and the actions needed?
- can 5G open up new possibilities and new benefits, and
- are different organizations (airlines, airports, ground service providers, and different subgroups within the group of ground service providers) willing to share the information, using a single platform that shows all the information in one place for the entire trip of every passenger? See the discussion on improving aircraft turnaround times in Chapter 3.

Could the Airport Collaborative Decision-Making (A-CDM) process be used not just to improve the balance between capacity and demand, but also for airlines, airports, and ground service providers to manage operations in real time? This collaboration would require not only the use of real-time data, but also an agreement on the objectives, tradeoffs, and measurements.[4] For their part, airports could develop sophisticated, but flexible, data platforms to work with data from collection to analysis to visualization to forecasts. Bob Kwik provides, in his article on AWS's website, three examples of airports that have begun to use such platforms—Nice Côte d'Azur Airport in France, Changi Airport in Singapore, and Toronto Pearson International Airport in Canada.[5] He also provides Siemens Logistics, a leader in airport baggage-handling systems, as an example of a business using its Baggage 360 system to monitor the baggage flow to be able to identify connections at risk, and to be able to predict processing times, not to mention the visualization of a bag on the arriving conveyor belt.

In a different subfunction within the commercial function, loyalty programs have been providing a lot of information to airlines, information that has not only enabled airlines to interact with customers but also to promote their products and services. However, in the past the loyalty programs promoted the value of frequent purchases, based on points, to lock travelers to a particular airline or an alliance partnership. In some ways, travelers were encouraged to buy from a particular airline based more on the financial incentives than on admiration of the products or services offered by the airline. Shouldn't airlines devote much time and creativity to redesign their loyalty programs to focus on customers' loyalty to the product features, seamless customer experience, and relationship with customers—affinity for the brand of an airline—rather than on the financial incentives offered by an airline? How about looking at creative ways to consider loyalty based on value perceived by customers and across the entire journey through engagement and communications? Similarly with low-cost and, especially, ultra-low-cost airlines, should loyalty initiatives be developed and promoted based on more than just low prices? Again, these questions bring us back to data.

To get value-adding data from loyalty programs, they need to be redesigned through the development of comprehensive customer management platforms that focus on

- the richness and granularity of the data on customers (their needs and preferences, for example),
- the real-time management of data and its analysis to derive meaningful and actionable insights,
- the ability to interact with customers in real time,
- the capability to provide real-time feedback to back-office systems to make it possible for them to take meaningful actions, and, in turn, and
- managing customer experience in real time and meeting travelers' emerging loyalty needs (see Chapter 2).

Airlines built their loyalty programs based on a customer's spending amount and some based on the use of the points earned to purchase a broad spectrum of products and services. These initiatives did provide some data. However, it is possible to get much more comprehensive data by going further—for example, by creating a currency that can be used to purchase anything, anytime, and anywhere. Think about the value of data generated through the use of loyalty currency. Loyalty programs are not only profitable for airlines but going forward the value of the first-party data generated by them is incredible. How about the data coming from sales and marketing groups that are analyzing customer acquisition and retention strategies? And, as far as personalization goes, the concept is excellent not only for providing customized products and services, but also for getting excellent data coming from targeted messages to the right customer, at the right time, at the right location, and through the right channel.

Relevant customer data helping different travel organizations make smarter business decisions is hardly a new concept. But deeper knowledge needs to be collected from sources such as credit cards with details such as not just what products are being purchased, but when, where, and through which channel. How about information from government agencies about times required to get visas? How about OTAs relating to booking patterns and packages? What are consumers streaming on TV and their mobile devices and what could the potential impact be on destination choices? However, getting deeper data from different sources does bring in the question of privacy and security.

How about the data needed for and the data generated by the use of self-service systems, which are gaining pace at the airport—for example, as airlines begin to replace check-in desks with boarding passes embedded in digital wallets (QR codes) along with automated boarding processes at the gates? The self-service initiatives are likely to be of much value to millennials and the Gen Z travelers. Keep in mind that a significant proportion of these generations are also connecting to social media channels (Instagram and TikTok, for example) to get travel ideas as well as to relay their input when there are problems such as flight delays and flight cancellations. However, despite the value of digital experience, we must not overlook the situations when digital channels break down (a mix-up in reservations, for example) and human intervention is need, especially situations requiring empathy. There is need for flexibility—different customers want different support capabilities, online chats, and conventional phone calls. This calls for the availability of relevant data at the right place, at the right time, and in the right form.

Since leading airlines are clearly interested in increasing their bookings through the direct channel, they can capitalize on the availability of first-party data that is available when shoppers are on airlines' websites, mobile apps, and, even, through social media channels. This data, on anonymous shoppers, can then be integrated with relational databases available from other sources to develop comprehensive customer profiles to create and offer more personalized services, leading to longer-term relationships with customers. The key to increasing direct bookings is the collection of first-party data and its effective use with AI technologies, especially now that there is a decrease in the use of data coming from third-party cookies. The key, of course, is not just the use of new data, but also new ways of using existing and new data. Two examples of new data sources are competitive web and app analytics, and credit-card spends.[6]

The point is to use real-time, relevant, and specific data to build direct relationships with known and unknown customers (on websites and apps) by offering meaningful solutions (outcomes over promises). These initiatives require zero-party and first-party data, especially now that the use of third-party cookie data is on the decline. These types of data, developed through collaborative partnerships, can then be used to develop AI-powered platforms. And it will be the use of AI-powered systems that will enable airlines to identify the precise needs of individual customers not only to deliver an elevated level of experience but to deliver it at scale.

In closing this section on data, it is worth noting two important points made in two forewords to this book. Frederic Deschamps, in his foreword, makes an important point about the availability of large quantities of data and now the low cost of processing the data. Complexity should not be increased, given the capability to slice and dice every aspect of the available data. Think about his example in the car-rental sector of pricing decisions where the business may have over three dozen types of cars to rent compared to one–five cabins in an aircraft and five to 20 types of rooms in a hotel. Excessive segmentation in the car-rental business may have given a short-term pricing advantage, but over the longer term the many different car types lost their values to consumers and introduced added complexity in managing an incredible number of pricing options.

Stephen Brobst, in his foreword, suggests that partners in the travel ecosystem should leverage a collection of Open Travel APIs that can radically disrupt the travel industry. There will be a need to standardize APIs within the industry that may even bring about regulatory pressure to accelerate adoption, as in the case with Open Banking APIs. These APIs will help the "design of next-generation travel services with innovative co-creation across industry partners" through the sharing of information.

Leveraging cloud-based technologies

The capability of cloud-based technologies is not just to store massive amounts of multi-dimensional data (on aircraft, crews, ground services, schedules, and, of course, passengers), but also to make data accessible to all authorized users in real time. The three major cloud-services vendors are Amazon Web Services, Google Cloud, and Microsoft Azure. Cloud-based technologies (data, "information-centric" platforms, predictive analytics, and communications) are now being used by different sectors of the aviation industry to enhance operational efficiency as well as to support GenAI (discussed below). Google has its new technology, Gemini, in its portfolio of AI initiatives and its Google Cloud network. Gemini is a sophisticated AI model with the capability of understanding and generating human-like text, images, audio, and video. It is developed to enhance user experience "with more intuitive and intelligent features."[7] Keep in mind the key value of GenAI is to create new content that can include text, images, audio, video, and even, simulations and code. And the process can be done in an incredibly short period of time, measured in seconds.

Leading airlines and airports are already beginning to use cloud-based technologies for the value they bring by themselves, but also their role in GenAI to improve their competitive positionings and provide step increases in customer experience. Cloud-based technologies also have the features to protect the data stored and analyzed in the cloud. However, based on best practices from outside of the aviation industry, it appears that working with cloud-based and GenAI technologies requires a shift in mindset. For example, cloud transformation is a journey rather than, for example, a migration of a data center. It is a process to move systems, applications, and data from, for example, an airline's or an airport's servers at each of their locations to the location of the servers of the cloud-based service provider. And there is a need to address talent and culture, not to mention numerous barriers that need to be removed to achieve business value from the investments in cloud-based and GenAI technologies. Relevant talent is called for not just in the cloud migration process (data, hardware, and software), but also in the cloud transformation process to upgrade and replace applications as well as on-demand scalability, for example. The goal is to identify and implement new business opportunities in the cloud environment.

Cloud computing can give forward-thinking managers in different sectors of the aviation industry the capability to improve productivity and efficiency by scaling resources dynamically and having better ways to communicate in real time to increase the speed of execution. Think about how in communications, there cannot be miscommunications or misinterpretations. To achieve the claimed benefits, airlines and airports must collect incredibly substantial amounts of data on customers and operations, including partners. The data needs to be at the elevated level of granularity. For example, in commercial areas there is a need to capture and adapt to consumer trends such as the increase in bleisure travel. In operations there is a value in being able to predict maintenance issues to prevent delays.

Think about GE Aviation's SmartSky Network and Mosaic ATM developing a way to connect a cloud-based flight management system with an airborne flight management system. The digital twins can get information from each other and integrate it with other information that can then be shared across a large ecosystem to address different scenarios. For example, the digital twins should be able to reduce any inconsistencies between ground-based systems that support flight operations and air traffic control.[8] Think about the value of such a system in evaluating time-based trajectories of aircraft managing air traffic in 4D (latitude, longitude, altitude, and time).

Cloud computing is transforming different sectors of the aviation industry across different functions—from commercial and finance to operations—while keeping a focus on customers (frictionless travel journeys) and employees (experience and productivity). At airports biometric and digital twins can add a lot of value to improve productivities and traveler experience. Five key features of the use of cloud technology are:

- collection and use of real-time data,
- scalability,
- integration of siloed data,
- fast and user-friendly accessibility of data, and
- data-sharing capability with other partners with a full agreement on which data can be shared and which cannot be shared.

Using GenAI responsibly

AI has been with us for quite a while—think about the development of smartphones and more recently autonomous-driving features in cars. Then came the introduction of ChatGPT. Now we have GenAI—that is, AI that has capabilities that the early versions of AI did not have, such as the ability to generate content. GenAI uses foundation models, part of what is called deep learning, enabling the processing of large quantities of unstructured data.

To put this discussion in perspective, deep learning is a subset of machine learning. Machine learning is a subset of AI through which a model gains capabilities after it has been trained. Machine learning algorithms detect patterns and then figure out how to make predictions and make recommendations. Foundation models are deep learning models trained on very large quantities of data, which could be structured or unstructured. Large Language Models

(LLMs) are a class of foundation models that can process huge amounts of unstructured text and learn the relationship between words, enabling the generation of natural-language text. These technologies can help to automate communications to provide personalized and relevant information that will enhance customer experience that, in turn, will increase customer loyalty, resulting in more profitable operations. Think about a traveler receiving a message that airport security lines are getting longer and to plan for an additional 15 minutes to clear security.

For some spot-on examples of the use of LLMs, see the thought leadership piece by Sean Smith in Chapter 8. Chili's is a large restaurant chain in the US. The restaurant chain was finding it difficult to measure quantitively the feedback from customers, the complexity related to the analyses of customer sentiments to provide actionable data. Management succeeded in finding a reasonable solution by leveraging an LLM for advanced natural language processing. Another example given related to the use of AI assistants by Klarna, a buy now, pay later service. Klarna was able to reduce 700 full-time agents and still have 2.3 million chat conversations in a month. AI assistants were able to provide incredible scale.

GenAI is transforming businesses, workplaces, and lifestyles of people worldwide. While this technology's potential benefits are well known, requirements for its effective implementation are less clear. Think about the investments needed in its implementation, not just in the technology itself, but also in the employees—relating to their own personal needs as well as their skills, their concerns and anxieties relating to the misuse of the technology, the potential biases imbedded in the systems, not to mention the potential of job eliminations. Keep in mind that employees cannot be expected to train themselves on how to use the new technology. It is therefore necessary to implement the necessary guardrails to protect businesses, employees, and customers.

The excitement about the opportunities arising from GenAI and LLMs and the speed at which they are being adopted is unparalleled, not just within commercial and operations planning, but also for the use of strategy planning. The developers of GenAI claim that these systems can make critical predictions with a high degree of accuracy. However, as stated earlier, the quality of predictions, solutions, and recommendations offered by these systems depends on the quality of the data used to train and validate the algorithms that provide the output. From this perspective, the accuracy of the output will depend on the accuracy of the date used as input. Otherwise, bias is likely to emerge. The question can even be related to how to determine the validity of the data in the first place. If the system is to predict the likelihood of a delay or a mechanical failure, what is the data that is being fed into the system? One way to feel comfortable about the solutions being offered could be to ask follow-up questions. Suppose the system suggests a recovery system that is more focused on customers than the resources required. A follow-up question could then be the additional costs. Or relating to a marketing strategy, the follow-up question could be the competitive reaction.

While the future of AI is irresistible, the real question is how to use it correctly and responsibly. AI can be used to develop ideas, to experiment, and to evaluate results. Relating to ideas, while humans can generate voluminous ideas, AI systems may be able to develop the ideas much faster and easier in the sense of avoiding the use of forming brainstorming teams. It is true that the system could generate many more ideas than humans and at a greater speed, but there is the question of practicality of the ideas generated. Could the system be overconfident in its estimate of practicality, given the possibility of erroneous input data in the validation process? Nevertheless, the solutions offered could add value in many other ways. If numerous solutions are being provided, the selection might be based on not only asking numerous questions, but asking them in the right sequence to establish the feasibility of the solution and to reduce the risks and develop contingencies. Then there is the question of priorities. Moreover, while it is impressive that the system can consider much more data than humans, does it have the ability to work without proprietary data, internal (for example, hidden agendas) and external (for example, competitors' plans)? From this perspective, strategies suggested are likely to be generic rather than specific.

Consequently, GenAI has clearly captured an incredible amount of interest of businesses and consumers, but has it begun to deliver value? Adoption of its use will require enormous investments (for example, in platforms) and changes in organizational structure and, even more important, organizational culture, as many business processes will need to be redesigned, not to mention the need to reskill employees. And let us not overlook the need to improve the quality of the input data needed. How will we develop systems to monitor the accuracy of the solutions being recommended and the need for retraining? Who develops monitoring capabilities—external vendors or internal groups within the organizations using the systems?

The capability of the GenAI system is not just to perform a task a human can do, but to do it at scale. Think about the complexity facing a flight operations group for building trips for pilots and crews for all the aircraft in the fleet, taking into consideration not only crews' legal duty limits and rest requirements, but also the requests of all crew members (bid processes) at all the crew bases! Think about the role of GenAI in maintenance where robots are quickly finding spare parts in warehouses. How about using machine learning and the Internet of Things (IoT) and sensors to track aircraft performance in real time to reduce unforeseen maintenance challenges? Today, GenAI-based systems are beginning to perform a broad set of tasks with only a few simple prompts. They can interpret questions from users reasonably well, then identify relevant insights from data and patterns, and provide answers as well as recommendations. These interactions can be in the form of normal conversations. Understanding questions in a conventional language accurately is an extremely powerful capability. Systems can even speak back in conventional language.

For business strategy decisions, however, humans use not only data and visual displays (charts and images), but also stories about data that can include subtle information on competitors and priorities. GenAI recommendations are likely to be based strictly on data and on patterns, both historical and predicted. On the other hand, it can be assumed that the next generation of these tools will include the systems making recommendations that would have considered both data and visual displays to the extent that such information is given to the systems in the learning and validation stages.

Relating to recommendations for business strategy decisions, should the system convey the insights used to make recommendations or simply make the recommendations? For example, make this investment or make this investment because ...? Obviously, it depends on the type of strategy decisions being made, like a business case for a new aircraft, a new route, or a new cabin configuration. For a new route, there would undoubtedly be multiple questions relating to traffic mix, customer preferences and loyalty, seasonality, competition, etc. As such, each recommendation needs to be supported by insights from numerous areas. The key is to combine the knowledge coming from the system and the insights of the human.

No question that AI systems have exceptional processing power and learning capabilities. While at the present time they are not constrained by emotions, is this a plus or a negative? Yes, the systems are consistent and faster and possibly more accurate (in terms of identifying patterns, for example), but they can be biased in different ways. The system is not affected by the user's mental stage. While the system cannot make strategy decisions at this time, it can support decision makers as they use their overall awareness of the situation and their intuition. The important point is to ask if the decision is based on data, analysis, and rationality (in terms of thinking) or based on all of these points plus the ability to see the bigger picture, based on experience and wisdom.

Just as GenAI is becoming pervasive in numerous business sectors, it has the potential to improve air travel, from planning to forecasting and predicting, not to mention traveler experience, given that it is at fragmented and incremental levels. Based on GenAI's role in these areas, it is relatively easy to imagine the systems helping airlines, airports, and travel intermediaries to collaborate, in the context of journey planning and delivery, for example, helping an airline or an airport to run multiple scenarios to manage the best way out of a disruption. One strategy is for airport and airline planners as well as distributors to consider the power of these systems in their operational design. Think about some organizational functions becoming obsolete and GenAI helping our understanding to create new capabilities. Similarly think about the role of biometrics to automate the verification process and the sharing of digital identities to accelerate the immigration process, not just to reduce congestion, but also to improve border control security.[9]

While advancing technologies within the space of biometrics, CT-scanners, and baggage tracking are already helping airports reduce their operating costs and improve traveler experience, airports can now develop a deeper understanding of these technologies to see how an airport's operational processes can be realigned to maximize benefits. As for airlines, the use of

GenAI has already begun to optimize the planning of networks, fleet, flight routing, and ground operations. In the case of travel agents, GenAI-embedded chatbots are beginning to handle general inquiries of travelers and guide them to a human travel agent for a complex travel inquiry. This technology can reduce the workload of human travel agents, allowing them to focus on complex and timely inquires.

Going forward, however, a holistic approach to the deployment of new technologies needs to begin with

1 a thorough understanding of the existing operational processes and the quality and quantity of existing disparate data,
2 a need to develop organizational and technology-focused capabilities, and
3 a need to have people who know how to use the relevant technologies and achieve scale.

The choice of technologies, the realignment of specific operational processes and the integration of data need to be considered simultaneously to reduce costs, enhance revenue, and improve traveler experience at the holistic level. For technology to deliver the expected benefits, users need to understand the changes required in their organizations to capitalize on the digitalization movement.[10] A recent report by McKinsey and Company provides an excellent collection of GenAI use cases across numerous functions within organizations and across different industries. Particularly interesting are the insights on the banking and the healthcare sectors.[11]

GenAI is a step change in the evolution of AI, augmented by machine learning and deep learning, and the availability of high levels of computational power, capacity, and speed. Machine learning algorithms can already identify patterns and, through a learning process (based on the processing of data and experiences), help users make reasonable recommendations and predictions. Deep learning relates to learning from unstructured data, which can be text, images, video, or audio. And now the needed high computational power (storage space and processing capabilities) is becoming available to read as much data as desired, to understand it, and to learn from it. And the computational power is not only becoming available in terms of the quantity of data to be analyzed, but also at lower costs. It is within this context that GenAI shows the potential to increase functional productivities by expanding the capabilities of planners and managers in different functions, such as marketing and sales as well as operations.

Think about the huge impact on marketing and sales that GenAI can produce to create different types of content along with text, images, and videos. Until now, travelers could only plan their itineraries and journeys within the framework of the planning tools provided by airlines and travel intermediaries. GenAI now enables travelers to make inquiries using natural language. And relating to text, the enhancement can be in the area of written answers to shopping questions. Think about how open-source LLMs can be used to read and understand information presented in unstructured forms to answer a broad spectrum of questions from travelers and provide meaningful answers to questions. American Express Global Business Travel illustrates the value of such systems to help stressed travelers on business, while conforming to their corporate travel polices and avoiding errors in the answers provided through the use of open-source LLMs. Very large machine learning models can be pre-trained on enormous amounts of complex data and are generally referred to as foundation models. From this perspective, GenAI can add a new dimension to personalized travel experience in light of the ability of the system to learn from large quantities of unstructured data.[12]

Moreover, GenAI can help travel service providers scale personalization with the use of data that service providers (airlines, airports, travel intermediaries) already have on travelers and with additional information that service providers can get on the travel intent from travelers themselves, and from third parties. The key to personalization is (1) the extent to which information is available on the situational intent, and (2) the ability to interpret words used to describe intent as well as travel habits. Take, for instance, Tripadvisor's announcement that it has enhanced its platform by including a travel itinerary generator that integrates its data with OpenAI's GenAI technology. The system can take "more than one billion user-generated reviews and opinions to create day-by-day itineraries based on a user's input of a destination, travel dates, who they are traveling with and the types of activities they are interested in."[13]

GenAI has the potential to transform not only how aviation businesses (airlines, airports, distributors) operate but also how the products and services are delivered to travelers, with holistic experience. What if an airline could design a new schedule, optimizing it not just from the perspective of customers, competitors, costs, and revenues, but also, as mentioned in Chapter 3, for minimum delay? From the point of view of businesses and their operations, these transformational changes will increase productivities of equipment and employees. Think about the predictive maintenance capability and its impact on managing disruptions. How about the ability of schedulers to produce more effective schedules with input from different groups inside and outside the airline using multi-dimensional and integrated data? From the perspective of traveler experience think about the additional value of much more intelligent virtual assistants (through conversational search) and much more knowledgeable call-center agents, loaded with vital information, to provide truly creative content and contextualized solutions, based on the travel history as well as traveler preferences. For example, while AI has been looked at as a way to predict the demand for air travel (and its impact on the development of schedules and prices, not just static but also dynamic scheduling and dynamic pricing), now data can also come from social media, based not just on conversations, but also on images. GenAI can be an important lever in personalizing travel itineraries that, in turn, will increase loyalty, based on personalized products as opposed to point-based, as discussed earlier. It is true that a human agent can provide somewhat personalized services, but the human agent can be assisted by a platform with embedded GenAI to take personalization to totally new levels.

As mentioned in Chapter 3, GenAI can add much value in managing disruptions from a traveler's perspective. Think about what happens when the last flight of the day is cancelled, and a traveler needs to get home. The traveler can look at their smartphone and do numerous searches. The airline cancelling the flight would offer availability only on its own flights as well as alliance partners. But the chances the airline would offer the services of competitors and other modes of transportation are slim. The use of GenAI (based on the benefit of situational awareness) can add much value by offering multiple options to a traveler to pick one based on not just costs and services, but also personal preferences. The challenge in this case is not the power of GenAI, but the willingness of service providers to make disruption management focused on the traveler more than operations, relating to crews and aircraft.

However, there are some questions relating to the use of GenAI. For example, will travelers trust the GenAI-driven algorithms to plan their trips? GenAI-driven systems can provide interesting recommendations, but not infallible recommendations. In light of this potential mistrust, will airlines and intermediaries make the necessary investments in this technology? What role would governments play? Would travelers have more trust in human planners of trips? Is there an ideal human–machine relationship?

It would be helpful if managers using GenAI had a good working knowledge of this powerful technology, including the machine learning and deep learning (a part of machine learning) aspects. Data scientists obviously have this knowledge, but users need to have sufficient familiarity since they know the intricacies in specific areas, such as revenue management and schedule planning. The first point is to grasp the criticality of the data and its quality, data that usually sits in different internal departments, to enable GenAI algorithms and systems to offer viable solutions and recommendations. Consequently, it is essential that the businesses maintain control over the data and provide the correct business rules (relating to pricing and flight scheduling within the context of offer and order management) for the system to provide meaningful recommendations. One key point is that these systems learn from their past decisions, what worked and what did not. As such, going forward, the systems may be able to do multiple simulations for the internal thinking before coming up with final recommendations.

There is very little in the way of evaluation criteria at the present time. Soon, it may be possible to ask for justification relating to a recommendation made by the system. But given the capacity of the systems and the speed with which they run, they are able to take into consideration many more variables than humans. But that again raises the question, what is the data that is being provided? As such, GenAI will have an effect not only in the planning and delivery of products and services, but also in the organizational structures and organizational cultures—to develop learning cultures. Some positions will become obsolete, and some new ones will be created. Within the context of planning GenAI can empower managers to become much more effective.

Of course, leading businesses have begun to use AI responsibly. There is now, in fact, a new term, Responsible AI (RAI). The caution comes into play, not only for internally developed programs, but also in the use of third-party technologies. Problems can arise not just from the use of poor-quality data, as discussed above, but also from the rush to develop and implement the AI programs. The use of RAI calls for the existence of the right corporate culture not only to use AI responsibly, but also to develop risk-management initiatives, given the movement within the regulatory landscape in the areas, for example, of consumer protection and data privacy. The change in culture requires, for example, not only ensuring that RAI applies across the enterprise, but also focusing on third-party systems, and the preparation for existing and additional regulations. For some insights on how RAI is being implemented across organizations worldwide, readers are referred to research reported in the *MIT Sloan Management Review* with participation by the Boston Consulting Group.[14]

In the final analysis, there are three thoughts, one on data, one on GenAI, and one on whether to build or acquire the technology for applications.

- First, there is much value in data, zero-party, first-party, second-party, or third-party. "Data-as-a-Product" can be used to add much value in developing aviation organizational capabilities. While different sectors of the aviation industry have a lot of data, (1) the data is fragmented, and (2) there is insufficient granularity. Keep in mind that data is knowledge, and knowledge is power.
- Second, as for GenAI, the question is not if it is coming; it is here. And it is not if it will have a major impact on the aviation industry, but when. Although the technology has started to produce some results, there are still some questions relating to the emergence of totally disruptive applications. Does an airline or an airport take a risk if it does start using GenAI right away, or is the risk in not using it? Or is the risk in not implementing it effectively (relating to the needed computing infrastructure and user interfaces, for example), and not using it effectively? Or is the risk in not innovating initiatives at a fast pace? So, it is necessary to monitor different risks. The challenge is not in using it but using it in a responsible way. According to a McKinsey report, "The risks associated with gen AI range from inaccurate outputs and biases embedded in the underlying training data to the potential for large-scale misinformation and malicious influence on politics and personal well-being."[15] A key consideration within the aviation sector would be to determine how much value an AI solution will provide from its implementation. Three researchers conducted an in-depth study within a healthcare organization that was actively developing and adopting AI for some decision-making tasks. The study involved data coming from in-hospital observations and

numerous long-form interviews. The conclusion was that an organization interested in using AI needs to look past performance reports and find the ground truth on which the AI has been trained and validated.[16] From this perspective, it might now be more important to raise the right questions than accept the right answers. And let us not overlook that, given the risks involved, rule makers are getting ready to get involved.

- Third, the question is if the organization (an airline, or an airport) should develop the technology in-house or acquire it from a vendor and use it for specific applications? Building the technology in-house would require enormous investments in data and technical skills, not just to build the technology, but also to maintain it. But the benefit would be the availability of customized solutions for specific applications. On the other hand, building applications on vendors' models can be cost-effective if the use cases are not extremely specific and there is trust in the vendor selected relating, for example, to security risks, such as misuse of proprietary data.

Ali Faruqi provides, in his thought leadership piece in Chapter 8, excellent examples of the use of AI. One example is the Commonwealth Bank's use of AI to support its call centers to answer complex questions by interrogating 4,500 documents on bank policies in real time. A second example is American Express using GenAI to predict customer behavior by using predictive analytics to gain deeper insights into customer patterns and behaviors. Based on the insights from these two case studies, Ali Faruqi then shows how airlines can harness GenAI and predictive analytics to enhance various aspects of their operations and customer interactions.

Innovative technology use case examples

3D visualization of airport operations and digital twins

Apple developed its Vision Pro, a mixed-reality headset, a "spatial computer," where digital media is integrated with real-world situations. It uses a 3D user interface. Then ForeFlight, a Boeing company, launched "Voyager" an innovative app designed for spatial computing that can offer an incredible 3D airport operational experience by combining "satellite imagery, high-resolution terrain and live traffic data" to display operations at an airport in a 3D environment in real time.[17] The display is presented on a virtual floating disc that a user can view from any angle. The system can provide a holistic, real-time view of airport activities that can help planners to streamline processes and help coordinate the activities of multiple stakeholders working at an airport.[18]

Airports can also consider deploying digital twins to optimize their capacities and operations, given the capability of this technology to understand multiple aspects of airports—car parks, stores, waiting areas, ground services, security, not to mention the handling of both passengers and cargo.

Consider just one aspect of a challenge—managing passenger traffic during busy hours. This is one area where digital-twin technology comes into play, with the ability to understand multiple variables such as capacity of different areas, staff constraints, early and late arrivals of passengers and their bags, and weather. Digital twins enable airport managers to visualize movements of passengers, staff, and bags and help airports optimize the allocation of their resources.

Digital-twin technology can also be used to simulate, experiment with, and eventually improve traveler experience. According to a McKinsey report, Daimler "has developed customer twins that allow customers to 'test drive' a vehicle without ever getting behind the wheel."[19] Imagine how such technology can be used by airlines to simulate passenger experience as passengers go through different stages of their trips.

Innovations on tracking bags

Tracking of bags has been an ongoing frustration for travelers and a high-cost item for airlines. One basic cause has been the lack of detailed data in real time and its sharing among three groups—airlines, airports, and ground-handling groups. The lack of data and its ineffective flow has resulted in bags being delayed and misplaced. Then the shortage of labor during COVID-19 made the problem more severe. However, changes in processes to manage bags and the use of advanced technology have begun to improve the situation. The starting point is an increase in the transparency of the location of a bag at any time. Airline apps are now beginning to enable travelers to track their bags in real time across an airline's entire system. Think about the value of integrating seamlessly among different systems within an airline, from booking to departure control to tail-to-tail transfers. The value of this integrated information is to provide real-time updates to all stakeholders, including, of course, travelers. Technology can be used to manage the process dynamically to maximize, for example, tail-to-tail connections. For example, AI can analyze flight histories and "predict which bags are most likely to miss their connection."[20] Some airports are also thinking about using baggage robots to help baggage handlers. And some airlines are also looking into what kinds of robots would add value in processing and tracking bags.

Next, the use of Radio-Frequency Identification (RFID) technology for tracking bags has been increasing. RFID technology is much better than traditional barcode scanning processes because this technology allows bags to be tracked automatically throughout the baggage-handling process instead of the direct line-of-sight scanning. There are, however, some limitations to the use of RFID technology, such as high implementation costs, a lack of standardized procedures between different airports and airlines, and a limited coverage in some areas. While even more technologies are emerging (for example, incredibly advanced conveyor belts, biometrics systems for bags, and cloud-based systems for integrating data and displaying it across the whole baggage journey), the critical success factor is still the collection of relevant data and sharing it in real time among all stakeholders.

An important aspect of the improvements needed in the handling of baggage is the totality of the infrastructure (conveyor belts, carousels, etc.) relating to the continuous operation of the complex baggage-handling system required to handle not only an extremely large number of bags, but also bags of different sizes, shapes, and weights. Maintenance issues relating to baggage-handling systems have become more critical due to the shortage of parts. Baggage-handling maintenance can now move from a reactive to a proactive basis, using (1) predictive maintenance solutions that use, in turn, real-time integrated data analytics, and (2) evolving information technologies.

Airlines are also investing large amounts to improve the airport check-in experience. Alaska Airlines announced an investment of US$2.5 billion in its airport lobbies "with the goal of getting passengers from the check-in hall and through security in five minutes or less."[21] The airline plans to remove traditional airport check-in kiosks and passengers can check in using their smartphone. The kiosks will be replaced with new bag-tag stations, where passengers can tag checked bags using iPad tablets, and put the bags on the belt themselves. Payments for transportation of bags can also be made at the bag-tag station.

UPS's use of predictive analytics

Eric Siegel in his book *The AI Playbook* provides an insightful example of how UPS predicts "tomorrow's deliveries."[22] UPS delivers over 20 million packages per day. A big question is which packages to load on which truck at a sorting station to maximize the utilization of each truck when it leaves the station. The challenge is that some packages do not arrive until after the packages–truck decision gets made. To deal with the incomplete information challenge, UPS developed its Package Flow Technology system, in which it used data and machine learning to predict deliveries. Initially, this technology, a combination of software and re-engineered process changes, developed almost 20 years ago, enabled UPS to automate the last leg of the delivery process.[23] Now, when actual data becomes available, the system is updated to produce better predictions. Next, to make deliveries more efficient, UPS developed the ORION (On-Road Integrated Optimization and Navigation) system to determine the optimal routing of each truck making deliveries. This system enabled the continuous optimization of delivery routes, based on traffic and pickup and delivery commitments, not to mention the achievement of final-mile efficiencies.[24]

UPS has also begun to use a GenAI system to streamline its customer-service operations with its initiative Message Response Automation (MeRA). On a typical day, UPS receives just over 50,000 emails from customers. The LLM-based system produced a 50 percent reduction in the time spent by agents responding to emails by giving the responses recommended by the system. This reduction in time enabled agents to spend more time on customers' more complex needs. The system enabled agents to access not only corporate policies and procedures, but also data to answer customers' questions, not to mention the system's sentiment analysis capability "to customize the tone of the response to customer questions." Agents need "to know how to respond to various scenarios."[25]

Airlines' movement towards becoming digital retailers

As mentioned in Chapter 2, significant consideration needs to be given to improving the booking process, given that a significant percentage of travelers are dissatisfied with the existing booking process and many travelers leave websites from the frustration relating to complexity on the one hand and lack of transparency on the other hand. There are two primary areas for potential improvements. The first would be the development and implementation of integrated platforms. These platforms would have the capability of dynamic content (including dynamic packaging) with a reasonable level of personalization based on the availability of near real-time information. The incorporation of NDC would be an essential part of the platform. The second part would be the simplification of the sales of ancillaries. The critical success factor is the ability to make the right offer at the right time to a specific traveler, more to enhance the traveler experience than to generate more revenue for the airline. Assuming that relevant and timely data is available, then it is possible to use GenAI to offer meaningful recommendations based on traveler profiles, especially through the use of conversations.

Other areas of improvements in retailing include the introduction of sophisticated apps that offer not only access to information on a broad spectrum of travel-related services, but also the capability to make reservations for an equally broad spectrum of events and activities.[26] Another example is the implementation of an electronic point-of-sales system that raises operational efficiency and customer experience. Data on passengers from the booking systems can be fed into the system that already has information on each flight (duration, time of the day, season, destination, etc.) to forecast the demand for onboard consumption of food and beverages as well as online sales. For cabin crews it updates inventories relating to products and meals, creating a more dynamic management of inventory.[27] And onboard retailing also includes the availability of new payment methods.

The retailing process of airlines is getting more sophisticated in terms of offering travelers more relevant and to some extent personalized offers while increasing revenue, using offer management and order management frameworks and technologies. However, a few forward-thinking airlines are beginning to raise two points. First, shouldn't airlines focus first on getting their basics right and the proper execution of these basics? Second, taking airline retailing to a new level will require a new level of collaboration among partners—not only airlines, distributors, hotels, car-rental businesses, and service providers at destinations, but also innovative start-ups.

Data-driven transformations

This chapter presented different ways to adapt and evolve with data and technologies. Based on the experience of some companies in other sectors, it is even possible to achieve data-driven transformation. Within the airline sector, Lufthansa is an example of one airline moving in this direction. However, the conclusion Lufthansa has reached is that in order to become a truly data-driven business, there is a critical role for leadership to become: data visionary, data transformer, data driver, data decision maker, data collaborator, and data coach. The leadership does not end with the Chief Digital Officer. It comprises other members in the C-Suite as well, including the Chief Executive Officer to establish a data vision to develop business value.[28] This is part of rewiring an organization, a topic discussed at length in the next chapter.

Finally, becoming a data- and analytics-driven business requires more than data scientists and the IT departments building the necessary models to accomplish certain tasks. Ganes Kesari discusses succinctly in his recent article in MIT's *Sloan Management Review* three factors that lead to the failure of IT projects and three actions for building better solutions.[29] A summary of Kesari's three factors to failure are:

- initiatives get run as technology projects with insufficient input from the user groups,
- user groups are used to their own way of doing specific tasks and feel uncomfortable with changing processes, and
- it is difficult to determine ROIs.

Kesari's three actions for building better solutions are:

- for technologists to work closely with the user groups on their major problems and priorities,
- to work with the user groups to identify and implement storytelling and gamification initiatives, and
- to define success criteria early in the modeling process.

Could a data-driven and an AI technology-driven mindset have detected and fixed CrowdStrike's issues?

Notes

1 Michael Chui, et al., "The Economic potential of generative AI: The next productivity frontier," *McKinsey and Company*, June 2023.

2 Veeral Desai, Tim Fountaine, and Kayvaun Rowshankish, "A Better Way to Put Your Data to Work: Package it the way you would a product," *Harvard Business Review*, July–August 2022. https://hbr.org/2022/07/a-better-way-to-put-your-data-to-work

3 "Catalysts for Change: Building the Hospitality Ecosystem of the Future," *Amadeus*, 2023, pp. 8–9.
4 https://www.iata.org/contentassets/5c1a116a6120415f87f3dadfa38859d2/iata-acdm-recommendations-v1.pdf
5 Bob Kwik, "From why to wow: How airports can use data to improve the passenger experience," *AWS Website*, February 22, 2023. https://aws.amazon.com/blogs/industries/from-why-to-wow-how-airports-can-use-data-to-improve-the-passenger-experience
6 "Airline Data Analytics: The Evolving Role of Analysis and New Data," *OAG*, March 18, 2024. https://www.oag.com/blog/airline-data-analytics-evolves-the-role-of-new-data
7 "Google's AI Model Gemini: A New Era in Artificial Intelligence & the Travel Industry," *MyTrip.AI by VoyagePort Inc.*, December 6, 2023. https://www.linkedin.com/pulse/googles-ai-model-gemini-new-era-artificial-intelligence-travel-erhle
8 "Cloud-based Flight Management Systems for Next-Generation Aircraft," *Connected Aviation Intelligence*, June 7, 2022. https://www.gcasummit.com/cloud-based-flight-management-systems-for-next-generation-aircraft
9 Jeremy Springall, "As travel surges, how do we drive down risk at the border?" *SITA*, August 8, 2023. https://www.sita.aero/pressroom/blog/as-travel-surges-how-do-we-drive-down-risk-at-the-border/?
10 Eric Lamarre, Kate Smaje, and Rodney Zemmel, *Rewired: The McKinsey Guide to Outcompeting in the Age of Digital and AI* (Hoboken, NJ: John Wiley & Sons, 2023).
11 Michael Chui, "The Economic potential of generative AI," *McKinsey & Company*, June 2023.
12 "AI Insights: Generative AI in Business Travel," *PhocusWire*, June 21, 2023. https://www.phocuswire.com/ai-insights-generative-ai-in-business-travel
13 Mitra Sorrells, "Tripadvisor integrates OpenAI for Travel Planning," *PhocusWire*, July 19, 2023. https://www.phocuswire.com/tripadvisor-travel-planning-tool-powered-by-openai?
14 David Kiron and Steven Mills, "Is Your Organization Investing Enough in Responsible AI? 'Probably Not,' Says Our Data," *MIT Sloan Management Review*, October 19, 2023. https://sloanreview.mit.edu/article/is-your-organization-investing-enough-in-responsible-ai-probably-not-says-our-data
15 "Implementing generative AI with speed and safety," *McKinsey & Company*, March 13, 2024. https://www.mckinsey.com/capabilities/risk-and-resilience/our-insights/implementing-generative-ai-with-speed-and-safety?
16 Sarah Lebovitz, Hila Lifshitz-Assaf, and Natalia Levina, "The No. 1 Question to Ask When Evaluating AI Tools," *MIT Sloan Management Review*, March 7, 2023. https://sloanreview.mit.edu/article/the-no-1-question-to-ask-when-evaluating-ai-tools
17 "ForeFlight Launches Voyager App for Apple Vision Pro," *ForeFlight News Hub*, 2024. https://blog.foreflight.com/2024/02/01/voyager-announcement
18 "Four Groundbreaking Innovations Transforming the Aviation Industry this Month," *OAG*, March 5, 2024.
19 "What is digital-twin technology?" *McKinsey & Company*, July 2023, p. 3.

20 Anna Giaritelli, "How AI is transforming the air travel experience in the US," *The Gazette*, March 15, 2024. https://gazette.com/news/wex/how-ai-is-transforming-the-air-travel-experience-in-the-us
21 Ben Schlappig, "Alaska Airlines Kiosks No Longer Print Boarding Passes," *One Mile At A Time*, March 13, 2024. https://onemileatatime.com/news/alaska-airlines-kiosks-boarding-passes
22 Eric Siegel, *The AI Playbook: Mastering the Rare Art of Machine Learning Deployment* (Cambridge, MA: The MIT Press, 2024), pp. 8–18.
23 "Package Flow Technology at UPS," *MH&L*, April 1, 2005. https://www.mhlnews.com/transportation-distribution/article/22046526/package-flow-technology-at-ups
24 "UPS To Enhance ORION With Continuous Delivery Route Optimization," *UPS*, January 29, 2020. https://about.ups.com/us/en/newsroom/press-releases/innovation-driven/ups-to-enhance-orion-with-continuous-delivery-route-optimization.html
25 Paula Rooney, "UPS delivers customer wins with generative AI," *CIO,* May 3, 2024. https://www.cio.com/article/2096052/ups-delivers-customer-wins-with-generative-ai.html
26 "AirAsia MOVE Launches MOVETIX, a Revolutionary Ticketing Platform for Global Events and Activities," *Breaking Travel News*, February 4, 2024. https://www.breakingtravelnews.com/news/article/airasia-move-launches-movetix-a-revolutionary-ticketing-platform-for-global
27 "Four Groundbreaking Innovations Transforming the Aviation Industry this Month," *OAG*, March 5, 2024.
28 Christian Haude, Ivo Blohm, and Xavier Lagardère, "How Lufthansa Shapes Data-Driven Transformation Leaders," *Sloan Management Review, MIT*, April 18, 2024. https://sloanreview.mit.edu/article/how-lufthansa-shapes-data-driven-transformation-leaders
29 Ganes Kesari, "Building a Data-Driven Culture: Three Mistakes to Avoid," *Sloan Management Review*, May 14, 2024. https://sloanreview.mit.edu/article/building-a-data-driven-culture-three-mistakes-to-avoid

7 Rewiring organizations for proactive and innovative collaboration

The aviation industry is not only a very complex industry, but it is also a high-stakes industry. The key message in this book has been that to become adaptable, resilient, and lean and to elevate customer experience in different sectors of this industry will require a much higher level of collaboration and coordination among partners. This chapter provides some thoughts on how successful collaboration can be achieved in different areas of different partners, especially when some partners are moving at a different pace in realigning their organizations relating to the use of technologies and data.

Some perspectives for productive collaboration

Let us begin by identifying four basic pillars for the development of a productive collaboration within different stakeholders in the travel ecosystem:

1 viewing performance through a new lens,
2 understanding the real problem holding back collaboration,
3 transforming the core parts of businesses, and
4 achieving scale by developing the required supporting capabilities.

Relating to the first pillar, a new lens to view performance, each organization in the ecosystem can look at performance beyond the traditional view and measurement. Many airlines are stuck in measuring performance (load factors, on-time performance, revenue per seat mile, aircraft and crew utilization, conversion rate of visitors to the website, etc.). It would add value to step back and explore new ways of performing through experimentation, extensive feedback, and learning, while doing.[1] Many groups operate under pressure to continue measuring performance using conventional processes and conventional mindsets. The view, according to Eduardo Briceño, should include the perspective of "growth and learning" that, in turn, calls for a change in mindset within the context of "experimentation and feedback." The idea is to "balance and integrate performance and learning."

DOI: 10.4324/9781003483960-7

For the second pillar, there is not only a need to clearly understand the roadblocks to collaboration, but also the steps needed to solve the problems. Examples of problems include: building and rebuilding trust in the organization, creating a culture for all organizations in the ecosystem to benefit, empowering the critical teams to eliminate roadblocks, and focusing on people who think differently. Leaderships need to change cultures so that high-performance collaborative partnerships can produce mutual benefits. According to the experience of Frances Frei and Anne Morriss, the goal is to "move fast & fix things."[2]

The third pillar is to rewire organizations for successful digital transformation. The objective for each stakeholder is not only to harness digital innovation for competitive advantage, but also to improve collaboration and coordination for mutual benefit. According to McKinsey partners Eric Lamarre, Kate Smaje, and Rodney Zemmel, rewiring an organization requires creating a transformation roadmap, building a talent bench, adopting a new operating model, using technology for speed and distributed innovation, embedding data everywhere, and getting users to adopt digital solutions and scale solutions across the enterprise. The authors provide three insightful examples of businesses that transformed their digital journeys. Freeport-McMoRan, a copper mining business, turned data into value. DBS, a multinational bank, gained insights from the top technology businesses from around the world to develop a clear vision to "Make Banking Joyful." LEGO, a global toy business, used technology to "reshape everything from customer experience to global supply chain management."[3]

While new ideas emerge from innovation and experimentation, the fourth pillar calls for the development of relevant capabilities to achieve scale. And three critical aspects for an airline to scale its business strategy are (1) a clear understanding of its value proposition, not to mention its uniqueness, (2) a clear identification of the customer base being targeted, and (3) an understanding and effective use of technologies. It is the development of innovative experimentation that will lead organizations to adapt and become more resilient and leaner.

All four pillars need to be explored within the context of both customer experience and employee experience, a strategy that requires a very different mindset, *an experience mindset*. As mentioned in a previous book, an improvement in customer experience cannot be achieved without a focus also on employee experience. And just as businesses explore reasons for customer dissatisfaction and disengagement, it is time to do the same for employees. While businesses obviously know about the "virtuous cycle" between customer experience and employee experience, the challenge appears to be how to dig deeper into the levers that have the greatest impact on employee experience and how to change culture, redesign processes, and use relevant technology to elevate employee experience. How about the development and use of relevant and effective metrics not only to measure employee experience, but also to improve it? Tiffani Bova, in her book *The Experience Mindset*, provides numerous excellent examples from such businesses as Pfizer, Salesforce, the Ritz-Carlton, and Unilever. As for the use of technology, ask just one question: Do customer-facing employees think that technology will make their jobs easier? The answer, according to Bova, is only 20 percent.[4] Joe Mull provides another perspective on employee experience. He has coined the term *employalty*, "to ignite commitment and keep top talent in the new age of work."[5] Mull clarifies the ingredients needed to retain employees and shows a framework not only to find and keep employees, but also to "unlock their commitment" to improve a company's performance.

One starting point is to develop a clear understanding on what the common goals and the values are to be co-created by each partner—airlines and airports on one side and airlines and intermediaries on the other side, to introduce not just incremental, transactional, and fragmented innovations in traveler experience, but a holistic approach for step changes. For instance, it is critical that not only airlines and airports come to an agreement on what needs to be done, but that each subgroup within an airline and each subgroup within an airport is onboard with the goals. In the case of an airline, it is not just marketing and sales, but also operations—ground, flight, and maintenance. In the case of an airport, it is not just the facility planners, investment planners and operations, but also concessionaires and ground service providers, not to mention providers of government services—ATC and security, both preboard clearance and border control. Similar considerations apply to the alignment of thinking between different groups of airlines (low-cost, hybrid, and full-service carriers) as well as different intermediaries (GDSs, OTAs, metasearch engines, and so forth).

These considerations assume the availability of full support from the CEO to enable strategies to get implemented, from making available the necessary budgets to the willingness to share data. Many reasons can justify the involvement and support of CEOs. For example, to bring about a step change in collaboration, airline and airport managers as well as travel distributors can innovate and co-create value through the use of new technologies that are likely to require changes in business models. Even the use of existing technologies may require an extension of the boundaries of existing business models.

Challenges, opportunities, and enablers

While challenges to collaboration continue to exist, let us not overlook the opportunities for proactive and innovative collaboration, not to mention the availability of a few real enablers to help airlines, airports, and travel intermediaries take big leaps in collaboration. Here are several examples of effective enablers:

1 making access easier to relevant, real-time, and integrated information not only on transactions, but also on behaviors,

2 enabling interdependent organizations not only to understand, predict, and visualize data, but also to share data and protect data, facilitated by emerging technologies and analytics,
3 providing the ability to share just the information each organization wants to share, and nothing else,
4 being willing to discuss the mutual value of data that different organizations have, the monetization of this data, and working with flexible technology platforms to adapt to the offer- and order-based retailing framework,
5 using new technology to obtain high-capacity and high-speed computing power to work with large volumes of multi-dimensional data,
6 capitalizing on open innovation through the use of external resources (partners, start-ups, customers, crowdsourcing platforms, etc.) and overcoming organizational barriers to open innovation,
7 deploying GenAI
   - to develop new ideas and new designs to collaborate to co-create value, responding to customers' unmet needs while reducing costs and enhancing revenues,
   - to make personalized offers based on data and the use of technologies to identify actual customers' needs and not customers' needs based on an airline's perceptions,
   - to reduce staff for back-office functions to work in customer-facing areas to create an emotional connection with customers, and
   - to offer personalized travel options to each and every passenger on a disrupted flight,
8 using digital-twin technology to help ecosystem partners (airlines, airports, distributors, etc.) simulate real situations and their outcomes to be able to make better decisions,
9 recognizing, based on the experience of high-end hotels, that travelers would pay more for truly meaningful experiences while delivering on the promises made,
10 collaborating to bring to reality disruptive thinking and radical approaches to sustainability,
11 working with user-generated reviews and opinions to suggest specific itineraries based on a user's input on a destination, dates of travel, and some types of activities of interest,
12 highlighting the experience gained from iterating and experimenting with initiatives to co-create value,
13 providing insights from best practices in other business sectors and spaces—for example, personalized and interactive wayfinding initiatives,
14 realigning culture and employees to create "employalty,"[6]
15 developing effective content marketing initiatives and sharing them with the travel intermediaries,
16 using more effective ideation techniques[7] (for example, cross-business innovation—that is, an airline and an airport innovating together),

17 finding effective payment strategies—given that the airline business is a low-margin business, taking even one percent out of the payment system would add a lot of value to the bottom line,
18 capitalizing on the *network effect* of different organizations within the ecosystem that are working to find solutions to the problems facing service providers and travelers,
19 increasing total revenue per passenger, not just by selling ancillary products and services, but also by enhancing traveler experience,
20 renovating organizations (for example, through digital transformation) to create value through the use of technology at scale, and
21 enabling passengers to take greater control of their travel itineraries themselves electronically.

Relating to point number 5 in the above list, the use of new technologies and technology service providers can enable management to rethink how airlines, airports, and travel intermediaries can build collaboration into their organizational and operational design. The NDC standards, for example, are enabling airlines to bring more personalized content to travel intermediaries. And new technologies in the areas of biometrics, CT-scanners, and baggage tracking can help airports improve traveler experience and reduce their operating costs. The benefit of using new technologies can, however, increase much more significantly when coupled with new thinking, such as using LLMs, touched upon in Chapter 6, to respond in real time to the feedback received from customers while shopping for air travel or during their actual travel, especially during disruptions (discussed in Chapter 3). Think about the potential value of being able to offer ancillaries based on real-time engagement with a customer, as discussed in Chapter 2.

Relating to point number 9 in the above list, think about the value of being able to respond to a customer's disrupted flight—ranging from a statement of an apology to an offer of discounts on future flights, with the amount of discount offered depending on a particular customer and a particular situation, based on real-time feedback—all made possible by the use of GenAI (discussed in Chapter 6). And, in the case of intermediaries, there is a clear need to explore new methods for intermediaries to generate new streams of revenue that represent win–win solutions for airlines and intermediaries. A change in thinking can also facilitate all four types of organizations (airlines, travel intermediaries, airports, and aircraft manufacturers) to focus more on travelers' holistic experience and less on products and services through the use of content marketing (creating information, not of interest to service providers, but information that is of significant interest to customers, enabling service providers to expand their customer bases).[8]

Expanding on point number 7 in the list above, think about what four major technology businesses (Amazon Web Services, Google, Meta, and Microsoft) are developing in their travel-related applications—for example, the capability to access internal data by the AI systems and for sophisticated chatbots to answer a much broader set of questions for planning trips, while assessing a shopper's behavior, and then making bookings. However, while these opportunities are real, there are also the concerns of (1) the privacy of the sensitive personal information being used, (2) any hidden biases in the algorithms, and (3) the potential for the chatbot to make mistakes.

Think about the 18th point in the list above within the context of virtual interlining (discussed in Chapter 4). Delta is already making huge investments in New York's LaGuardia Airport and the Los Angeles International Airport to improve customer service and experience. Think also about Delta's collaboration with Joby Aviation to provide home-to-airport transportation, a collaboration that includes the two airports. To quote Delta, in a "first-of-its kind arrangement, the companies will work together to integrate a Joby-operated service into Delta's customer-facing channels."[9] Now airlines, airports, aircraft manufacturers, and distributors need to collaborate much more to provide frictionless and convenient connections, as discussed in Chapter 5.

Collaboration does not need to be achieved only through disruptive innovation; it can be achieved, in turn, through the use of new technologies. Think about some examples of disruptive innovation in the aviation industry—jet engines, computer reservation systems, deregulation of the commercial airline industry, loyalty programs, revenue management systems, development of digital twins, and more recently GenAI. However, it has also been possible to create value in many areas without having to wait for the emergence of disruptive innovation. Think about inflight connectivity. Airlines have been offering some level of Wi-Fi depending on their business models and available technology. The capacity and bandwidth have been limited and while some airlines have offered the service for free, others have charged various prices, ranging from US$5 to US$20. Now, the demand for inflight connectivity has increased significantly. It is not just the desire of a few passengers interested in checking their text messages and emails, but also a lot of passengers wanting to watch movies or do whatever they wish. The challenge now is five-fold:

1 to make a connection between the satellite and an aircraft that is flying at 30,000 feet,
2 to provide sufficient capacity and bandwidth for all the passengers and their usage,
3 to get older-generation aircraft upgraded by installing new Wi-Fi systems,
4 to deal with the high costs associated with connected technologies and hardware, and
5 to tighten data privacy norms.

On the other hand, technology has also improved for service providers to overcome some of these challenges. For example, the number of satellites has increased to handle the capacity. There are now numerous companies operating in the satellite space, including Inmarsat, Intelsat, Panasonic, SpaceX, and Viasat. And the connections are getting better. There is a significant improvement in the connections going from users' devices in the cabin (through wireless access points) to the main servers and modems in an aircraft's belly hold, which are connected to the antennas on top of the aircraft to communicate with satellites that communicate with the ground systems. And more satellites and better connections are enabling airlines to provide:

1 greater availability of Wi-Fi on a worldwide basis,
2 sufficient capacity and bandwidth,
3 sufficient reliability, and
4 lower charges.

A few airlines are also thinking about offering Wi-Fi services that not only have high capacity and high bandwidth, but also are free. Such a strategy will undoubtedly enhance customer loyalty, providing airlines the possibility of charging slightly higher fares. But there needs to be cross-functional integration. First, from the perspective of revenue management, the greater loyalty and the potential for higher fares might be better than the conventional sale of ancillary products and services. Second, in addition to an increase in loyalty, let us not overlook the value of additional data that can be gathered to provide valuable information on traveler behavior.

In addition to the four pillars of proactive collaboration discussed above, on a broader level, collaboration within the travel ecosystem could also be achieved through nondisruptive innovation, using existing or new technologies or through the use of existing or new data to co-create value for all stakeholders—win–win solutions, as opposed to win–lose solutions. This point about nondisruptive innovation is elaborated comprehensively by W. Chan Kim and Renée Mauborgne in their book *Beyond Disruption*.[10] The authors call this way of innovating ***nondisruptive creation***. Nondisruptive creation in collaborative strategies to improve traveler experience through a holistic approach can be achieved through the use of well-designed workshops that address how to innovate and achieve collaboration without displacing the existing spaces of airlines, airports, and travel advisors. Such teams can also identify ways to collaborate with agility and resilience in the extremely dynamic marketplace in the aviation sector. For example, a higher level of collaboration between airlines and travel intermediaries does not need to wait until breakthrough technologies become available. They could start with an agreement on the costs of distribution (relating to the makeup of different revenue streams for travel intermediaries) and on the co-creation of value. The co-creation of value can come through a reduction in the complexity of airline shopping, and the exploitation of the NDC to benefit sellers, buyers, and distributors of air travel services.

The point about collaboration with agility and resiliency in a dynamic marketplace is elaborated at length by Des Dearlove and his contributors in the book *Certain Uncertainty*.[11] If airline and airport managers and travel advisors accept that going forward the marketplace is likely to be extremely volatile, then effective collaboration and cooperation need to be designed carefully to bring about step changes in the travel experience, not to mention reducing costs and enhancing revenues. Conventional marketing models may not be sufficient. A new proposal is to think about using an "Omnihouse" model that "puts the entrepreneurial and operational aspects of marketing at the center of action." There are usually two major groups (entrepreneurship and professionalism) and four subgroups within each of these two major groups. The components of the entrepreneurship group are creativity, innovation, entrepreneurship, and leadership. The components of the professionalism group are productivity, improvement, professionalism, and management. The goal is to integrate the activities of each group and subgroups within each group.[12] Another proposal is to start developing frictionless organizations that deliver a high level of customer experience with lower levels of effort. It can be done, but "It requires detailed and perceptive analysis, effective sponsorship, cross-departmental conflict resolution, smart design, and persistent implementation."[13]

Finally, besides data, technologies, and a change in processes, the success of holistic collaborative strategies to bring about a step change in traveler experience will also require the existence of an "experience mindset," as mentioned earlier in this chapter. In the new era, huge investments in customer experience will be necessary, but they will not be sufficient. Managements in all partnerships will also need to invest in employee experience. As mentioned earlier, Tiffani Bova provides numerous examples of best practices derived from such businesses as Pfizer, Ritz-Carlton, Salesforce, and Unilever to strengthen both employee experience and customer experience.[14] The understanding is clear that a high level of employee experience is really important for the delivery of a high level of customer experience. The challenge is how to achieve it. The implementation step requires deep changes in "people, processes, technologies, and culture," creating a "virtuous cycle." Businesses, including within the aviation sector, say that employee experience is important. But how much focus is placed on the four components of the virtuous cycle, not to mention on the metrics for measuring employee experience?

The rate at which technology is changing requires that employees in most categories may need to be reskilled—a monumental challenge. Here is a summary of what business researchers are concluding, based on the experience of successful businesses, particularly relating to automation and AI:

"1. Reskilling is a strategic imperative.
2. It is the responsibility of every leader and manager.
3. It is a change-management initiative.
4. Employees *want* to reskill—when it makes sense.
5. It takes a village."[15]

In the case of airlines and airports, the point needs to be a strong alignment between the strategic goals of the organization and the innovations needed to meet these goals.[16] The new era, described in Chapter 2, calls for CEOs to redesign their organizations not only to create and deliver relevant value, but also to become resilient. However, the need for redesign is not a new need resulting from the events of the last three years. Two business researchers[17] point out the experience of Procter & Gamble, which created six industry-based sector business units in 2019, in which its CEO described the situation as "the most significant organization change we've made in the last 20 years."[18] Consequently, if businesses are entering a "never normal world," then there is a clear need to adapt rapidly through innovative collaboration within partnerships that calls for highly adaptive organizations, re-allocation of resources, and fast learning with relevant data and emerging technologies.

Collaborative partnerships: examples from outside the aviation sector

Healthcare sector

Collaborative partnership initiatives in the healthcare sector are on the rise to improve processes and efficiencies, not to mention patient care, patient engagement, and health outcomes. Collaboration in the healthcare sector has begun to go beyond the competitors in the healthcare landscape. Also being included now are technology businesses and communities to offer a high-quality integrated delivery system with lower costs. This means not only picking the right partners, but also developing a collaborative mindset that will require changes in organizational cultures. As for technology, improvements can be facilitated by purchasing more than some software. It is working with technology businesses to develop and implement platforms, for example, that make use of AI (to analyze big data), advanced search capabilities, data interoperability, and scaling. One such business is MEDITECH, which, in turn, is collaborating with Google Cloud. Another example of collaboration is between Nuance Communications and NVIDIA. This partnership plans to "bring medical imaging—specific machine learning development frameworks directly into clinical workflows."[19] However, deep collaboration with a technology business requires much more than simply a transaction—purchase of software, for example. It requires a change in organizational culture. Similarly, partnering with communities served requires understanding what they are trying to do, such as addressing the broader health needs of their people. Benefits are obviously the greatest when partnerships are symbiotic.[20]

Kristin Shores highlights five areas that are important to the success of partnerships in the healthcare sector:

1 "Trust & Mutual Respect,
2 Shared Vision & Goals,
3 Open Communication,
4 Flexibility & Adaptability,
5 Celebrate & Educate."[21]

Some of the insights from the best practices in the healthcare sector would also add much value for the aviation sector. Think about the statement above that benefits are obviously the greatest when partnerships are symbiotic. In the aviation industry think about the relationships between airlines and airports. Would the partnerships not be symbiotic? As for the five areas identified by Kristin Shores, they would apply equally well to the aviation industry. Think about, for example, the need for trust among airlines, airports, and distributors for the expertise and capability of each partner. Similarly, the visions and goals of just these three partners need to be aligned to drive creativity by reducing complexity, increasing flexibility, and sharing information to improve traveler experience and reduce costs.

Automotive sector

Transformation of the automotive sector is accelerating to adapt to the vision of mobility in the future—rapidly changing consumer preferences, availability of advanced digital technologies, and emerging environmental regulations. These views of the future of mobility have led to the development of not only electric vehicles, but also vehicles that are connected and vehicles that are autonomous. Adapting to these trends requires the development of collaborative partnerships. Rainer Mehl identifies the following five areas of transformation in the automotive sector: softwarization, autonomous driving, EV charging, vehicles as mobile power packs, and in-vehicle experiences. He further identifies four reasons for the need for collaborative partnerships: "Speed and scale of transformation requires external support. Entrepreneurial burden needs to be shared. Access to specialized skills and services. Niche players can provide differentiation."[22] Relating to the first point, since auto makers can hardly become software-driven businesses, they clearly need to develop collaborative partnerships. Tesla doing a large part of software development in-house might be an exception. Think about the role the collaborative partnerships, relating to specialized expertise and capabilities, have played in the development of autonomous vehicles. Think about the partnerships among Waymo + Volvo, Stellantis, Jaguar, and Renault-Nissan in Google's development of its self-driving car.[23]

Consider next the desire and expectation of drivers and passengers for seamless connectivity, similar to their smartphones. This connectivity includes not only access to high-quality entertainment, but also assistance in driving and parking, not to mention direct payments from the dashboard of the vehicles. This level of connectivity calls for innovation in such areas as sensors and communication technologies for vehicles to communicate with each other and the surrounding infrastructure. As an example of collaboration, Volvo partnered with Ericsson to develop connected vehicles to meet the desires and expectations of drivers and passengers. It is reported that over the years, this partnership has proven to be mutually beneficial: "Volvo uses the industrialized Ericsson Connected Vehicle Cloud (CVC) platform to deliver top-notch digital features like full-scale automation, telematics, entertainment, navigation and other vital services to all vehicles."[24]

Think about NVIDIA, a solution provider to the automotive industry relating to the future of driving. Think about the value of in-vehicle AI assistants and the validation of autonomous-driving technology. See a case study on how the BMW Group is transforming its manufacturing using AI-enabled digital twins.[25]

Telecommunications sector

The telecommunications sector is all about connectivity and while traffic is increasing at an incredible rate, revenues are not. And businesses have been exploring how to support consumers who want more effective and efficient, not to mention affordable, telecommunications services, while businesses have been dealing with the complexities of their networks. Just think about how 5G and AI alone could impact this sector. But different companies in this sector realized that to seize these opportunities would require effective collaboration to capitalize on these two developments alone. The starting point being considered was how telecommunications operators could monetize 5G effectively. The second question was how AI and machine learning could be used to recognize consumer behavior and to offer personalized services while managing the network more efficiently.[26] Just three areas of collaboration that began to be discussed were cloud computing, shared scheduling and routing software, and software-as-a-service (SaaS) systems. However, there were ongoing discussions on how to overcome challenges to collaboration, such as competition, data security, and regulations. But progress began to be made, facilitated by technology, for example in the area of sharing scheduling and routing software. The concept was to use a platform that allows different companies to plan, schedule, and route their resources more effectively and efficiently to reduce operational costs while improving customer service. However, using a platform to share scheduling and routing software required the establishment of standards and protocols, a complex and time-consuming process, given the needs of privacy, security, and interoperability relating to customers' data, not to mention the existence of fragmented data.[27]

Here are just two examples of collaborative partnerships. Given that there are still some gaps in network coverage provided by operators of telecom services, especially in rural and remote areas, AT&T and Verizon have been collaborating with satellite players to plug connectivity gaps. This collaboration has been facilitated by satellite broadband, which has grown into a full-fledged industry, led by SpaceX's Starlink.[28] A second example is that Vodafone and Telecom Italia Group (TIM) created a network-sharing partnership for 4G and 5G and the expansion of their existing passive sharing agreement to enable a more rapid deployment of 5G over a wider geographic area. The goal is to provide better telecom services to consumers and at lower costs to both Vodafone and TIM.[29]

Financial sector

Michael Sindicich, Forbes Councils Member, describes eloquently how the financial sector is undergoing a substantial transformation with the emergence of fintech companies. These are companies that offer financial services or applications, relying heavily on innovative technology to offer creative user-centric products and services that meet and exceed consumer expectations, as well as transparency and speed. However, some fintechs need help in scaling their innovative ideas, building customer trust, and dealing with complex regulatory and compliance environments. Then there are traditional legacy financial institutions, such as banks, which have large customer bases, solid infrastructures, and the trust of customers, not to mention their understanding of the industry and the complexity of regulations. However, these strengths of some national banks can make it difficult for them to change their business models quickly to adapt to the changes in the marketplace. For example, it is difficult for a large national bank to meet the diverse needs of its large customer base, and to change its legacy infrastructure that is built on outdated technology and inefficient systems. Given the limitations and strengths of both the fintechs and the national banks, think about the value of collaborative partnerships. As Michael Sindicich points out, "fintech firms can inject innovation, speed and novel perspectives into legacy systems, while these established institutions offer scale, reach and deep regulatory insight."[30]

Collaborative partnerships can facilitate fintechs' access to resources and customer bases that would take them a long time to build, while traditional banks can access technology to become relevant in the digital age, for example, relating to digital payment systems, while enhancing customer experience. One example of a collaborative partnership is between Centime and First National Bank of Omaha. This collaborative partnership is formed to "help small and mid-sized businesses gain visibility and control over their cash flows, empowering them to thrive and grow." Implementing Centime's Cash Flow Control solution into SMEs' planning systems can help them monitor their cash inflows and outflows, providing them with the capability to undertake real-time cash flow forecasting, not to mention access to cost-effective credit solutions. First National will add Centime's AI-driven Cash Flow Control solution to its online banking services for business clients.[31]

In the financial ecosystem there are two distinct groups, lenders and brokers. Cubefunder, a fintech lender, based in Windsor, UK, provides flexible financing solutions relating, for example, to repayment models, to SMEs. Then, there is the National Association of Commercial Finance Brokers, whose members can help lenders reach a diverse range of businesses. These two have formed a collaborative partnership in which Cubefunder has been able to provide funds to a large number of businesses in England and Wales. "The shared objective is clear—to facilitate smoother, more transparent, and effective financial transactions for businesses of all sizes."[32] The relationship between the partners can extend beyond financial transactions.

Here are three more examples of collaborative partnerships reported by Faster Capital:

1. "Stripe, a payment processing startup, partnered with JPMorgan Chase to enhance its payment infrastructure. The collaboration allowed JPMorgan to offer seamless payment solutions to its corporate clients.
2. The Ant Group (formerly part of Alibaba) collaborated with Chinese banks to create Alipay, a digital payment platform. This partnership transformed the payments landscape in China.
3. Revolut, a neobank, collaborated with Barclays to offer its customers faster international transfers. The partnership leveraged Barclays' existing infrastructure."[33]

The insight is that innovative fintech start-ups can collaborate with established financial institutions and access valuable resources (customer base and distribution channels, for example) as well as their industry and regulatory expertise. As for the traditional financial institutions, they can gain insights into the use of cutting-edge technologies and processes to become agile and more competitive. Collaboration can take place in the areas of product innovation, regulatory compliance, or data gathering and sharing to develop contemporary platforms and improve operations. Key requirements for successful collaborative partnerships are to find ways to enhance end customers' experience by recognizing each partner's capabilities and strategic goals, to offer integral solutions, maintain open communications, focus on the need to protect data and its privacy, and build trust.

Consider another business, FICO (Fair Isaac Corporation), well known for its FICO Scores, credit scores used by about 90 percent of lenders in the US.[34] In some ways, this score represents the identity of a consumer. However, FICO is also involved in the area of detecting fraudulent credit-card transactions. FICO's initiative, called Falcon, is a software business that requires enormous data, collected "from across a global network of banks."[35] Keep in mind an important point, namely that FICO is not a bank and does not process credit-card transactions. However, it collects data from multiple banks that have decided to "cooperate [rather] than compete" to reduce the fraud rate. FICO's Falcon fraud detection system collects data from a huge number of banks, integrates the data, and then uses an AI machine learning system to develop a model that detects fraudulent transactions. It "monitors transactions end-to-end to detect and prevent fraud in credit cards, debit cards, prepaid cards, commercial cards, digital payments."[36]

Athletic footwear and apparel sector

Think about Nike, an American athletic footwear and apparel company with revenue now over of US$50 billion. A critical success factor was for Nike to develop partnerships with a broad spectrum of brands, artists, and influencers which not only extended its customer base by reaching new audiences (outside the customers for athletic shoes), but it "surprised its loyal customer base with unique new products." These partnerships helped Nike grow exponentially into an enormously popular sports brand worldwide.

Let us start with 1984 when Nike signed a five-year contract with Michael Jordan, a young newcomer in the National Basketball Association (NBA), that lead to the development of the Air Jordan brand in 1985. Think about the brand awareness of Nike's shoes. Think about the price at which a complete set of Michael Jordan championship Air Jordan shoes, worn by him during the victories of his six NBA titles and six NBA Finals MVPs, sold: $8,032,800. This sale was reported as a global auction record for game-worn shoes, according to Sotheby's.[37] Then Nike's Jordan brand and Gatorade partnered to develop a Gatorade-themed capsule collection to promote Gatorade's 1991 "Be Like Mike" campaign. The "Be Like Mike" campaign was created by an advertising agency that had been working with Gatorade, a giant in the sports-drink space.

In 2006, Nike developed its partnership with Apple that was still in place at the end of 2023. Through this partnership Nike reinforced its sports and fitness leadership position while Apple added to its brand recognition, not to mention sales of its devices, such as the Apple Watch. This partnership took Nike's relevancy to a new level through the creation of the Nike Run Club app, which helped propel Nike in the digital fitness space.

Also in 2006, Nike began to partner with CLOT, "a cult streetwear brand from Hong Kong." Nike and CLOT bridged the gap between Eastern and Western fashion by releasing a special edition of Nike's Air Max 1. This product was inspired by Chinese acupuncture, a significant cultural icon that was incorporated in the Air Max 1 silhouette. "Its bold toe box design is constructed from the transparent plastic, giving an unobscured view into the insoles that feature the feet's pressure points."[38]

In 2013, Nike developed a partnership with Beats by Dre, a headphone company, that moved Nike into the music space to "get in front of people who use their sportswear as a symbol of culture." Back in 2006, famous hip-hop producer Dr. Dre believed that people listening to music outside of a studio should be able to get the same high-quality sound that they would experience in the studio. He partnered with Jimmy Iovine, a former record executive and a media proprietor, to create Beats by Dre. The connection in this partnership was "through the storytelling of high-profile athletes and musicians."

Nike developed creative brand partnerships with a broad spectrum of brands, artists, and influencers to extend audiences outside of its loyal mainstream customer base. This partnership strategy enabled Nike to grow its brand in the world by innovative co-marketing initiatives that led to incredible growth across multiple sectors.

Moving forward

The theme of this book has been that different sectors of the aviation business need to adapt and become resilient and lean in to face changes in the marketplace where the rate of change is accelerating. Moreover, businesses, especially airlines and airports, need to offer a much higher level of customer experience while becoming much more productive and efficient. One way to achieve these goals is not only to become much more frictionless, but also to collaborate much more effectively with existing and new partners in the ecosystems, including innovative start-ups. Leading airlines already have accelerator programs to explore innovative initiatives. The challenge is to create new solutions at scale. The points made in this book for the aviation sectors are supported by the insights available from the examples from numerous other business sectors. FICO's fraud detection platform is just one example of the value of collaborative partnership. The key in the success of collaborative partnerships is to recognize each partner's capabilities and strategic goals, reduce complexities, understand the changing preferences of customers and employees, and then develop meaningful solutions to travelers' problems through their entire journeys.

Notes

1 Eduardo Briceño, *The Performance Paradox: Turning the Power of Mindset into Action* (NY: Ballantine Books, 2023).
2 Frances Frei and Anne Morriss, *Move Fast & Fix Things* (Boston, MA: Harvard Business Review Press, 2023).
3 Eric Lamarre, Kate Smaje, and Rodney Zemmel, *Rewired: The McKinsey Guide to Outcompeting in the Age of Digital and AI* (Hoboken, NJ: Wiley, 2023).
4 Tiffani Bova, *The Experience Mindset: Changing the way you think about growth* (NY: Portfolio/Penguin, 2023), front jacket flap.
5 Joe Mull, *Employalty: How to Ignite Commitment and Keep Top Talent in the New Age of Work* (Canada: Page Two, 2023).
6 Joe Mull, *Employalty: How to Ignite Commitment and Keep Top Talent in the New Age of Work* (Canada: Page Two, 2023).
7 Sheena Iyengar, *Think Bigger: How to Innovate* (NY: Columbia University Press, 2023).
8 Joe Pulizzi and Brian Piper, *Epic Content Marketing* (NY: McGraw Hill, 2023).
9 Staff Writer, "Delta, Joby Aviation partner to pioneer home-to-airport transportation to customers," *Delta News Hub*, October 11, 2022. https://news.delta.com/delta-joby-aviation-partner-pioneer-home-airport-transportation-customers
10 W. Chan Kim and Renée Mauborgne, *Beyond Disruption: Innovate and Achieve Growth without Displacing Industries, Companies, or Jobs* (Boston, MA: Harvard Business Review 2023).
11 Des Dearlove, *Certain Uncertainty: Leading with Agility and Resilience in an unprecedented World* (Hoboken, NJ: John Wiley & Sons, 2023).
12 Philip Kotler, Hermawan Kartajaya, Hooi Den Huan, and Jacky Mussry, *Entrepreneurial Marketing: Beyond Professionalism to Creativity, Leadership, and Sustainability* (Hoboken, NJ: Wiley, 2023), p. 1.
13 Bill Price and David Jaffe, *The Frictionless Organization* (Oakland, CA: Berret-Koehler, 2022), p. 249.

14 Tiffani Bova, *The Experience Mindset: Changing the way you think about growth* (NY: Portfolio/Penguin, 2023).
15 Jorge Tamayo, Leila Doumi, Sagar Goel, Orsolya Kovács-Ondrejkovic, and Raffaella Sadun, "Reskilling in the Age of AI: Five new paradigms for leaders—and employees," *Harvard Business Review*, September–October 2023.
16 Haijian Si, Christoph Loch, and Stelios Kavadias, "A New Approach to Strategic Innovation: A tool for connecting your projects with your goals," *Harvard Business Review*, September–October 2023.
17 Herman Vantrappen and Frederic Wirtz, "CEOs Can Make (or Break) an Organization Redesign," *Sloan Management Review*, August 2, 2023.
18 "P&G Accelerates Pace of Change for Shareholder Value Creation," *Procter & Gamble*, November 8, 2018, https://news.pg.com
19 https://www.google.com/search?q=Nuance+Communications+and+NVIDIA+Bring+Medical-Imaging+AI+Models+Directly+Into+Clinical+Settings&rlz=1C1GCEA_enUS1000US1000&oq
20 Fred Bazzoli, "Moving healthcare forward: The power of collaboration," *Health Data Management*, October 25, 2023. https://www.healthdatamanagement.com/articles/moving-healthcare-forward-the-power-of-collaboration
21 Kristin Shores, "A Blueprint for Success: The Vital Role of Collaborative Partnerships in Healthcare Technology," *InterlaceHealth.com*, November 29, 2023. https://interlacehealth.com/a-blueprint-for-success-the-vital-role-of-collaborative-partnerships-in-healthcare-technology
22 Rainer Mehl, "Partnerships Accelerating Automotive Transformation," *Capgemini*, June 3, 2022. https://www.capgemini.com/insights/expert-perspectives/partnerships-accelerating-automotive-transformation
23 "The Role of Partnerships & Collaboration in Autonomous Driving," *Y-Mobility*, May 2, 2023. https://www.y-mobility.co.uk/the-role-of-partnerships-collaboration-in-autonomous-driving
24 Naveen Josh, "Co-innovation in the Automotive Industry: Creating the Next Generation of Vehicles Through Collaboration," *Allerin Tech Pvt Ltd.*, June 25, 2023. https://www.allerin.com/blog/co-innovation-in-the-automotive-industry-creating-the-next-generation-of-vehicles-through-collaboration
25 "See How BMW Group Is Transforming Manufacturing," *NVIDIA*, n.d. https://www.nvidia.com/en-us/lp/omniverse/how-bmw-group-transforming-manufacturing-thank-you.html?
26 Cheryl Knight, "Telecom's tipping point: Monetization, AI and the power of partnership at MWC," *Silicon ANGLE and CUBE Research*, February 26, 2024. https://siliconangle.com/2024/02/26/telecom-tipping-point-monetization-ai-power-partnership-mwc24
27 Sem Jemsu, "Can we expect any collaboration among telecom companies for shared scheduling and routing software by 2024?" *Field Squared*, February 17, 2024. https://fieldsquared.com/blog/can-we-expect-any-collaboration-among-telecom-companies-for-shared-scheduling-and-routing-software-by-2024
28 Jordan McDonald, "How connectivity giants are embracing the space race," *Tech Brew*, February 1, 2023. https://www.emergingtechbrew.com/stories/2023/01/31/how-internet-incumbents-are-embracing-the-space-race

29 "Vodafone finalises network sharing partnership with Telecom Italia and agrees to combine italian towers with INWIT," *Vodafone*, July 26, 2019. https://www.vodafone.com/news/services/network-sharing-partnership-with-telecom-italia
30 Michael Sindicich, "Collaboration Paves The Way For Next Big Innovation In Fintech," *Forbes Finance Council*, January 25, 2024. https://www.forbes.com/sites/forbesfinancecouncil/2024/01/25/collaboration-paves-the-way-for-next-big-innovation-in-fintech
31 "Centime and First National Bank of Omaha announce strategic partnership," *Centime*, July 19, 2021. https://www.prnewswire.com/news-releases/centime-and-first-national-bank-of-omaha-announce-strategic-partnership-301335985.html
32 "The Power of Collaboration: Crucial Role of Collaborative Partnerships in SME Finance," *UK Finance*, February 29, 2024. www. ukfinance.org.uk/news-and-insight/blog/power-collaboration-crucial-role-collaborative-partnerships-in-sme-finacial#:
33 "Collaborations and Partnerships with Financial Institutions," *Faster Capital*, March 14, 2024. https://fastercapital.com/topics/collaborations-and-partnerships-with-financial-institutions.html
34 "What is a Credit Score?" *MyFICO*, n.d. https://www.myfico.com/credit-education/credit-scores
35 Eric Siegel, *The AI Playbook: Mastering the Rare Art of Machine Learning Deployment* (Cambridge, MA: The MIT Press, 2024), p. 135.
36 "FICO® Falcon® Fraud Manager," *FICO*, n.d. https://www.fico.com/en/products/fico-falcon-fraud-manager
37 "Michael Jordan's championship sneakers sell for record $8M," *ESPN*, February 2, 2024. https://www.espn.com/nba/story/_/id/39444603/michael-jordan-championship-sneakers-sell-record-8m
38 "Air Max 1 'Kiss of Death'," *Nike*, 2021. https://stockx.com/nike-air-max-1-clot-kiss-of-death-2021

8 Thought leadership pieces

Chapter 8 offers five thought leadership pieces that provide international perspectives relating to the theme of the book. These pieces are written by a diverse group of practitioners with extensive experience, both in the aviation domain and in other business sectors. The contents of some of the thought leadership pieces suggest that managers now need to consider new ways to look at and implement proactive collaborations to "cross-pollinate ideas from both technical and strategic stakeholders" to build adaptable and reliant organizations that are more productive and to elevate customer experience to much higher levels.

DOI: 10.4324/9781003483960-8

The first step to an AI-driven maintenance operation

Get clean to improve the odds of a successful AI initiative

Cameron Byrd

CEO, AIXI

Barry Lott

Director Aircraft Records and Maintenance Reliability, Southwest Airlines

A comprehensive AI-driven maintenance operation is the logical next evolution for the airline industry. Tools such as chronic aircraft and rogue part identification, prescriptive maintenance, and predictive maintenance will be installed in every airline. A variety of moderately successful implementations of these tools are out there already, but they aren't living up to the hype. Successful implementation and deployment of these tools could be game-changing, launching an airline to industry-leader status in operations, efficiencies, and customer satisfaction overnight. Conversely, failure can lead to blown budgets, increased costs, lower efficiency, loss of brand reputation, and poor decision-making, sinking an otherwise stable company. Across all industries, the odds are just barely above even, considering "54% of AI projects make it from pilot to production."[1] Leadership knows they need AI, as "79% of leaders agree their company needs to adopt AI to stay competitive".[2]

However, there is uncertainty in almost all aspects of an AI implementation. People don't know what problems should be tackled first, how much it will cost, will it be successful, what it takes to maintain an AI model, buy vs build, and how to measure success. With huge budgets, unclear direction, high-stakes outcomes, and only 50/50 odds, executives are hesitant to move forward: "60% of leaders worry their organization's leadership lacks a plan and vision to implement AI."[3] This thought leadership piece intends to highlight the most important, most difficult, and often overlooked first steps to a successful AI-driven maintenance implementation along with information on proper execution.

Know your data

The first step in any AI implementation is understanding your data. This is not just a preliminary task. It's crucial and sets the foundation for the entire AI system – especially in how clean your data is. Your data foundation mirrors the maxim: "garbage in, garbage out."

Clean data holds powerful characteristics:

- It accurately represents the real-world constructs it models.
- It is complete without any missing data.

- It is valid and conforms to the data domain while maintaining relationships and hierarchies.
- It is consistent, without variation in how it is recorded.
- It is uniform, using the same format and units of measurement so that it can be aggregated.
- Finally, it is timely and available when needed, which in today's world is usually close to real time.

The urgency and necessity of addressing clear, reliable data should be felt by executives, as it is the first crucial step towards a successful AI implementation.

Clean your data

Unclean data affects everything downstream. Data quality directly impacts quality decisions. Using unclean data in analytics can adversely impact analysis outcomes, decision-making, and overall business operations.

- **Inaccurate results:** Unclean data can lead to incorrect conclusions and faulty analytics results. This might include errors in statistical calculations, misleading trends, and incorrect predictions or forecasts.
- **Loss of credibility:** If stakeholders discover that data-driven decisions are based on flawed data, they may lose trust in the data analytics process and the teams involved. Rebuilding credibility can be costly and time-consuming.
- **Poor decision-making:** Decisions based on incorrect or incomplete data can lead to ineffective strategies and actions, potentially causing financial losses or missed opportunities.
- **Increased costs:** Identifying and correcting errors after data has already been used for decision-making can be resource-intensive and expensive. Additionally, operational inefficiencies driven by incorrect data can indirectly increase costs.
- **Reduced efficiency:** Time and resources may be wasted on analyzing and making sense of poor-quality data, leading to delays and decreased productivity.
- **Compliance risks:** In aviation, similar to finance, healthcare, and telecommunications, where data accuracy and handling are regulated, using unclean data can lead to compliance violations, resulting in fines and legal issues.
- **Damage to brand reputation:** If poor data quality leads to public errors or exposes customer data inaccurately, it can damage an organization's reputation and lead to loss of customer trust and loyalty.
- **Resource drain:** Continuously correcting errors due to unclean data requires additional resources, which could be better spent on more strategic tasks.

Investing in proper data management and cleansing techniques is crucial for any data-intensive organization.

Use case: Historical maintenance logs

Almost every airline today runs at least part of its maintenance program using historical maintenance logs. This data informs reliability programs, creates reports, and helps troubleshoot maintenance issues. The FAA even collects this data from operators in order to identify safety issues. However, the current practice of assigning a single four-digit ATA code to each log entry, which is used throughout the industry and across all OEMs for congruency, has flaws.

If you observe any technician doing a log history search, you will notice that they only use the first two digits of the ATA code. When asked why, the response is something akin to, "I only trust the first two digits, the rest is garbage!" Looking deeper, we find that this data is around 80% accurate for the first two digits and at best 60% accurate using all four digits. The aviation industry is currently and knowingly running its maintenance programs with unclean data. It's a "mostly garbage in, definitely garbage out" scenario for airline maintenance teams. But it doesn't have to be.

The fact that this data is already being used in maintenance programs means that there is a rare opportunity to increase efficiencies and outcomes by just cleaning the data. That's it – nothing more. Clean the data and the reliability and use of all downstream tools will improve and set the foundation for AI implementations. From our example above, maintenance records already have many characteristics of clean data, but they lack consistency and uniformity.

At a high level, the aviation industry is on the right track by assigning ATA codes to each log entry, which will create consistency and uniformity. However, the industry has failed to do this effectively and there's a lack of trust in the data that is captured. Some operations recognize the problem and have human experts manually re-coding log entries. Unfortunately, this process takes time – a lot of time – and reduces the timeliness of the data. In addition, humans are not inherently good at coding or large pattern matching. Plus, it is boring, requires training, has a high turnover rate, and is inconsistent from human to human. This represents a perfect opportunity for an AI implementation.

AIXI, a company specializing in creating AI-driven solutions for airline operations, uses its industry-specific language model to automatically assign ATA codes to maintenance records in real-time using its ATA AutoCoder. It codes all historical records creating the clean, consistent data foundation needed to empower technicians and optimize MRO procedures. Southwest Airlines has been using AIXI's ATA AutoCoder for more than two years in an effort to "dramatically improve engineer access to defect trends, most likely fixes and more to support better maintenance." The ATA AutoCoder has proven to be around 97% accurate and can execute in real-time. AIXI's ATA

AutoCoder is able to assign five codes to each maintenance record instead of just one:

- One ATA code is associated with the discrepancy,
- Another code is associated with the fix, and
- Three human-readable codes represent the object, failure, and action taken to fix the problem.

Consider this example: a technician might enter 'NGS [nitrogen gas system] degraded' as the discrepancy and 'R/R L/H pack flow' as the fix. The ATA AutoCoder converts this shorthand to 4741 for the discrepancy ATA code and 2530 for the fix ATA code. It would name the object as the NGS System, classify the failure as degraded and classify the fix as removed/replaced. The resulting entry is then much clearer for later retrieval and analysis. And it happens in a matter of seconds.

The accuracy of AIXI's ATA AutoCoder takes "garbage" maintenance records and makes them gold. The five fields add fidelity to the data that has never been there before, revealing insights about airline operations that were previously unobtainable.

The gains from installing AIXI's ATA AutoCoder are immediate and significant. Humans don't have to labor over manually assigning ATA codes to records and are free to focus elsewhere. In addition, all teams within the airline that rely on historical records for their operations and decisions now have access to clean, actionable data that empowers them to work more accurately and efficiently.

- Technicians can look up historical records using all four digits rather than just two. The extra code assigned to the discrepancy allows them to see the relationships between discrepancies and fixes. They can look up a particular discrepancy and find all fixes that have been applied to that problem, as well as how often a fix was applied to that problem.
- Reliability teams can complete studies in hours instead of weeks and feel confident that the results are accurate.
- Finally, the human-readable codes empower anyone in the organization to use the data for insights without training on ATA codes.

The next steps to a fully realized, AI-driven aircraft maintenance program consist of a multitude of tools that will require clean, consistent maintenance logs in order to work effectively. These tools include algorithms for prescriptive maintenance, chronic aircraft identification, rogue part identification, long-term planning, and predictive maintenance. Many implementations of these algorithms exist or are in development. However, they all work off of the original maintenance logs and the ATA codes assigned by the mechanics. That puts us back to tools using "garbage in" data. In short, the best tools, including those with AI-supported intensions, are doomed to fail without clean data.

This message to executives cannot be stressed enough. Initiatives that rely on maintenance logs will fail unless that data is cleaned up before moving forward to using a tool like AIXI's ATA AutoCoder.

Southwest Airlines is proving the power of clean data when coupled with targeted AI implementation and AIXI's ATA AutoCoder is providing their foundation. Barry Lott, Director for Aircraft Records and Maintenance Reliability at Southwest Airlines, says that clean data is also opening new possibilities for his teams. "Accurate aircraft and fleet trending, prescriptive maintenance and, in the future, predictive maintenance would not be possible without AIXI's technology," according to Southwest Airlines.

AIXI is improving on previous implementations of prescriptive maintenance, chronic aircraft and rogue part identification, and long-term planning tools by building them using the output from their ATA AutoCoder. AIXI's tools offer unmatched versatility based on the data accuracy that is used as its input. In addition, the extra codes allow them to filter, aggregate, drill down, manipulate and find important insights in ways that were previously impossible with only one ATA code per log entry. These tools are easily integrated into airline operations and provide immediate ROI for airlines in efficiency and cost savings.

All current and future AI, machine learning, and analytical models rely heavily on data and their success is based on data cleanliness. Maintenance and reliability operations are no different. Not only can clean data improve all current operations that rely on that data, but it is imperative that data be cleaned properly before any kind of prescriptive maintenance, chronic aircraft or rogue part identification, long-term planning or predictive maintenance can become a reality in any meaningful way.

Embracing modern retailing

Paving the way forward

Hanife Hilal Demirtaş

Vice President (IT), Distribution and Sales Solutions, Turkish Airlines

In this book, the author shares his deep knowledge in harmony with the changing industry dynamics and evaluates the need for the collaboration of four basic players across the industry: airlines, seller intermediaries (distributors), aircraft manufacturers and airports. This thought leadership piece addresses one of these players—distributors.

For decades, distribution has been one of the key concepts of the aviation ecosystem, profoundly shaping the evolving landscape of travel. Passenger Service System (PSS) integrations in legacy distribution networks facilitated airline sales to reach out to wide geographical regions. With the help of distribution systems, airlines have had the ability to partner with travel agencies, Online Travel Agencies (OTAs), and Global Distribution Systems (GDSs) which enable airlines to reach potential passengers worldwide. Standard sales and servicing processes also provided seamless booking and servicing experiences for customers. On the other hand, payment and settlement requirements of different third parties in the airline ecosystem were facilitated by the Billing Settlement Plan (BSP) and Airlines Reporting Corporation (ARC). This enabled new stakeholders to set up quickly and append themselves to the airline distribution networks.

"Legacy" distribution networks, interconnected to the airline PSSs, facilitated airlines to maximize sales and provided standard customer experiences for years. Now the old technology and distribution constraints, such as Full Content Agreements (FCAs) of GDSs, have started to restrict airlines that want to innovate to compete more effectively and adapt to the changing market conditions. For instance, airlines willing to create personalized offers could not do it through legacy GDS integrations. On the other hand, changing customer profiles and digitalization were forcing airlines to enhance their offers and create better processes. These restrictions created a need for modern distribution technologies, such as the New Distribution Capability (NDC), and the creation of Modern Airline Retailing (MAR) initiatives.

NDC, now a distribution standard for the airline distribution ecosystem, facilitates parties to work together. A critical change in an NDC-enabled distribution ecosystem is the transfer of the responsibility of creating offers to airlines. This transfer of responsibility requires airlines to invest in technology not only to sustain their systems, but also to invest to extend further their capabilities. Another important aspect is about variability. It is the way of using NDC standard schemas differently by applying workarounds for flows or extending NDC schemas in order to address particular functional needs of airlines. While the NDC framework provides standardization, sellers need to manage variability issues for integrating different versions of NDC. And even if the NDC versions are the same, there are differences between different web services. These variability issues need to be addressed by related parties given the fact that they bring complexity to the travel intermediaries. It is NDC that enables MAR by enabling airlines to present airline personalized offers to travel intermediaries.

As discussed in this book, given the fact that the aviation marketplace is expected to be unpredictable and given that airlines have a perishable product that is affected by frequent changes, airlines try to manage their risks and reach out to their potential customers in the world in many different ways. For instance, airlines can both promote airfares from direct channels and also provide NDC APIs to some big players like Expedia, booking.com and support competitors. This setup puts airlines and travel intermediaries in a position to be both competitors and collaborators. Yet, it is a familiar concept for airlines and GDSs that also provide PSS systems to airlines, for airlines to serve direct channels and also compete on indirect sales. In essence, the distribution concept depends on different parties to work together in harmony, connecting airlines with travelers and facilitating the exchange of value that drives the global travel economy. IATA's Global Passenger Survey 2023 has shown that aviation customers want convenience and speed during their travels[4]. Sellers need to develop easier processes for passengers who also want speed at airports. This means that airlines and airports need to work together to provide frictionless experiences for their customers. For years, in both the direct and the indirect distribution spaces, collaboration has been needed between airlines, travel intermediaries, technology providers, and other industry stakeholders. There is a critical question raised in this book: to what extent do these different stakeholders collaborate? Are they collaborating enough for providing better customer experience? I believe that we will see new initiatives to compete and collaborate to provide better passenger experiences.

Booking.com and Expedia.com are popular OTAs, offering airline fares together with hotel bookings, car rentals and other travel services. Customers who seek various flight options from different airlines or bundled deals including accommodation or other travel services may use those sales channels. Additionally, these OTAs also present loyalty programs for their customers that affect buying decisions of their customers. Google Flights is a flight search engine, showing different options, but does not directly sell. To complete the sales process, it redirects to the airline sites or relevant OTA sites. Passengers can compare and discover different flight options and Google is able to bring traffic to airlines or other intermediaries, which makes Google Flights an important contributor to the ecosystem. Travel management companies (TMCs) are other parties who contribute to the ecosystem by integrating their systems either directly to airlines or to other intermediaries such as GDSs. TMCs facilitate airline sales by positioning themselves in between airlines and corporate/individual customers. TMCs are well positioned for corporate customers by enabling hotel, car rental and related services for corporate customers' particular needs.

As the NDC framework began to be incorporated in the modernization of airline retailing systems, the phrase "to provide Amazon like shopping experience" began to appear. Formerly, industry professionals used to say that aviation processes were complex, and it was not easy to set up frictionless processes for passengers. Now it seems that there is a perspective shift towards providing seamless experiences for passengers. Increased digital shopping experiences of customers after the pandemic period also made sellers think about providing better customer experiences like e-retailers. Changing customer expectations made the industry embrace higher servicing standards and modern distribution technologies provided better functional capabilities to support higher service levels. Putting a customer focus to the aviation business is very valuable given the fact that the industry has been driven by the legacy technology and its constraints for decades. For example, it takes months to integrate a new fare to sales channels or add a name change process to sales channels because it is actually a reissue process for PSSs. Airlines are not only motivated by becoming free of current legacy restrictions, but they can also seize new opportunities that are about to emerge. Not only new offers can be controlled better, but dynamic pricing capabilities can be deployed in all channels.

In the last decade, the industry has been preparing itself to become free of these restrictions and deploy wider capabilities under the roof of Modern Airline Retailing Transition to introduce more innovation. Modern Airline Retailing, also named "One Order" transition, will make customer processes easier by providing just one document. It will make all processes easier to handle beyond any doubt. In the legacy distribution world, the ticket of a passenger and the ancillaries are on separate documents, making the management of disruption and after- sales processes highly complicated and subject to errors. Passengers usually need to reach out to customer service departments and manage their ancillaries even if they have already paid for them. Sellers will be able to manage the "Order" of the customer more easily in a modern retailing ecosystem from all channels. Providing a rich set of payment options such as credit cards and digital wallets in a modern retailing ecosystem is another benefit for customers, given the fact that they need sellers to increase convenience during their shopping process and delivery of the service.

In the last couple of years rapid digitalization and shifting traveler expectations caused airlines to adapt their distribution strategies to changing market conditions. Many airlines invested in their direct channels to provide better customer experiences, tried to control their offers better, and made moves to create a closer relationship with their customers and yet increase their customers' loyalty accordingly. "Data," being a very precious source, is one of the commodities that airlines want to differentiate and innovate. Airlines need to use data better and implement new technologies using their data better to compete in the changing marketplace. As a result, any airline's direct channels may not only include airline ticket offices, call centers, websites, and mobile apps, but also include new-generation channels like LLM-enabled chatbots from the revolution of Generative AI.

Another concept that the whole industry is talking about is "Personalization." Presenting personalized services to passengers, from imagination to the post-travel phase, is a challenge. After GDPR defined the personal data and relevant rights clearly, all stakeholders needed to keep a balance between using the data and breaching any personal rights. On the other hand, it is also possible to differentiate content according to various parameters like customers' locations, their shopping preferences, itineraries or regional parameters before using any critical personal data. Airlines have been investing in their systems to provide more personalized experiences, by taking their customers' consent to use their data.

One of the use cases about personalization is how to recognize a specific passenger even if the airline does not recognize the customer? There are techniques where sellers in the aviation industry use rule-based systems to analyze intent of the customer with the help of behavioral data, customer trends or using some other anonymous inputs. Another critical question is even if you have relevant information, how to establish a system and perform effectively in real time to support personalization effectively? One thought around this problem is not to integrate all relevant data to the personalization systems but to create a central customer data-hub for personalization purposes[5]. However, keep in mind that restrictions around distribution channels have caused airlines to work with incomplete customer data.

Personalization without breaching personal rights is a sensitive subject. After Covid-19, contactless travel studies had gained momentum in the world, which also contributed to the personalization pain points by providing a secure way of sharing personal information with stakeholders. IATA's Digital Identity Initiative providing contactless travel experience will overcome the problem by securely sharing personal information, such as digital passport, biometrics, frequent flyer IDs of the passenger, which could be stored in a passenger's personal device in a digital wallet. The initiative adds value by overcoming the bias about working with a customer's personal information in a secure way. I believe the rest will follow suit; some other improvement areas will appear for stakeholders to collaborate for providing a better customer experience.

In summary, if the industry is moving forward in an unpredictable way with competition increasing, and disruptions increasing, aviation stakeholders need to do something differently. At the same time, to act like modern retailers, players will have to adapt to the changing customer needs and provide them with better experiences. This cannot be handled solely by modernizing systems. Players also need to think about new processes and new ways of doing things to provide frictionless holistic experiences to their customers.

Collaboration in the age of AI

A perspective from the financial services industry

Ali Faruqi

IT Manager, Wells Fargo

Collaboration is central to innovation, and AI is no exception. Successful AI implementation requires the cross-pollination of ideas from both technical and strategic stakeholders.

A survey by Dataiku reveals that 54% of Financial Services and Insurance (FSI) organizations are embedding or expanding their AI adoption efforts, surpassing the industry average of 48%.[6]

The use of data science and AI has extended beyond central teams, permeating various functions and departments across organizations. This widespread adoption has fostered increased collaboration and the cross-fertilization of ideas.

In the FSI sector, the departments leading AI adoption include IT, Customer Service, Marketing & Sales, and Operations.

Some notable examples of recent AI usage in the FSI include but are not limited to:

Commonwealth Bank and AI for call center support

At Commonwealth Bank's call centers, a Generative AI model assists staff in answering complex customer questions by interrogating 4,500 documents on bank policies in real time. They can input customer questions into a chatbot during conversations to quickly determine loan eligibility and address complex inquiries within seconds. This reduces the need for investigations and callbacks, presenting a valuable use case for companies with large customer bases.[7]

Furthermore, AI is making 53 million decisions daily, utilizing 1,000 models and processing 157 billion data points throughout the bank, making the Commonwealth Bank the largest corporate AI user in Australia.

According to Matt Comyn, the CEO of Commonwealth Bank, "the [AI] technology that we have seen over the last six to nine months has the potential to be quite transformational."

In addition to this, the bank collaborates with 49 external AI model developers, including Microsoft. It has also partnered with and invested in the leading global AI platform H2O.ai to facilitate the rollout. This shows the commitment of the bank to support and collaborate with the growing ecosystem of AI companies, which is essential for business growth.

American Express and AI for predicting customer behavior

AmEx Digital Labs is investigating the potential of generative AI to enhance predictive analytics, aiming to gain deeper insights into customer patterns and behaviors. Their AI applications are focused on predicting customer performance over time to improve financial planning and decision-making. Additionally, they are prioritizing customer sentiment analysis and interactions.

AmEx's approach to AI is by emphasizing its impact on customer experience, aiming to simplify and enhance it. AmEx Digital Labs is exploring the use of Large Language Models (LLMs) to analyze customer feedback and inquiries from service portals and social media to provide appropriate and helpful responses.

While the exact details of how customer feedback is quantified and incorporated in the models are not publicly shared by AmEx, there are some standard analytical approaches to do that.

Sentiment analysis is one such approach to categorize comments into positive, negative, or neutral sentiments and assign a sentiment score. For instance, a comment like "The customer service was excellent" might receive a high positive sentiment score, whereas "The app is too slow" would get a negative sentiment score.

Topic modeling is another approach that can identify and count the frequency of specific themes or issues mentioned, such as "transaction speed" or "customer service."

When adopting new technologies, especially AI, AmEx Digital Labs aims to enhance their "3Ps": making products more personalized, proactive, and predictive for individual customers.[8]

For personalization, AI can be leveraged to build detailed customer profiles based on transaction history, preferences, and behaviors. This can be used to tailor product recommendations and offers to individual customer needs and preferences such as providing personalized credit card offers based on spending habits and interests in travel and dining.

AI can also help in being proactive and predictive by predicting potential issues in services or products before they affect the customer, such as detecting fraudulent activities or potential account issues. Incorporating such predictions in customer notifications and alerts can proactively suggest steps for customers to take to secure their accounts.

Commonalities with the airline industry

The use cases explored by Commonwealth Bank and American Express are interesting examples of an AI-driven approach that can work across industries, including the airline industry. Airlines can harness generative AI and predictive analytics to enhance various aspects of their operations and customer interactions. For instance, AI can be used to predict flight demand, optimize pricing strategies, and manage crew schedules efficiently. Additionally, AI-driven sentiment analysis can help airlines better understand passenger feedback, both from customer service portals and social media, enabling them to address issues proactively and improve the overall travel experience. Personalized travel offers and tailored in-flight services can also be developed using AI, ensuring that each passenger's journey is customized to their preferences and needs. By adopting such AI technologies, airlines can not only improve operational efficiency but also significantly enhance customer satisfaction and loyalty, ultimately leading to a more competitive and resilient industry.

By examining these use cases, it becomes clear that the successful implementation of AI hinges on more than just technology; it requires a robust framework of collaboration and strategic alignment. The value of collaboration becomes even more evident as we explore how cross-functional teams can drive innovation and efficiency through AI. To harness the full potential of AI, organizations must implement a collaborative AI strategy that integrates insights from diverse stakeholders, ensuring that AI initiatives are not only technically sound but also aligned with overarching business goals.

The value of collaboration

In order to extract maximum value from AI efforts and create business impact, the leadership team should create a collaborative and cross-functional environment for technical talent to innovate and deliver.

Integration of diverse expertise

Risk management, customer service, compliance, and finance are examples of diverse expertise needed to develop solutions in the financial services industry. For instance, developing an AI tool for fraud detection requires input from data scientists for the technical build, from risk management professionals who understand the nuances of banking fraud, and from legal teams to ensure compliance with regulatory standards. Collaboration ensures that AI tools are not only technically sound but also practically relevant and compliant.

Enhanced problem solving

When improving customer experience through AI, a team comprising members from IT, customer service, and marketing can use their combined insights to create solutions that are technically feasible, aligned with customer expectations, and strategically marketed.

Driving digital transformation

When teams from IT, digital banking, and branch operations work together, they can better align AI technologies with both the bank's digital strategy and its traditional branch-based approach, thus ensuring a cohesive customer experience across all channels.

Risk management

Cross-functional collaboration between AI technical teams and risk management professionals ensures that these models are not only advanced in terms of technology but also fine-tuned to reflect the real-world financial environments and compliance requirements they operate in.

Implementing a collaborative AI strategy

Establish innovation labs

Many banks have set up innovation labs where employees from different functions can come together to experiment with new technologies. These labs provide the space and resources necessary for innovative thinking. Capital One Lab is one such example where they have developed virtual card numbers, fraud data protection systems and Machine Learning infrastructure. An example of collaboration at Capital One is exploring the intersection of AI and design. As Capital One's Chief Design Officer, Daniela Jorge, says: "In designing products, what we have to do is understand broad segments of users and then find common patterns. With AI, I think there's that opportunity to have a much more one-to-one solution between humans and the system."[9]

AI can enhance human-centered design by clearly identifying user pain points and priorities with minimal friction, enabling designers to reach more effective solutions efficiently.

Regular cross-departmental workshops

Workshops and regular meetings that involve multiple departments can facilitate better understanding and cooperation across the bank, aligning various functions with the bank's AI objectives.

Leadership and governance

Most importantly, establish a governance model that includes leaders from various functions to oversee AI projects. This can ensure that all potential impacts, risks, and opportunities are considered.

Conclusion

To summarize, AI collaboration extends beyond the internal functions of an organization to include strategic external partnerships. This approach is essential for driving innovation and achieving competitive advantage in today's rapidly evolving financial landscape. While there exists a great overlap in the AI technology and solutions that can be utilized by both banks and airlines, there is also overlap in our products and services that can be developed by both banks and airlines with the help of AI-powered collaboration. One prominent example of such partnerships is co-branded credit cards. These collaborations offer significant advantages to both parties and their customers. For banks, co-branded cards provide access to a new customer base and opportunities to offer tailored rewards programs enhanced by AI-driven insights. For airlines, these partnerships enhance customer loyalty by offering travel-related perks and benefits, powered by predictive analytics and personalized recommendations.

By exploring the potential of collaborative efforts, banks and airlines can pave the way for a future where innovation and customer-centricity are at the heart of their success. The journey towards this future is one of continuous learning, adaptation, and partnership—a journey that holds the promise of transformative change and enduring impact.

Technology, innovation, and collaboration are the foundation of air travel

Bob Kwik

Worldwide Head of Airport and Ground Transportation Solutions, Amazon Web Services

On December 17, 1903, Wilbur and Orville Wright achieved the dream of powered, sustained, and controlled flight with the Wright Flyer at Kitty Hawk, North Carolina, USA. This invention was the culmination of years of innovation and marked the birth of aviation and sparked an entire industry. At its core, the Wright brothers' accomplishment was driven by technical ingenuity, problem-solving, and a relentless pursuit of innovation through determination and collaboration. Aviation continued to advance and evolve through the creation of organizations such as airports, airlines, and ground handling agents; built on a foundation of technology and collaboration, these organizations enabled the industry to scale globally and reshape the world.

While innovations in aircraft design and aviation technology have been crucial enablers, the seamless operations of the air travel industry rely on collaboration between a multitude of organizations and stakeholders. Passenger air travel as we know it could not exist without the coordinated efforts of airlines, airports, air traffic control, ground handling services, security agencies, and many other entities. Effective collaboration between these interdependent players is vital to ensuring the efficient flow of aircraft, passengers, baggage, and cargo through the complex aviation ecosystem on a global scale.

As the aviation industry continues to grow and confront new challenges, emerging technologies promise to elevate collaboration to unprecedented levels. Data analytics, artificial intelligence, and secure information sharing have the potential to synchronize operations, optimize resources, mitigate disruptions, and enhance the overall travel experience. However, realizing the potential of this transformation is dependent on the leaders in aviation to foster a culture of collaboration within and across organizations.

The enabler of effective collaboration in the aviation industry lies in the leadership of key players such as airports, airlines, and ground handling agents. It is their vision, strategic alignment, and commitment to breaking down silos that will determine the industry's capacity to harness the power of collaboration and technology to drive innovation, efficiency, and customer satisfaction in the years to come.

Technology can enable collaboration

> Airport data sharing and collaboration key to improving passenger satisfaction.
>
> Airports Council International[10]

Data platforms, data sharing initiatives, and artificial intelligence (AI) can play a crucial role in fostering collaboration among aviation stakeholders. By establishing secure and standardized platforms for data exchange, stakeholders can share real-time information on flight operations, passenger flows, baggage handling, and resource allocation. This shared data can enable synchronized decision-making, proactive planning, and coordinated responses to disruptions, supported by AI-powered insights and automation, ultimately leading to more efficient operations and an improved travel experience for passengers.

Sharing a relatively small amount of data can have a high impact on the passenger experience. For example, Manchester Airport Group's real-time gate information sharing with Ryanair means that passengers have accurate gate information on their mobile app if there are any unplanned gate changes.[11]

Data clean rooms offer a secure and privacy-compliant environment for stakeholders to collaborate on shared data sets without directly exchanging or exposing sensitive information. By bringing together and analyzing aggregated and anonymized data from multiple sources, such as passenger booking records, flight schedules, and airport operations, stakeholders can gain valuable insights and identify opportunities for process optimization, resource allocation, and service enhancements. Data clean rooms can facilitate collaboration while maintaining data privacy and security.

For example, ATPCO uses clean rooms to aggregate fare data, shopping data, and pricing data to give airline partners access to comprehensive, aggregated, and anonymized information to generate the most relevant offers improving the customer experience.[12]

Artificial intelligence and machine learning technologies can be powerful enablers of collaboration by automating processes, analyzing complex data sets, and providing intelligent recommendations. For instance, AI can be employed to predict passenger flows, optimize staffing levels, and streamline baggage handling processes across multiple stakeholders. Additionally, AI-powered predictive maintenance can help airlines, airports, and ground handlers coordinate equipment maintenance schedules, minimizing disruptions and ensuring seamless operations.

The Cincinnati airport uses data from security screening checkpoints, social media, nearby traffic, flights, and weather to predict passenger arrivals in 15-minute intervals and make predictions six days in advance. This helps the airport improve day-to-day planning and scheduling and prepares airport stakeholders for upcoming passenger arrival volumes and demands.[13]

Generative AI (GenAI) technologies, such as large language models, can revolutionize collaboration by facilitating natural language interactions and enabling seamless communication across stakeholders. GenAI systems can assist in generating reports, summarizing complex data, and providing intelligent recommendations based on real-time operational data. GenAI can also help with customer service, providing personalized travel assistance and responding to passenger inquiries in a more efficient and consistent manner.

Delta Airlines is building a GenAI tool to answer customer questions in a more conversational style, using data from Delta's travel policies, real-time flight schedules, customer rebooking options, and airport conditions.[14]

By leveraging these technologies, aviation stakeholders can break down silos, share information more effectively, and collaborate in real time to address operational challenges, improve resource utilization, and ultimately deliver a superior travel experience for passengers. However, the successful implementation of these technologies requires a strong commitment to data governance, cybersecurity, and a culture of collaboration across the entire aviation ecosystem.

Think about collaboration through the lens of disruption

Too often, we think about collaboration when nothing is going wrong. However, in the dynamic and complex world of passenger air travel, disruptions are inevitable, and it is during these moments that the need for seamless collaboration among stakeholders becomes most apparent. Rather than focusing solely on collaboration during periods of smooth operations, we must start from the point of disruption and work backwards to build resilient systems capable of self-healing that minimize the impact on passengers.

The ultimate goal of collaboration in the aviation industry should not be the unrealistic pursuit of eliminating disruptions altogether, but rather the development of self-healing systems that can rapidly adapt and recover when disruptions occur. This could involve the real-time re-routing of flights, the efficient reallocation of resources, and the seamless communication of contingency plans to passengers and staff alike. By fostering a culture of collaboration that extends beyond organizational boundaries, stakeholders can collectively respond to unforeseen events with agility and ensure that the passenger experience remains as seamless as possible, even in the face of adversity.

While the vision of self-healing systems may seem like a distant goal, the important step is to initiate the journey towards this goal by tackling high-impact problems one by one. This could involve addressing common pain points such as flight delays, baggage mishandling, or airport congestion, which can have cascading effects on the entire travel ecosystem. By bringing together the collective expertise and resources of airports, airlines, ground handlers, and other stakeholders, collaborative efforts can yield innovative solutions that not only mitigate disruptions but also enhance the overall passenger experience.

By embracing a mindset that starts from the point of disruption and works towards building self-healing systems, stakeholders can create a mechanism that solves high-impact multi-stakeholder problems while inventing and iterating towards self-healing systems.

Enabling a better door-to-door journey

In the era of modern air travel, the passenger journey extends beyond the confines of airports and aircraft. It encompasses the entire door-to-door experience, from the moment a traveler leaves their home, hotel, or office until they reach their final destination. Collaboration among aviation stakeholders, including ground transportation providers, is crucial to ensuring a seamless and convenient travel experience throughout this end-to-end journey.

Effective collaboration can enable seamless connections between air travel and ground transportation, such as taxis, ride-sharing services, or public transit. By integrating real-time flight data with transportation scheduling and routing, passengers can be offered convenient and reliable transportation options that align with their travel plans. This not only reduces the stress and uncertainty associated with ground transfers but also minimizes the risk of missed flights or delays getting to their final destination.

Collaboration can build situational awareness for both passengers and aviation staff, ensuring that everyone has access to the right information at the right time. Real-time updates and forecasts of flights, baggage, traffic congestion, wait times, and ground transportation availability can be shared across service providers, empowering passengers to make informed decisions and adjust their plans as needed. Similarly, airport and airline staff can leverage this shared situational awareness to proactively address potential disruptions and provide personalized assistance to passengers, enhancing the overall travel experience.

In today's fast-paced world people are increasingly willing to pay for convenience and peace of mind. The popularity of services like food delivery, ride-sharing, and subscription-based models demonstrates that consumers value seamless experiences that simplify their lives. By collaborating to offer a truly door-to-door travel experience, aviation stakeholders can tap into this demand for convenience and potentially unlock new revenue streams by providing premium services that cater to passengers' evolving needs and preferences.

Enabling a seamless door-to-door journey begins with collaboration among aviation stakeholders, ground transportation providers, and other relevant parties. By creating situational awareness and leveraging data-driven insights, stakeholders can anticipate and address potential pain points, streamline processes, and deliver a travel experience that exceeds passenger expectations.

Collaboration, and innovation, is ultimately about people

Driving change to improve collaboration in the passenger air travel industry is not solely a technological challenge but also a human one. While technological advancements can enable collaboration, it is the people – operational staff, leaders, and stakeholders – who must embrace and champion these changes. However, this transformation can face resistance.

At the operational level, there is a natural reluctance to add more complexity to already complex processes. Frontline staff, such as airport personnel and airline staff, are focused on ensuring smooth operations and may perceive new collaborative initiatives as potential disruptions to their well-established routines. They may be hesitant to adopt new systems or workflows that could introduce unfamiliar challenges or learning curves.

Similarly, leaders within air travel organizations may also be reluctant to drive collaborative changes, albeit for different reasons. One crucial factor is the perceived risk associated with sharing data and information across organizational boundaries. Leaders may be concerned about potential security breaches, competitive disadvantages, or loss of control over sensitive information. Additionally, the fear of disrupting existing business models and revenue streams can act as a barrier to embracing collaborative initiatives that may require significant operational or cultural shifts.

To overcome these challenges and unlock the full potential of collaboration, a multi-stakeholder approach to innovation is essential. By bringing together diverse perspectives and fostering open dialogue, stakeholders can collectively address concerns, build trust, and co-create solutions that align with their respective goals and priorities. This collaborative innovation process can help to identify win–win scenarios, mitigate risks, and ultimately earn the trust and buy-in of operational staff and leaders alike.

According to the SITA Air Transport IT Insights 2022 report,[15] which surveyed airport leaders globally, 25% of airports will invest in innovation labs to drive digital transformation and foster collaboration with industry partners. While these innovation labs often include innovation partners, such as startups, they frequently don't include other stakeholders in airport operations and the passenger journey, such as airlines, handling agents, retailers, rental car companies, and ground transport providers. This can limit the innovation to what the airport can directly control and therefore limit the scale and impact.

By creating dedicated innovation hubs or test labs that include the airport stakeholders (similar to what you would see in an airport operational control center), airports can collaborate with their stakeholders in a safe and controlled environment to explore new collaborative technologies, processes, and business models. These spaces can facilitate cross-functional collaboration, rapid prototyping, and iterative testing, allowing stakeholders to experiment, learn, and refine their collaborative approaches before scaling them across their operations.

Driving change to improve collaboration in passenger air travel requires a holistic approach that addresses not only the technological aspects but also the human factors. By fostering multi-stakeholder innovation, earning trust, and engaging operational staff and leaders, the aviation industry can overcome resistance and unleash new ideas that can transform the travel experience for passengers worldwide.

Embracing the collaborative future: A call to action for aviation leaders and technologists

We find ourselves at an inflection point in the passenger air travel industry, where the barriers to experimentation and collaboration are lower than ever before. Technological advancements have opened up new avenues for stakeholders to explore innovative approaches to collaboration in a safe and secure manner, paving the way for transformative changes that can elevate the travel experience.

At its core, effective collaboration is about intelligently sharing information and leveraging collective knowledge to drive continuous improvement. By embracing a culture of data sharing and breaking down silos, aviation stakeholders can unlock insights that were previously siloed or obscured, enabling more informed decision-making and proactive problem-solving.

As we look towards the future, it is crucial that industry leaders seize this opportunity to foster cross-organizational collaboration and empower their teams to experiment with cutting-edge technologies. Data platforms offer the potential to establish secure and standardized channels for sharing real-time operational data, enabling synchronized decision-making and coordinated responses to disruptions. Data Clean Rooms provide privacy-compliant environments for stakeholders to analyze shared data sets and uncover valuable insights without compromising sensitive information.

Artificial intelligence and machine learning technologies can automate processes, analyze complex data, and provide intelligent recommendations, driving efficiency and optimization across the aviation ecosystem. Furthermore, Generative AI holds the promise of revolutionizing collaboration by facilitating natural language interactions, enabling seamless communication, and providing intelligent assistance based on real-time operational data.

As we stand on the precipice of this transformative era, it is time for leaders to embrace a collaborative mindset and empower their organizations to experiment fearlessly with these technologies. By fostering a culture of innovation and cross-stakeholder cooperation, we can collectively unlock the full potential of collaboration and usher in a new era of seamless, efficient, and delightful travel experiences for passengers worldwide.

To the visionary leaders and technologists driving this change, the call to action is clear: collaborate, innovate, and unleash the power of shared knowledge and cutting-edge technologies. Together, we can transcend organizational boundaries, overcome hurdles, and create a future where the journey is as seamless and memorable as the destination itself.

Opportunities and challenges with large language models (LLMs)

Sean M. Smith

Machine Learning Engineer, Amazon

It would be hard to reach this chapter without having at least heard of Large Language Models (LLMs). Potentially the most hyped technology of the century, for both good and bad reasons, LLMs have survived at least a year of hype. While the technology presents a lot of opportunity there are also challenges that need to be considered.

In this thought leadership piece, we'll overview some key topics that surface in the discussion of LLMs. We'll cover some key terminology that's important to consider when discussing Artificial Intelligence (AI) and LLMs. We'll then apply these concepts to relevant case studies that outline and expose other topics. We'll see the opportunity and risk that's inherent in these solutions. Finally, we'll consider what key things need to happen to set the organization up for success.

What is Artificial Intelligence?

It's probably worth unifying around some common terminology that is used in AI. While many researchers will debate on what the most appropriate definition is to describe this field of study, generally it is safe to think of AI as a class of algorithms that make machines think and act like humans.

One effective way to think about AI is to consider it a tool set. These algorithms are useful when we need some level of reason and logic to solve a problem. When deciding if AI is useful for a problem you are solving, you can propose a colloquial test I like to refer to as an intern test. I ask myself "Would I trust an intern to solve this task and is it okay if they mess it up sometimes?" An intern comes to us with basic levels of reasoning and logic, so they loosely resemble the utility we get from AI. If the answer is yes, then it's okay to reach into the AI tool bag; otherwise I may try to reformulate the problem or suggest a different tool for the problem.

Some may be familiar with the field of Machine Learning (ML) but confused where it fits into the field of AI. Machine Learning is a subfield of AI that studies algorithms that learn from data. One way we can use data is by training a model to take an input and produce an output. This approach is referred to as supervised learning and represents the largest class of algorithms inside of Machine Learning. The majority of Machine Learning algorithms that are used today fall into this category of supervised learning.

An example of supervised learning for an airline would be predicting if a flight will be delayed. We could have inputs such as weather, how many flights previously were delayed, or which airport we are at. The output would be True or False if the flight is delayed. Using this formulation of inputs and outputs we can build powerful algorithms. Even LLMs have a step of training that involves supervised learning.

With these definitions we can turn our attention to the most hyped field, which is Generative AI. This class of algorithms refers to methods that can generate content, such as text, video, images, speech, or other forms of content. While there are many active areas of research that are making great progress, businesses are most ready to adopt methods that generate text. The most popular tool to accomplish this task is a Large Language Model.

LLMs are the new powerful tool driving innovation in AI products. LLMs are typically used as robust assistants that understand language and can follow instructions. Anyone who has spent a few hours studying how to exploit a language model is ready to have a positive business impact. However, the opportunity most people are missing is that the technology can radically change traditional Machine Learning workflows for Natural Language Processing (NLP) problems.

Let's examine a traditional workflow for an NLP problem with and without an LLM. Before the LLM, an AI project could span 3–6 months. This would include 1–2 months of collecting and cleaning 10,000 to 1 million data points, 1–2 months to train and validate model performance, and then 1–2 months to expose the model to end users. With Generative AI workflow, we can spend 1–2 hours collecting just enough data to validate our performance (100–1000 data points), 1–2 hours building a prompt, and 1–2 hours to deploy the model.

This is the biggest opportunity LLMs present for a business: it is easy to go from zero to one and anyone in the business can accomplish this. Because the interaction with the model is all through natural language, everyone is prepared to create value using this technology. With minimal training an accountant can rival the results of a seasoned ML practitioner. While this democratized access is a great new thing, it creates new challenges businesses need to be aware of.

As discussed, anyone in the business is positioned to deploy AI products with minimal training. However, there are some challenges with AI products these individuals will not be prepared for. For example, testing AI products has unique challenges. We can extensively test software with a selection of 5–20 individual tests to handle our edge cases. However, for AI applications, we test across thousands of examples and look at an average over these examples. If the average is satisfactory, then we move onto deployment and have specific strategies to make sure things don't go wrong. With generative products, the end user may be an adversary and attempt to get our product to do unintended things. A person leading AI products should consider these things and have the training and experience to understand how to anticipate these problems.

Chili's Story

Topics: Zero-to-one, scalability

Chili's is an iconic restaurant chain located in the United States with select global locations. To deliver superior customer experience, Chili's is frequently testing the performance of menu items and policy changes that affect guest experience. Chili's recognizes the need to measure the success of these changes to understand their impact on customer satisfaction.

One significant challenge faced by Chili's was the difficulty in quantitatively measuring customer feedback. The need to answer specific questions, such as the performance of a new spicy margarita in a given month, required measuring customer opinions from the restaurant. Chili's already collected thousands of customer reviews each day but did not have an efficient way to be actionable using this information.

Chili's initially tackled this challenge with a manual approach involving two analysts who crafted text-based rules or manually reviewed and cleaned data. Unfortunately, this process was not only time-consuming but also prone to errors. The complexity of analyzing customer sentiments demanded a more sophisticated and streamlined solution.

Recognizing the limitations of the existing approach, Chili's adopted a solution that leveraged an LLM for advanced natural language processing. The problem was formatted as a text extraction problem that extracted key elements in the following schema:

- Entity Extraction:
  - Identification of main entities in a review, such as specific menu items like margaritas, chicken crispers, etc.
- Property Extraction:
  - Extraction of text associated with each entity to determine context; this can be words like tasty, gross, contains hair, looks, and tastes like mold, etc.
- Sentiment Analysis
  - With the entity and property, we can determine if sentiment is positive, negative, or neutral
- Classification of Entity/Property
  - Using the entity and property, we can classify it into a category from a preset list. This leverages an idea referred to as Zero Shot classification.

The adoption of this approach allowed Chili's to seamlessly integrate customer feedback analysis into its decision-making processes. Analysts could now track sentiment changes associated with specific menu items or categories, ensuring that any modifications to the restaurant's offerings did not significantly impact customer satisfaction.

The implementation of the LLM-based solution yielded remarkable results for Chili's:

- Efficiency Gains: Drastically reduced the time and effort required for analyzing customer feedback, enabling a more agile response to changing market dynamics.
- Error Reduction: Minimized the risk of errors inherent in manual review processes, ensuring the accuracy of customer sentiment analysis.
- Data Granularity: Provided analysts with the flexibility to generate custom reports, offering detailed insights into specific aspects of customer feedback.
- Continuous Improvement: Enabled Chili's to make informed decisions by ensuring that changes in the restaurant did not result in significant fluctuations in sentiment or category satisfaction.

Klarna

Topics: AI assistants, scalability, guardrails

A great example of a conversational assistant having profound help for customers is Klarna. Klarna is a buy now pay later service that has over 3 million monthly chat conversations with its customers. With this volume it's important to be able to scale the interaction very quickly. This led Klarna to partner with OpenAI to create a solution that could handle a large amount of its customer service volume.

Klarna built an AI assistant that now handles two-thirds of its customer service chats, a total of 2.3 million conversations in just one month. This represents the equivalent work of 700 full-time agents. Because of its effectiveness, the assistant is estimated to drive $40 million USD in profit for the year of 2024. The assistant is available 24/7 and is fluent in 35 languages. It resolves errors in 2 minutes, compared to 11 minutes with a human agent. Looking at satisfaction scores the AI assistant is on par with human agents solving the same job.

This has profound implications for call centers since they can scale their operations in two ways. First is to hire more employees and the second is to make their employees more effective. With the AI assistant, it's possible to scale on demand. They do not have to deal with the seasonality of demand facing the call center to create trained agents. When they need more agents, they just need to allocate more servers.

A key reason the Klarna assistant is so effective is because of the reduced operating complexity created for the AI assistant. For customer service requests, most are related to simple questions about properties of the order. This is an easy task for the AI assistant since the information is easily retrievable. When tasks begin to get more complex the AI assistant will likely fail to be helpful. In this case it would be good to transition the user to work with a human assistant once the AI assistant has failed. This will still reduce operating complexity and cost since the AI assistant can handle a majority of the requests.

One of the things Klarna did a very good job of is the implementation of guardrails, an important and often overlooked feature of AI assistants. Guardrails can be thought of as general safety features that are placed on top of or inside of the AI assistant to keep the model on task. For example, Klarna will reject your requests to talk about topics that are too far away from the exact things it is prepared to help you with.

Air Canada

Topics: Retrieval Augmented Generation, Red-Teaming

We saw how Klarna created a positive customer experience with a customer facing chatbot but is this success always the case? We can look at an example from Air Canada where we see that there is a lot to learn about edge cases that can happen when deploying AI solutions.

Jake Moffat booked a flight on Air Canada for a next-day flight after his grandmother had passed away. Air Canada advertises a policy that offers customers a reduced rate for booking last-minute travel under tragic circumstances. Jake was connected with the company's chatbot and asked what the policy was, and it confidently answered him as long as he applied within 90 days of the original purchase.

The problem with the chatbot's response is that this is not Air Canada's policy. The policy requires that the company will comply if the request is filed before purchasing the flight. The airline went on to distinguish the chatbot as a separate legal entity and the company would not be responsible for its actions. Moffat filed a claim with the Canadian tribunal regarding this circumstance and was awarded the appropriate amount of money for the policy according to the chatbot.

There are some good takeaways from this story. Outside of the AI system itself, it's important to first consider the user experience. When creating any interaction between a company and a customer, the company should always take responsibility for the interaction. In this case Air Canada could have avoided the damage to their reputation by offering Moffat the money he was owed, an amount around $483 USD. They could then take the actions to remove their chatbot while it undergoes "maintenance" to prevent a similar situation. This surely would have resulted in less damage than the way the actions played out.

This story also highlights an important quality of LLMs referred to as hallucinations. A hallucination occurs when an LLM confidently responds with an answer that is not grounded in any known fact. In this case, the LLM hallucinated about Air Canada's policy on bereavement flights. Unfortunately, there is no known way to completely remove this feature of the language model; however, there are things we can do to reduce this.

One way to accomplish the reduction in hallucinations is to use a system design called Retrieval Augmented Generation (RAG). When building a system like this, it's important to bring your own knowledge and information to fuel the LLM's ability to answer relevantly. When we retrieve relevant knowledge documents from a company FAQ and use them as context for an LLM to answer questions, we call this process Retrieval Augmented Generation (RAG). It exploits a well-known quality of LLMs called In-Context Learning, the ability for the LLM to adapt to new information in real time.

This process of RAG has profound implications for businesses. The first is that it is not necessary to train your own AI system but just provide it with relevant information. This is the power of In-Context Learning. When we write prompts or provide examples of what we want the language model to do, it is learning in real time. The second implication is that you drastically reduce the likelihood that the LLM will hallucinate. There is good academic research that RAG reduces hallucinations on open domain question answers. On closed domain question answering, like the Air Canada case, the reduction in hallucinations is much larger. The LLM comes to your business with zero knowledge, and in the chance that it does have knowledge you should presume it is all incorrect. You want to supply existing knowledge to the LLM before it answers questions like shown in the example below for the reasons discussed above.

Consider, for example, a prompt for Retrieval Augmented Generation:

> Please answer the following question using ONLY information provided in the following context.
>
> Question: I would like to book bereavement travel.
>
> Context:
> To book bereavement travel
>
> Step 1:
>
> Please *contact us by phone* to request a bereavement fare. We will ask you to provide us with the name of the dying or deceased family member and your relationship to them, as well as:
> ...

Another trouble with conversational AI products like the one Air Canada released is the presence of adversarial users. The adversarial user has different intentions than the user that cooperates. An adversarial user will try to exploit the application to do things that the product should not do. An example where this is particularly damaging is if the user exploits limitations in the AI to get it to say incorrect things. If I trick the AI into giving me an incorrect refund this is quite damaging to the brand and needs to be accounted for.

To make sure the application is protected from adversarial attacks it is common to go through an exercise referred to as Red-Teaming. Red-Teaming involves hiring a team of experts that work to expose problems with the applications and test to make sure good guardrails are in place. There are plenty of examples where good Red-Teaming has been skipped. Looking up examples of Google's Gemini creating insensitive depictions of Nazis or Microsoft's Tay spreading offensive and inflammatory tweets shows examples of where Red-Teaming would have been extremely valuable. Companies like Meta have realized the importance of Red-Teaming and actually have in-house labeling teams that are expertly trained in the process.

Going beyond LLMs with specialized language models

As mentioned previously, LLMs are great tools for going from zero to one. They are convenience models and there are cases when it makes sense to move away from them to get specialized technology. As an organization becomes more mature there will be general interest in training specialized language models to complete specific tasks. With this in mind, let's cover some common pitfalls that can happen when pursuing an approach like this.

Before considering building specialized models, you must consider if you have the data strategy and talent to handle this task. Building this requires careful planning and must be taken care of far in advance of the model building project. This process can be outsourced to specialized firms; however, be careful of the leaders you hire to handle this process. The vetting process should be very careful. When considering if someone is an AI expert, I like to ask some variation of the following questions (these are relevant as of writing):

- What is Quantization of Language Models and describe some algorithms that are state of the art for the task?
- Which library or framework would you use to run a Language Model for Inference?
- How many bytes does a floating-point number take when loaded in half-precision?
- What are the general phases of training an LLM?
- What is the difference between Encoder, Decoder, and Encoder-Decoder architectures?

If someone is pursuing this specialized training process, they should be able to answer some variation of these questions. Training specialized language models is challenging, and in the wrong hands can end in disaster. A great team will not only be able to answer these questions, but they can explain them to you in terms you understand. These aren't overly complex questions, but they are things practitioners will know the answers to.

The role of open source in AI strategy

An emerging trend in AI strategy for companies on the frontier of building LLMs is to open source the models they have built. This seems counter-intuitive since companies like Meta, Mistral, Cohere, and others lose a competitive advantage by releasing these models. This strategy actually highlights an important aspect of where we derive value from language models in the business and it's worth spending time to consider.

First, it's important to consider what it actually means to open source a model. This terminology is actually quite contentious, since LLMs have many moving parts. Typically, when a company open sources the model, they make their model available to the public, but do not share the data they used. Strong proponents of open source will say this is not enough, and they are right to a certain extent; however, the community is very grateful for what we have been able to build with the models that have been released.

The implication of this being a valid business model shows that LLMs themselves are not valuable, but the experience they create is what is valuable. Meta is a great example of this with their series of language models called LLaMA. These models were first released to the community in February of 2023. Since their release the community has built many different variations and improvements on this series of models. Because of the community contributions Meta has ended up with better core models. Another case comes from Google open sourcing its Gemma series of models. Within a few hours, key players in the community discovered several problems with the model and quickly fixed them. When these companies adopt these changes into the AI experience in the platform their users win big.

This works for Meta because the value the model provides is not the model itself, but the integration of the model into their platform. When the business identifies key processes involving humans that can be augmented and improved with language models, they are in a great position to create value. Netflix, years ago, had an interesting approach where they famously created an open challenge with their dataset competition. Looking past the problems with this project (really scary data privacy problems that are easy to work around) companies could implement similar challenges to avoid the challenge of finding high-quality AI talent.

Key steps to integrating LLMs in the business

If you want to get started integrating LLMs into the core business, it is important to determine why you want to do this. The fear of being left behind is not a great answer; it has to be deeper. Fortunately, with the ease of access and general interest in investing in the technology, it is easy to find ideas and use cases that are worthwhile.

A great place to start off is with investing in training your employees to responsibly use LLMs. Your employees are a great asset and can have amazing ideas for your business. In 2023 I was visiting the Google NYC office and was surprised by how much they valued their employee input for Gemini. Outside of the cafeterias there were submission boxes where employees were asked for their ideas to generate value for Gemini. Google understands that spreading the responsibility of idea generation is a winning strategy for innovating in a competitive playing field.

Earlier I mentioned investing in the right leaders, but you should also invest in educating employees. Finding good quality training programs for your employees to learn about AI will help find potential opportunities where you can leverage AI. Andrew Ng, a legendary figure in the field of AI, started a company called DeepLearning.AI which offers courses to people at any place in their journey to understand AI. I would recommend his courses for anyone who is interested in learning how to interface with LLMs or any AI technology. In general, you want to look for courses that have been in the field for a long time and have pursued advanced studies. There is an industry joke to avoid "leaders" who have previous startups in Web 3.0 or Blockchain. These are trend followers, not trend setters.

The next critical step is getting the right leaders. From my experience the individuals most prepared to lead AI strategy are those that come from strong technical tracks. Previously we covered questions for those who are implementing specialized language models. While a leader of strategy does not necessarily need to intimately understand these questions, it's indicative of someone who has studied the field as a whole. If they can't create value themselves, they will not attract individual contributors who are industry leaders.

After establishing the leaders it's important to set a top-down and build AI strategy. Companies that don't follow this end up with pockets of strong technical minds and enthusiasts. Enthusiasts are those that are excited about AI but don't have the practical experience to drive strategy. When enthusiasts lead AI projects it can be challenging to discover which pockets are truly generating a return on value for AI projects. When a top-down AI strategy is set it is easier to avoid the forming pockets of enthusiasts.

The next step is to establish the data strategy. Depending on the projects and key features you are pursuing you need to establish how you will collect feedback from your customers and what you collect. This information will help iterate on your products and go past the zero-to-one phase. When you have enthusiasts in the company, they are often afraid of data collection projects. If all you are comfortable with is prompt engineering, your value as a leader goes away. I have seen this firsthand, that enthusiasts are often afraid of these projects because they perceive them as a shift in control. This is a dangerous culture to build and something to be avoided.

Conclusion

It's an exciting time for businesses in the age of AI. In this age of LLMs we will see many companies soar to new heights and some companies get left behind. While it's intimidating to get started in the AI race it's important to begin thinking about the strategy to avoid getting left behind. Customers will grow to expect certain experiences powered by AI and it's important to set up the business processes to make sure we can meet the customer where they expect us to be.

Notes

1 Meghan Rimol, *Gartner Survey Reveals 80% of Executives Think Automation Can Be Applied to Any Business Decision*, August 22, 2022, retrieved May 15, 2024 from https://www.gartner.com/en/newsroom/press-releases/2022-08-22-gartner-surveyreveals-80-percent-of-executives-think-automation-can-be-appliedto-any-business-decision#

2 *AI at Work Is Here. Now Comes the Hard Part*, retrieved May 15, 2024 from https://www.microsoft.com/en-us/worklab/work-trend-index/ai-at-work-is-here-now-comes-the-hard-part

3 *AI at Work Is Here. Now Comes the Hard Part*, retrieved May 15, 2024 from https://www.microsoft.com/en-us/worklab/work-trend-index/ai-at-work-is-here-now-comes-the-hard-part

4 "Global Passenger Survey (GPS)," *IATA*, n.d. https://www.iata.org/en/publications/store/global-passenger-survey

5 Alberto Guerrini, Gabriele Ferri, Stefano Rocchi, Marcelo Cirelli, Vicente Piña, Antoine Grieszmann, "Personalization @ scale in airlines: combining the power of rich customer data, experiential learning, and revenue management", *Journal of Revenue and Pricing Management*, 2023.

6 AI, Today in FSI: Survey Report (dataiku.com).

7 James Eyers, "CBA goes all in on generative AI," *Australian Financial Review*, May 24, 2023.

8 AI in FinTech: 7 use cases market leaders pursue, 8allocate, August 2, 2023. AmEx is experimenting cautiously with generative AI for fintech, *VentureBeat*, May 29, 2023. https://venturebeat.com/ai/amex-is-experimenting-cautiously-with-generative-ai-for-fintech

9 AI and design: Exploring the synergy of creativity and technology, *VentureBeat*. https://venturebeat.com/ai/ai-and-design-exploring-the-synergy-of-creativity-and-technology

10 "Airport data sharing and collaboration key to improving passenger satisfaction," *ACI*, January 27, 2020. https://aci.aero/2020/01/27/airport-data-sharing-and-collaboration-key-to-improving-passenger-satisfaction

11 "How Manchester Airports Group and Ryanair worked alongside AWS to provide a better customer experience," *AWS*, February 9, 2023. https://aws.amazon.com/blogs/industries/how-manchester-airports-group-and-ryanair-worked-alongside-aws-to-provide-a-better-customer-experience

12 ATPCO Leverages AWS Clean Rooms to Enable Airline Dynamic Offers Functionality at Scale, *ATPCO*. https://www.atpco.net/press/atpco-leverages-aws-clean-rooms-enable-airline-dynamic-offers-functionality-at-scale
13 Calming airport data turbulence with EASE. https://aws.amazon.com/blogs/publicsector/calming-airport-data-turbulence-ease
14 Amazon's New AI Tools: How Travel Companies are Using AWS, *Skift*. https://skift.com/2023/11/29/amazons-new-ai-tools-for-travel-how-delta-ihg-and-others-are-using-aws
15 "Air Transport IT Insights 2022," *SITA*, n.d. https://www.sita.aero/resources/surveys-reports/air-transport-it-insights-2022

About the author

Nawal Taneja, whose experience in the aviation industry spans more than five decades, has worked for and advised worldwide major airline and related aviation C-Suites and their Boards. His experience also includes the presidency of a small airline that provided schedule and charter services with jet aircraft and the presidency of a boutique think tank that provided advisory services to the air transportation community throughout the world. On the government side, he has advised worldwide high-ranking government policy makers on matters relating to the role of government-owned, government-controlled, or government-facilitated aviation-related businesses. Within the academic community, he has served on the faculties of the Massachusetts Institute of Technology and the Ohio State University. He has also served on the advisory boards of both public and private organizations. Currently, he serves as an Executive-in-Residence in the College of Engineering at the Ohio State University and on the Advisory Board of the Nault Center for Entrepreneurship at the University of South Florida. In addition to his ongoing work with C-Suites of airlines, he is now asked to engage with innovative start-up groups to help them commercialize and scale their initiatives.

Encouraged by practitioners in the global aviation industry, he has written a series of 16 books to move the arc of thinking about aviation businesses to develop, capture, and deliver new value by pursuing creativity and collaboration to drive change. Each contains numerous and lengthy forewords by C-Suite executives in airlines, airports, aircraft manufacturers, technology businesses, trade associations, and investment groups. The book series also contains multiple thought leadership pieces that provide international perspectives relating to the theme of each book. These pieces are written by a diverse group of practitioners with extensive experience, both in the aviation domain and in other business sectors. He has also been asked by practitioners in the aviation industry to organize and chair the International Airline Symposium, an annual, small, and private event, to generate cross-industry conversations. The ambitious objective throughout the book series and the International Airline Symposium series (now in its 29th year), as well as through his advisory assignments, is to stimulate leaders to explore multiple perspectives by asking challenging and provocative questions rather than simply looking for answers.

He holds a bachelor's degree in Aeronautical Engineering (First Class Honors) from the University of London, a master's degree in Flight Transportation from MIT, a master's degree in Business Administration from MIT's Sloan School of Management, and a doctorate in Air Transportation from the University of London. He is a Fellow of the Royal Aeronautical Society of Great Britain.

Index

9781032776019